Harford Flemming

A Carpet Knight

A Novel

Harford Flemming

A Carpet Knight
A Novel

ISBN/EAN: 9783337026929

Printed in Europe, USA, Canada, Australia, Japan

Cover: Foto ©Thomas Meinert / pixelio.de

More available books at **www.hansebooks.com**

A CARPET KNIGHT

A Novel

BY

HARFORD FLEMMING

AUTHOR OF "CUPID AND THE SPHINX"

Nothing is there to come, and nothing past;
But an eternal now does always last.
COWLEY, *Davideis*

BOSTON
HOUGHTON, MIFFLIN AND COMPANY
New York: 11 East Seventeenth Street
The Riverside Press, Cambridge
1885

A CARPET KNIGHT.

CHAPTER I.

AFTER THE BALL.

"A mighty maze, but not without a plan."
POPE.

THE lights were brilliant still, although the flowers were fading. The music had ceased, and the hunchbacked violinist was putting his instrument into its case. The flageolet player and the pianist and the two French horns were gone.

The gay entertainment had come to an end, and the hostess stood meditatively before a tall mirror, at one end of the room, which reflected her white satin dress and all its elaborate embroidery, from the low-cut neck to the point of the train, with uninterrupted accuracy.

She had been said to resemble Titian's Flora on account of the fashionable color of her hair, and perhaps from an impressive serenity of demeanor. She was a striking-looking woman and dressed to perfection, which can hardly be said of Titian's masterpiece; but she was no longer young, and al-

1

though her figure and complexion were still fine her small red-brown eyes and a lack of delicacy in the shape and expression of her mouth interfered with her title to be considered handsome.

She seemed to be looking at herself, although she was not consciously doing so, any more than she was aware of the ironical smile with which the hunchbacked musician regarded her, as, after having carefully packed his instrument, he bowed and departed.

The whole of the ball-room was as perfectly reproduced in the mirror as the lady's toilet, and the gaze of the hostess was fixed on a certain yellow satin sofa, which furnished an alcove on her left, formed by a deep bay window, the opening of which was partly screened by a stand of flowering plants and shaded by heavy curtains.

The two persons who occupied the sofa were so closed in by their surroundings that it was not to be wondered at that they had not perceived the gradual departure of the company in general, and were yet unaware of the emptiness of the room.

One, a young girl in a dress of marvelously interwoven stripes of blue and gold, was sitting well back in the farther corner. She was slight, with dark hair, a dark skin, and very clearly cut features. Her head was a little bent, and her eyes were cast down, with an amused smile about the corners of her mouth. She seemed to be submitting rather than listening to the somewhat labored speech of her companion, a youth not much older than herself, who was leaning a little towards her, and talking earnestly. The lady of the house could only see the reflection of his back, a fine broad one, and judge by his attitude of the expression of his face ; but she could see enough to satisfy her.

" He is doing very well," she said to herself. " She may smile now, but she will not smile always. If he only does not change his mind, he will win his way at last. I have known men succeed who were twice as stupid and not half so good-looking, where they were determined. The great thing will be to get her guardian's consent "— She started, for at this moment her interesting study was broken in upon.

" Ah, Mr. Drayton," she said aloud, as she turned to greet a tall, handsome man in evening dress, who approached her without noticing the two whom she was watching. " So you have escaped from Mr. Davering at last, and are ready, I fancy, for a little supper with which to end the evening."

" No more supper, thank you. I came to look for Julia," said Mr. Drayton. " I had no idea it was so late. Your husband beguiled me into his sanctum, and there we have been smoking and re-calling old college days for the last hour. I hear the ball was delightful, Mrs. Davering. How charmingly your rooms look ! "

" Yes, I think the party went off fairly well," said Mrs. Davering, not without some of the " pride that apes humility ; " " but you really shall look at nothing until I have shown you your own beautiful gift, — these lovely Jacqueminots. Do they not look well in this corner? I hung them here that every one might see them."

She drew his attention, as she spoke, to a basket of dark red roses, with green vines of smilax trailing from it, which hung on the carved props of an easel, the support of a little landscape in water colors, which brightened the corner of the room farthest from the alcove and its occupants.

"It seems to me that every one has gone," said Mr. Drayton rather absently. "I must find Julia. I am afraid she will be wondering where I am."

"Perhaps we shall find her in the library," said Mrs. Davering, slipping her arm through that of her companion. "How well Julia looked this evening!" she continued, as she led him unsuspectingly towards the door through which he had entered; "she has so much ease and charm of manner, too, one would not imagine that this was her first ball."

"Julia has seen some society at home," said Mr. Drayton, smiling, "and then traveling does a great deal in that way for young people, I think."

As they left the room the young man on the sofa said, "I am really obliged to you for letting me explain it. It is awfully interesting to me, you know, and I can't understand why so many girls don't care a fig for what a fellow takes an interest in."

"Perhaps they don't take an interest in the fellow, you know," said the young lady, with a frank smile.

" Well, no, I did not mean that; that would be natural, of course," said the youth, turning red.

" But I mean that I think it would be very unnatural."

" I wish I could tell what you really do mean, Miss Prescott," he answered bluntly.

" I really do mean that so far as I can see the people are all gone, and so far as I can hear the music is stopped, and the party must be over ! "

" By Jove, I believe it is ! " exclaimed her companion, springing up. He was a strong, active-looking fellow, with brown curly hair, a ruddy complexion, and a pair of very stolid blue eyes. " What a bore to have it end ! " he said.

" I do not agree with you, Mr. Hazzard. It was pleasant, but do you not think we might really have been bored if it had kept on forever ? "

" Oh, I don't know about that," said Mr. Hazzard. " I think I could have stood it; that is, I would not have minded sitting on as we were."

" For how many years ? " asked the girl, looking up at him gayly as he stood before her. " Imagine my growing old and wrinkled in my ball-dress, and your losing all your teeth, and still sitting on, on this sofa, until you could not get up without a cane."

" Oh, I only meant if we could remain unchanged, of course," said Mr. Hazzard, with a troubled look. It seemed to him that his conversational ship had sailed into unknown waters, and he was afraid of hidden reefs.

" I really think that would be more of a bore,"
said Miss Prescott. " To be always sitting on a
yellow satin sofa, and always the same, just think!
Now growing old is not cheerful, but still it might
divert our minds a little."

She looked very pretty as she said this, and very
saucy. Poor Mr. Hazzard, who was evidently a
captive to her charms, sighed deeply.

" I should not want anything to divert my mind,"
he said, gloomily.

"Nonsense! You would be dying to go shooting, or rowing, or skating, or anything that you are
fond of doing. But I wonder where Mrs. Davering
is. I must go and say good-night. And I thought
I heard my guardian's voice a moment ago."

" So you did. I think he went into the next
room with my mother."

"Shall we go and find them?" asked Miss Prescott. She appeared, as she stood up, to be of about
medium height, lithe and well proportioned, her
figure seeming to imply a certain reserved strength,
which was also felt to be half hinted in her face.

" How glad you seem that your first ball is over,"
said the young fellow, jealously.

" Until it is over, how can my second one begin?" she asked, philosophically.

As Mr. Drayton and his ward were being driven
home from Mrs. Davering's ball, he said, —

" Well, dear, was the party a success?"

"Oh, yes, it was rather pleasant."

" Is that all?"

"I know it sounds ungrateful," she said, depre-catingly.

"You would have enjoyed it more if Philip had been there," said Mr. Drayton. "He could have introduced some of his friends. I was very sorry that he had to go to Washington just at this time, but it was a choice of evils ; either he or I " —

"And you knew how unhappy I should be if you went," broke in Julia. "What should I have done? It would have been rather ungracious to disappoint Mrs. Davering, when she insisted on considering that the party was given for me ; and yet I never could have had the courage to go with-out you to take care of me."

"I suppose it was hardly a matter of courage," said her guardian. "In fact," he added resignedly, "I fancy that this was one of those occult occa-sions when I was bound to play propriety for your benefit."

"I suppose so," replied Julia, with equal meek-ness.

"I confess that I sometimes get a little mixed up between the conflicting duties of the charac-ters I am called upon to assume," said Mr. Dray-ton. "That of a gossiping chaperon, if I may so describe my rôle to-night, suits me admirably ; but I can't help thinking that if I had not been so busy in this capacity I might have been of more use to you as a society man."

"You might, if you had talked to me," said Julia, "for then we should have entertained one another,

and there would have been no doubt about my enjoying the evening; but as for playing master of
ceremonies and introducing other people, I could
quite well dispense with your services."

"Did you have as many people as you wanted,
to dance with ? "

"Oh dear, yes, and to talk to ! — sometimes two
or three at a time; but they were not very interesting, or perhaps I was not. And then Charley Hazzard would insist upon my going to look at the
flowers in the bay window ; and when we got there
he asked me to sit down, which I did unsuspectingly, for I began to think afterwards that we never
should get out again."

"Oh ho ! " cried Mr. Drayton. " So that was
where you were, when I could not find you ? It
was not so bad, was it, to have to talk to a handsome young fellow, while you looked at the flowers
and listened to the music ? "

"But I did not have to talk. I had to listen;
and not to the music, either, but to a minute description of the way men train for boat-races."

"That was very instructive."

"It was very destructive to one of my bouquets !
I pulled it almost all to pieces out of sheer desperation."

"The form which your desperation took was not
very flattering to the sender of the flowers."

"The sender? Perhaps it might not have seemed
so, if he had been there; but I am almost afraid he
would not have cared."

" Afraid ? "

" I mean that I suspect he sent them only because he has been asked to the house so often."

" Why, what a little skeptic you are getting to be ! I wonder there is anything left of the lilies of the valley I gave you," he said, laughing, as he glanced down at a fragrant bunch, which she still held in her hand. " They were a direct return, I assure you, for many an evening's entertainment."

Julia laughed, too.

" On the contrary," she answered, " I used to be a skeptic, but now I am learning to distinguish." She looked up into his face, which she could see quite plainly by the aid of a street lamp, with a bright, trustful gleam in her dark eyes which contrasted strongly with their usual self-contained expression.

" And who is the person whom you have distinguished so unflatteringly ? "

" Oh, as for that," said Julia, " he is not here at all. The bouquet which I demolished was sent from Boston, by Philip's friend, Dr. Carey."

There was a short silence.

" Julia ! " said Mr. Drayton, suddenly, in a graver tone than he had used before.

" Well, sir ? "

" It troubles me that you seem to take so little pleasure in the society of your young friends."

" I have very few," said Julia.

" But there is no reason why you should not have many."

" I do not care for most people enough to make friends of them."

" That does not seem natural at your age."

" Does it seem unnatural, at yours, that one should not care to trust every one ? "

" No, not at mine."

" Then would you have me stupid, just because I am young ? "

" No, dear, not stupid, but with more of the freshness of youth, its beautiful faith and happy belief in things at their best."

" I am sorry," said Julia. " I have no illusions. If I ever had any, they must have been nipped in the bud."

" And yet there is a great capacity for faith in your nature," said Mr. Drayton, thoughtfully.

" Do you think so ? "

" I know it."

" And if there should be — for I am not sure — would you have me expend it on people whom I know to be shallow and selfish ? "

" How can you know it, child ? You judge people too hastily and too harshly."

" Perhaps I do ; but if I cannot think them nice, how can I want to see much of them ? "

" Try to be more charitable. You will find that there is some good in every one ; at least, so I think. It may be an old-fashioned doctrine. Meanwhile, is there no one — no young girl of your own age, for instance — whom you do feel attached to, and would like to see more of ? "

Julia was silent for a moment.

"Yes," she said, "there is one, — an old school friend. I would give a great deal to see her again!"

"You have only to say the word, my dear. I am delighted that there is a friend whom you would like to have with you." And thus encouraged Julia did say the word.

CHAPTER II.

"For Art may err, but Nature cannot miss."

DRYDEN.

THE face of a young girl, seated in an American drawing-room car, had attracted the attention of a fellow-traveler, who watched her with some interest. It was a sweet, fair face, with wide blue eyes and a very tender little mouth. It did not suggest the idea of any great depth or breadth of intellectual capacity, but it filled one with a certainty that its owner was pure and good. She had, besides this, an air of extreme youth and inexperience, which, together with an evident desire to seem at home in novel circumstances, was almost touching.

She was, apparently, unused to traveling, and nothing about her escaped careful notice, but she was very quiet in the study of her surroundings. It was, perhaps, as much the well-bred reserve of her manner as her face which held the attention of her observer; but he had a nice eye for effect, although not quite equal to understanding the detail of female attire, and he had been struck with the elegant simplicity of her dark green traveling dress, fitted faultlessly to her pretty, slender figure, even before he saw her face. A small plush bonnet, of the same dark color, had at first been a source of .

intense aggravation to him, as all that he was permitted to see beyond the bonnet was a stray lock
of curling light brown hair and part of a smooth
white cheek.

Occupying the arm-chair directly behind his fair
neighbor, his situation was not a very favorable one
for observation, but the revolving liberty allowed
to his otherwise fixed position enabled him to turn,
presently, so as to face the large window at the side
of the car, through which she was looking; and
then it chanced that a swift little backward motion
of her head, as her eyes followed some retreating
object in the landscape, gave him at length a very
complete impression.

He was himself a gentlemanly-looking young fellow of about five and twenty. He wore an overcoat
of a very light shade, although it was winter, and
carried a cane. He had also carefully suspended
his black silk hat in a kind of crate overhead,
which seemed to be intended for that purpose, and
put on a small camel's-hair cap of a pale brown
tint, embroidered with silk of the same color.

The journey, which had been begun at about
four o'clock of a December afternoon, happened,
as the event proved, to be prolonged much beyond
its expected length; for instead of reaching their
destination, which chanced to be the same, at a
little after six, the two travelers found themselves
scarcely one third of the way when that hour arrived, in consequence of an accident somewhere on
the line of the railroad.

The news of the disaster was telegraphed along the road, but the conductors were too well drilled to show anxiety in their faces. They passed about cheerfully from car to car, answering all inquiries with a calm assumption of ignorance, which, as the minutes grew into hours of waiting, became intensely aggravating to uneasy persons, who saw their dinner hour and their journey's end receding farther and farther in opposite directions.

There was no one who felt the unfitness and impropriety of such a divorce more keenly than the young man in the light overcoat. He got out of his seat and left the car. He came back to it again with an air of forced resignation. He changed his cap for his hat, and his hat for his cap, many times. When the conductor appeared he asked him penetrating questions as to the nature and vicinity of the accident, which he cleverly assumed to have occurred, and treated the evasive answers which he obtained with the contempt which they deserved.

It soon grew too dark to see beyond a large red light before the station where they were delayed, and thus the diversion of inspecting the scenery was denied, and he was cut off from all amusement but that of watching the occupant of the arm-chair in front of him.

The girl had turned away from the window as the shades of evening fell, and, the lamps being lighted within, had drawn a paper-covered volume from her canvas traveling-bag, which she seemed to be perusing with much interest.

She did not exhibit the least sign of uneasiness, impatience, or alarm. One would have suspected from her manner that she almost enjoyed the delay, since the little incidents to which it gave rise were evidently of as much interest to her as the more active events of the journey.

She looked up when any one passed through the car, or any of the passengers spoke near her. She listened to all that the conductor had to say, and was very friendly with a little Scotch terrier belonging to an actress, who was seated just opposite; but between all her little upward glances, which were as earnest and unconscious as those of a bird, she returned to the novel she was reading, with the air of one whose individuality was quite apart from those of her fellow-travelers.

After watching her with attention for some time, thinking that she might happen to turn towards him, or that chance might offer him some opening for conversation, — which he intended, be it understood, to conduct after the most courteous and respectful manner, — her neighbor became hopeless of the attempt. There was something in the young lady's manner which precluded it.

At last, at nearly ten o'clock, they reached their journey's end. The young lady in the dark green traveling dress collected her book, her shawl, and her bag, and stepped out of the train, in a well-known railway station, in the midst of a very large, very flat city, where almost all the houses were built of red brick, and were approached by white marble steps, and where many of them still retained the white painted doors and shutters of a former fashion; where the streets crossed each other at right angles in the most proper manner, and four green squares, at justly measured intervals, planted with solemn rows of trees, bounded the older, more central, and more intensely respectable portion of the metropolis.

These stately attractions had not yet dawned upon the young lady, who was a stranger to the city of brotherly love, and was surprised and confused at the size and bustle of the huge brick station in which she found herself.

She was evidently expecting some one to meet her, — probably an old gentleman, for she glanced anxiously at the face of every elderly man whom she saw, as she walked along the platform, and scanned still more wistfully those who were standing outside the railing which separated the trains from the waiting-rooms and offices.

As her fellow-passengers filed slowly through the iron gateway, formed by an opening in this railing, she saw many of them greeted by an expectant friend or group of friends, and eagerly hurried away. Those who were not met by any one appeared to be old travelers, accustomed to look out for themselves, or natives returning to their homes, who trudged off with an air of ease and familiarity with the surroundings which denoted that they knew just where to go and what to do.

Unfortunately for the stranger, she belonged to

no one of these classes. She was alone, in an unknown city, not at all accustomed to traveling, and
everything about her was new and untried. She
had been so certain of being met and welcomed
that it had not occurred to her to consider her best
course of action in case she were not, and she began to fear that her uncertainty and perplexed expression would attract attention.

At this moment the young man who had occupied the seat behind hers approached and touched
his hat.

"Can I do anything for you?" he asked.

"Thank you — no," she said, coldly. "I am
expecting my friends to meet me."

"Perhaps I can find them for you," said the
young man, who really wished to be of service.

"You are very kind, but I think they will be
here in a moment."

He touched his hat again, and was passing on,
when a glance at her face arrested him. Its
troubled expression quite belied the quiet decision
of her words. He hesitated and stood still.

"I should be very glad to help you," he said, in
a tone of embarrassed sincerity, which appealed to
the girl more successfully than his former more
confident address had done.

"There is nothing you can do," she said, relent-
ing a little, "unless," she added shyly, "you could
find me a carriage."

"I will do so with pleasure. Let me take you
first to the waiting-room." He led the way as he

2

spoke, carrying her bag, which he had taken from her hand. She followed him without a word, and waited in the ladies' room until he reappeared at the door, when she came hastily out.

" How about your trunks?" he asked, in a business-like tone, as he helped her into the carriage he had summoned.

" I have only one."

" Would it not be well to give your check to the driver, and take it with you?"

" I think it would."

A silence fell between them when the man had gone for the trunk.

The young lady was seated in the cab. Her accidental protector stood gravely by the open door, until the cabman came back with her trunk, which was a large one, and lifted it to its place in front.

" Will you get in, sir?" he asked, holding the cab-door open.

" No. Wait a moment. Where shall I tell him to take you?" the young man inquired.

" To Mr. Algernon Drayton's, 1822 Meredith Square. I am very much obliged to you."

The young man started.

" Then you are a friend of Mr. Drayton, or of Miss Prescott!" he exclaimed, forsaking the constraint into which her reserve had forced him for his more buoyant natural manner.

" I am a friend of Miss Prescott's."

" I am so glad that I chanced to meet you. I am Mr. Wilmott, a friend of Miss Prescott's, too,

and Mr. Drayton is my uncle. May I not see you
safely to the house?"

And without waiting for an answer, he gave the
number to the driver, jumped into the carriage, and
closed the door.

The young lady was surprised, relieved, and embarrassed. It was a comfort to know that she had
some claim, even the most distant, on the attention
and kindness of her escort; but his suggestion of
going with her, and the *tête-à-tête* which it involved,
of uncertain duration, in a four-wheeled cab, appeared to her extremely awkward.

If she was impressed with this view of the subject, however, nothing seemed farther from the
mind of her companion. He spread her shawl,
which he had taken it upon himself to carry, on
the front seat, stowed away her traveling-bag un-
derneath it, and advised her to put her satchel on
top of the shawl. He then suggested that the window on her side had better be open, and, having
gained her assent, proceeded to open it.

"That enables you to see something," he said
cheerfully. "Now I can tell you about the streets
as we go along. Have you ever been here before?"

"No, never."

"Really? That is delightful. Then you have a
great deal to see. I suppose you went to school
with Miss Prescott?" he added presently.

"Yes. We were at school together for several
years."

" In New York ? "

" Near New York."

" I wonder if I have not heard her speak of you? Do you live in New York ? "

" I live at New Rochelle."

" Then you must be Miss Arnold."

" Yes," she said, smiling at his persistency.

" I knew you must be," he rejoined, in a tone of great satisfaction. " Now, Miss Arnold, if you will look out, please, you will presently see the buildings for the new city offices."

She turned in the direction he indicated, and caught a confused glimpse of a white mass of masonry.

" Why, how large they are! " she remarked, with mild surprise.

" They are large, of course," replied Mr. Wilmott complacently, and began giving her some local information with regard to them, of which she did not hear a great deal, as she was gazing rather absently out of the window.

Suddenly it occurred to her that she had not expressed sufficient gratitude for the spontaneous courtesy of her new acquaintance.

" I really feel very grateful to you, Mr. Wilmott, for your kindness," she said, looking into the darkness of the carriage as she spoke, where her companion's face was only faintly visible. " I should have been much at a loss to know what to do with myself, if you had not decided the matter for me."

" Of course you would," said Mr. Wilmott.

" Miss Prescott had written that Mr. Drayton would meet me at the station," she continued, " or I should not have been allowed to come."

" The train was delayed, you know. There was an accident on the road. We were three hours late," said her companion briskly.

"Yes," said Miss Arnold, " I know we were. They must have given me up. The truth is that I have hardly had enough experience to venture to travel alone."

" They ought to have been able to find out about the accident. I can't understand how such a clever man as my uncle can have made such a stupid mistake," said Mr. Wilmott energetically.

" Perhaps he was prevented from coming, in some unexpected way."

" I should have thought that in that case Julia — Miss Prescott, I mean — would have tried to meet you herself."

" She may not have known of his having been prevented."

" I see you are determined to be charitable."

Just then the cabman began to drive faster, and conversation became impossible, owing to the plunging and rattling of the cab over the cobble-stones, a form of pavement with which the young lady from New Rochelle was not familiar.

" It will be better when we get on to the track," called her new friend reassuringly ; and she needed reassurance, for there was an excitement and sense of adventure in this strange arrival which made her heart beat faster and faster with expectancy. She distinctly associated the jar and hollow grating sound with which the wheels of the cab sank into the iron grooves of the tramway with her first impression of Philadelphia, although she did not learn until afterwards that the careful fitting of the wheels of all carriages to this unyielding road was one of the peculiarities of the Quaker city.

They stopped at last at the house in Meredith Square, and the cabman asked if he should ring. Miss Arnold looked out anxiously.

" I suppose so," she said, in a perplexed tone.

"Yes, ring the bell, of course," said Mr. Wilmott cheerfully. He was troubled with no agitating doubts.

The house was dark and silent. The man's footsteps resounded, as he climbed the steps, with a distinctness characteristic of very cold weather. He struck his hands together impatiently after he had rung, and then buried them in the depths of his coat pockets. He walked back and forth on the top step for a few moments, and then rang again. This time a window of the second story was cautiously opened, and a female head protruded.

" Wait a moment," said a voice, in a subdued tone. " I will come down," and the head mysteriously disappeared.

" Something must have happened! " cried Miss Arnold, no longer able to conceal her perturbation at such a strange reception. " What can it be? "

" I will go and find out," said Mr. Wilmott,
with a quick appreciation of her distress which was
comforting. He went rapidly up the steps, and the
cabman came back to his horse. The next moment
the door was opened by a slender figure holding a
lamp, and a whispered colloquy was held in the
entry. Then Mr. Wilmott returned to the carriage.

" It is all right," he said. " Julia is there, and
she is delighted that you have come ; only my uncle
met with an accident."

" An accident ! "

" Yes. He was thrown from his horse, it seems,
yesterday, in the Park, and fearing the worst Julia
wrote to you not to come until she knew how badly
he was hurt ; but Mr. Drayton is doing so well that
she had already sent a telegram urging your coming to-morrow. It is odd that I knew nothing of
all this, but I have been away for several days."

" How strange that I did not get the letter ! "
said Miss Arnold uneasily.

" Oh dear, no, not the least strange. Letters are
delayed or go astray every day. Julia may have
misdirected it, in her anxiety, or more probably it
reached your home just after you left to-day. Will
you not let me help you out? She is waiting for
you, and greatly pleased that you have come so soon.
I have no doubt it will be a comfort to her to see
you."

" How kind you are ! " said the girl impulsively.
He helped her out of the carriage very gently,

and then followed with her shawl and bags, while she ran up the steps, and was soon folded in the arms of her friend.

"You are a dear thing," said Miss Prescott, laconically. "I am delighted to see you! Bring that trunk in very quietly, please, and put it down here in the entry," she continued to the cabman, who was advancing with Miss Arnold's trunk on his shoulder. "Oh, he is much better, thank you," she added, in reply to a hurried question about her guardian.

"Good-night, Julia," said Mr. Wilmott. "Where shall I put these things?"

"Anywhere. Don't go, Cecil. Will you not come in and get warm?"

"No, not to-night, thank you. I will see you to-morrow. Good-night; good-night, Miss Arnold."

Then, when the cabman was paid and had departed, the two girls were alone.

CHAPTER III.

"He had not the method of making a fortune."
GRAY.

MRS. DAVERING was not naturally a clever woman, if the word implies intuitive perception of
that which may or may not lie beyond the surface
of human nature, for she lacked insight; but the
meaning of the epithet has been much questioned,
and in its commoner acceptation — that of a person
who makes the best of themselves — she deserved
it, for her powers of observation were not incon-
siderable, and of such cleverness as might be acquired by a careful use of them, at the age of forty,
she possessed a fair amount.

She could not judge of other people's motives
apart from her own, or form any idea of what parts
they would play in entirely new situations; but taking herself as a model (which she was always
ready to do), and coming to the conclusion that the
inhabitants of this globe were at bottom much
alike, she calculated with a good deal of confidence
how they would or would not act in circumstances
with which she was familiar, and it chanced sufficiently often that her calculations proved correct.

People thought her extremely well satisfied with
herself and her fortunes, and she chose to appear

so, because she reasoned that the more prosperous any one appeared to be the more would that one be sought and admired; but in reality she was not quite contented with anything.

What life had so far offered she hardly deemed worthy of her expectations. It had certainly been more than fell to the share of many people, but that was of course, while it had not been by any means all that she would have been able to enjoy and turn to advantage.

She had married young for love, and on the death of her first husband had married again for money. She had also secured, in this second venture, an amiable, lackadaisical companion, somewhat younger than herself, who was so rich that he could afford to treat his profession as a mere gentlemanly occupation yet she would have liked him to enjoy the respect which belonged to a man of energy and ambition, and never could understand why he failed to do so.

She was the mother of several sharp little girls, who had inherited her own eagerness in the advancement of their interests, and she would have liked them to be pretty, which she could plainly see that they were not. Above all, she had a handsome, reckless son, born of her first marriage, who was the joy and the anguish of her existence. He possessed a fine figure and a magnificent development of muscle, but was a trifle less well endowed with brains. He excelled in all active manly sports, but had never been able to get beyond the simplest studies at school, and when it came to the question of an occupation in life found himself entirely unable to solve it. Yet he was indebted even for the education which he had wasted to the bounty of his stepfather, and Mrs. Davering knew only too well that some career must be found for him.

Meanwhile he was amusing himself. Mr. Davering, who, to do him justice, was as generous as he was rich, had made no objection hitherto to meeting his bills, and Charley Hazzard was known far and wide as the best-hearted fellow, the most careless, and the most well meaning in existence. He was a capital shot, a fine oarsman, a champion player at lawn tennis, much to his mother's pride; but she realized with a bitterness of spirit, in strong contrast to the complacency of her outward aspect, that these talents would never gain him a living.

What was to be done? After pondering all the possible ways by which money could be acquired, Mrs. Davering reverted to her own experience. Why should not Charley marry well? It was thus that the lady expressed it to herself, and then she began to lay her plans. If she could only succeed in finding him a suitable wife, one with sufficient wit and judgment to balance his muscle, and with sufficient wealth to satisfy his rather expensive tastes, what a triumph it would be! She cast her eyes about her far and wide on every likely maiden of her acquaintance, but of all whom she noted Julia Prescott found most favor.

Julia was an orphan. That is to say, her father was dead, and she lived with her guardian, at the head of whose table she had been allowed to preside from the time that she was quite a little girl. Chance had first thrown her in Mrs. Davering's way. In fact, they had met abroad under rather peculiar circumstances.

It happened that Mr. Drayton was passing the summer in Europe with his ward, during one of her long vacations, when she was overtaken, at Florence, by a malarial fever, in consequence, it was supposed, of having imprudently gone to Rome rather late in the season.

When the girl fell ill Mr. Drayton was at his wits' end to decide what to do for her, but some kind English ladies came to the rescue. They sent him a physician and engaged a nurse for Julia, whose united efforts, with his own devotion, brought her through.

Just as he was congratulating himself on her recovery, however, and they were preparing to set out for Switzerland by way of the Italian lakes, letters reached him from America which made it necessary that he should return immediately. The question what to do with Julia again perplexed him sorely, and at this critical moment Mrs. Davering glided upon the scene.

She, too, had been belated in Italy, and was hurrying northward. She had met Mr. Drayton, who was a widower, more than ten years before, and hastened to recall herself to him, although she

had not seen him since the death of his wife. He
was a man whom women were apt to remember,
and as his chief charm consisted in a certain loveliness of nature time did not impair it.

Mrs. Davering suggested that Julia should be
left with her while Mr. Drayton returned, and offered to bring her safely back to America in the
autumn, when it was her own intention to fly homeward. She promised to take her journey in easy
stages, such as would suit the invalid, and as her
husband and her son, with whom she was traveling,
were submissive in all things to her she commanded
the situation.

. The party of four were thrown very constantly
together until they reached the Tyrol, but here
Charley Hazzard, who was barely sixteen, fell in
with a congenial set of English boys, fresh from
Eton, and fond, like himself, of making a labor
of pleasure. He accordingly went off on long
mountain excursions with his new friends, leaving
Mr. Davering to smoke and talk politics in the
hotel, and his mother and Julia together.

On these occasions the older lady would congrat-
ulate herself upon having secured so pleasant a
companion, and one who could suit herself quite
easily to the society of a person so much older
than herself; for Miss Prescott, at the early age of
fifteen, was acquainted with a great many grown-up
gentlemen and ladies who were also well known to
Mrs. Davering, and her powers of observation were
quite as keen as those of her new friend, who en-

joyed drawing out the girl's opinions on account of
their freshness, and was surprised at the quickness
with which she saw into people and estimated them
for what they were worth. She often wondered
how one so young had come to be so wise ; but
Julia had not attained her precocious development
without paying for it. There had been an event
in her life which had given painful impetus to her
perception of human failings, and had made her
sadly skeptical of sincerity and disinterested goodness.

She enjoyed Mrs. Davering's easy temperament,
appreciated her good nature, and found a charm
in her manner which many others had felt. She
never talked of herself to her new acquaintance,
and would have found little encouragement if she
had attempted to do so ; but there grew between
them a cordial companionship which answered many
of the purposes of friendship, and, on the whole, it
had worn well. In truth, Mrs. Davering took good
care that it should.

At last it appeared to the older lady that the
time had come for action. Julia Prescott was nineteen years old, she would soon be twenty, and Mrs.
Davering's son admired his mother's young friend
as much as even his mother could desire. Accordingly she intimated to Mr. Drayton that it was
quite time for his ward to enter society, and then
proceeded to suggest that she herself should give a
ball for the purpose of introducing her.

He consented very readily, glad of so pleasant a

plan for Julia's presentation to the world, and to be himself saved an effort to which he hardly felt equal.

Mrs. Davering was delighted. She flew off to break the news to Julia, who would be happy, she felt sure, at the prospect of becoming a young lady of fashion. Perhaps the girl did not meet her project with as much enthusiasm as its projector hoped for, but if so her opposition was passive, and was overcome by amusement when Mrs. Davering proceeded to explain that "coming out" with a ball was no longer a commonplace affair; for most of the young ladies who found their way into society nowadays were like the unfortunate "Maria" discussed in "Punch," whose attractions were thought only worthy of an afternoon tea.

CHAPTER IV.

"Oh, Mirth and Innocence! Oh, Milk and Water!
Ye happy mixtures of more happy days!"
BYRON.

THERE was a great deal to be said between the two girls on the evening of Edith Arnold's arrival, when they were safely closeted in Julia's room. Miss Prescott had to reassure her friend a hundred times as to the nature of her guardian's accident, which proved to be so much less serious than she feared at first.

"There is no danger now, the doctor tells me. Indeed, there never was any but in my imagination. But tell me how you fell in with Cecil Wilmott," she continued. "You must have thought it very strange that neither Mr. Drayton nor Philip were at the station to meet you."

"I expected Mr. Drayton," said Edith.

"I would not have had it happen so for the world!" cried Julia. "You know I telegraphed to-day that all was well, and urged your coming through to-morrow, and I had told Philip to be sure to meet you at the train to-morrow evening."

"Philip is a son of Mr. Drayton?" asked Edith doubtfully.

"Why, yes, of course. Have you never heard me speak of him?"

" Not that I can remember. I was thinking as
we drove along that I had never heard you speak
of any one but your guardian."

" That is odd," said Julia, giving a speculative
poke to the sea coals in the grate, in front of which
the two girls were sitting, while a tray containing
several empty plates before Miss Arnold showed
that she had done justice to her supper.

" Philip was away a great deal when we were
younger," resumed Julia after a short silence; "and
then he is rather a reserved fellow. I do not
know him very well, although he is as good to me
as if he were my brother. The family here consists of Mr. Drayton and Philip and myself, and
then there is Miss Ruthven, Mr. Drayton's aunt,
who has come lately to take care of us all ; but I
am afraid she is almost in despair of ever making
me respectable. You know I always was something of a Bohemian, Edith."

" I know that you never were very fond of obey-
ing the powers that be," said Edith, " but I should
not think you required any one to make you respectable. As for being *respectful*, that is another
matter."

" Oh, I try very hard to be respectful to Miss
Ruthven. I could never hold up my head again if
I were not, she is so dignified ; but I sometimes
sigh for the old days when I did just as I pleased,
without stopping to wonder what she would think
of me."

" She is a sort of Mrs. Grundy, then ? "

3

"To me she is, for I have a feeling that she does not approve of me ; but she has the highest respect for Mr. Drayton, persisting in looking up to him, although he is her own nephew, and she loves and admires Philip more than any of us: so you see *their* difficulty consists not in making her think well of them, but in so conducting themselves as to be worthy of the high esteem which they inspire. It is quite different with me."

"Why do you think she does not approve of you ? "

"It would be hard to say. It is as if she knew something which made her very hopeless of my ever proving to be worth much, one way or another; but she is the least obtrusive person in the world. She has come, of course at my guardian's request, to be a nominal duenna for me, but only calls it a visit, which she must always be persuaded to prolong or renew. She will have nothing to do with the housekeeping, which devolves upon me by common consent, and goes home in the spring to her old house in Germantown very gladly, I think. On the whole, I do not doubt that she is a necessary institution. Now, Edith, tell me something about yourself. How are your mother and sister ? Was it very hard for them to let you come away?"

"They are both quite well, thank you. Gertrude is always interested in her painting. Her last picture was much admired in the exhibition to which she sent it. I thought it was too lovely for anything, but then I am prejudiced."

" And is she painting another one ? "

" Yes, she is hard at work. I so wished to see her finish it ! "

" Then it was *you* who found it hard to come ? "

" Ah, no, I wanted to come, too. I was wild with delight, when your letter reached me, at the thought of seeing you and seeing something of the world, besides. I think it was rather hard for them to let me come away, but they will get over that."

" Which do you care for most," asked Julia, " your mother or your sister ? "

" What a strange question ! "

" Tell me," persisted Julia, in an eager tone.

" I cannot tell you," answered Edith, and then added very gravely, " I think perhaps it is my mother."

" How I envy you for having a mother ! " said Julia ; " and a sister, too, for that matter."

Edith looked up quickly as though surprised, but the words which she was about to utter were arrested by the expression of her friend's face. She knew that Julia's mother was not dead, although her daughter did not live with her ; she knew very little more, but she judiciously refrained from asking any questions.

In the pause which followed Julia rose, and began walking impatiently up and down the room.

" How handsome she is ! " thought Edith ; but her beauty might not have excited the admiration of an unprejudiced observer, although she formed a striking picture as she paced to and fro, in a long maroon-colored dressing-gown, with her black hair hanging loose over her shoulders.

Her eyes were large and dark and brilliant, ready to express anger or amusement most effectively; but they were not melting eyes, and rarely tender. They almost seemed to rebel against the softer emotions, as though their owner, young as she was, had had some hard experience of the world, and was determined to be even with it. Her mouth was large, also, with beautifully shaped lips, over which there played too often a touch of scorn, and her manner of moving was abrupt rather than graceful, but her friend watched her with a keen inward stirring of sympathy.

" You do not know what it is, Edith," said Julia presently, " to belong to no one ! "

Edith was silent for a moment.

" Have you not a happy home," she asked at last, " and all that money or the world can offer, to satisfy your tastes ? Can you not study what you please, and have you not traveled almost everywhere ? "

Julia smiled sadly. " Hardly ; but if I had," she said, stopping suddenly in front of Edith, " would you change your mother's love for all these things?"

" Of course not."

" And yet you are a sensible little body," said Julia, touching Edith's hair softly as she spoke, " and you have had to deny yourself some of these advantages, which leads one often more fully to appreciate them."

"That is quite true," assented Edith. "But, Julia, you have your guardian. I am sure he must love you, from all you have told me of him."

"Mr. Drayton? Ah, yes; no one knows what he has been to me, Edith!" she cried impetuously. "Without him, I could have killed myself more than once, I believe, for very misery and want of patience."

"It is strange," said Edith dreamily, "but your face reminded me, just then, of the way you looked when I first saw you."

"When you first saw me? Why, that was when we were children, at school."

"Yes."

"How can you remember what I looked like then?"

"It seems to me," said Edith, "as if I had forgotten nothing connected with our school-days. They are always coming back to me. I often wish that I could live them over again."

"Do you, really?" asked Julia wonderingly. "I suppose your life has been very quiet at New Rochelle."

"I suppose it has," said Edith simply.

"And do you actually look back with pleasure to the routine of school?" inquired Julia.

"Not so much to that as to the companionship," replied Edith. "The life which we led in common; our jokes and our scrapes, are all pleasant to recall."

"I remember the priory, too, of course," said

Julia. " What a picturesque old humbug it was,
with its make-believe Elizabethan gables and its
stately trees ! But I cannot remember the time
when you and I were not friends."

" We began as soon as we could," said Edith,
laughing, "for I had just come to school when I
first saw you. It chanced to be a rainy day, and
the girls were sitting about the room rather de-
jectedly, or romping in a noisy way, during the
hour for recess. I felt a little strange among them
all, and I noticed you standing with your back to
the others, looking out of the window. I can see
you now in my fancy as if it had been yesterday."

Julia laughed. " Well," she said, " you are welcome to the charming vision. I was an ugly child,
I know."

" Not as I remember you," cried Edith earnestly.
" You were slight and dark, with a broad, low forehead, from which the hair was drawn away and
braided in two long plaits which hung down your
back. I liked your looks, but you were quite alone,
and I fancied from something in the expression of
your face that you had been crying."

" What was the matter?" asked Julia carelessly. " I did not often cry."

" I know it, and I recollect thinking that perhaps you had had some bad news, for I noticed that
you held a letter crumpled up in your hand."

" I don't know who the letter could have been
from. There were very few people who took the
trouble to write to me, at that time."

"I did not know, either, and I should not have dared to ask you any questions, for there was an air about you which seemed to proclaim that you wished to be left to yourself; but you told me afterwards, when I knew you well, that you had had a letter to tell you that you must pass your summer holidays at the school, and I always fancied that this was the one."

"That was deep tragedy to a school-girl, and if so the letter was from my mother," said Julia, with a sudden frown. "She was going to stay with some friend, I believe, who did not like children," she added, in an explanatory tone. "Of course to spend one's holidays at the school seemed to you the most terrible of misfortunes," she continued, attempting to return to her former tone of banter.

"I thought it was very hard indeed," said Edith warmly, "and I remember some of the other girls told me that you had passed several vacations there."

"And so you took pity on me."

"What do you mean?"

"Why, have you forgotten how you and your sister came and insisted on my spending my holidays with you?"

"Oh, no, I have not; or what trouble we had to induce you to come to us. I think mamma had to get one of the teachers to write to your mother about it."

"Did she? I dare say. I suppose I did not like being an object of charity."

"Charity! O Julia, it was the happiest summer of my life!"

"Well, so it was of mine," said Julia. "At least it was the first happy summer I had ever known. I have not forgotten your pretty home, or how good you all were to me."

"Do you remember how we planned and hoped to be together at Christmas?" asked Edith; "and then" — she suddenly paused, and added, "you went away, I think about a month before the Christmas of that year."

"Yes," said Julia, quietly. "I went because my mother was married again."

Edith made no answer. The recollection had suddenly flashed on her of how the school-girls had whispered about mysteriously that Julia's mother had married an Italian, and perhaps she would go abroad to live.

"I was so much afraid that you might not come back," she said at last, shyly.

"But I came," returned Julia, in the same quiet tone.

"Yes, you came, but you were different."

"How different?"

"I do not know; you looked older, and you were very reserved and grave. I remember you told me quite coldly that for the future you were to live with your guardian, Mr. Drayton, and that was all you would say."

"Ah, yes," said Julia, with a touch of bitterness in her tone, which was evidently not intended for her friend. " I think I was not allowed after that to spend my vacations at the school."

"No, or with us, either, I am sorry to say," responded Edith, smiling.

After this some one looked at a watch, and declared that she had " had no idea that it was so late," and after a little more talking the two girls parted for the night.

CHAPTER V.

"A man he seems of cheerful yesterdays
And confident to-morrows."
                              WORDSWORTH.

CECIL WILMOTT was a young man of moderate
means, who had studied a profession by way of
having a nominal occupation, but was more often
found at his club than his office.

He was not handsome, but well made and easy
in his movements, of medium height, an excellent
dancer, a ready talker, with a genial manner and
a pleasant smile. He was a favorite in society,
where, although still young, he had been known for
some years, at the time when he befriended Miss
Arnold at the railway station.

He was at breakfast with his mother and sister
on the morning after this adventure, when a letter
was brought him which evidently caused him much
annoyance.

"What the dickens am I to do about it?" he
said to himself impatiently, as he perused the page
with clouded brow, and added aloud, "I don't see
what the fellow writes to me for!"

"What is the matter, Ceci?" asked his anxious
mother, from behind the tea-urn.

"Oh, nothing; a stupid trouble which a man
has got into about a dog," said Wilmott. "Give

me a good strong cup of coffee, so that I may forget about it."

" What does the man want of you?" asked his sister, curiously.

" He wants me to help him out of it," said Cecil, " so far as he can be helped. I suppose that I shall have to do it."

" I hope you will not get into any trouble yourself, dear," said his mother.

" Not on this occasion, I fancy. By the bye, Charlotte, I should like you to go some time to-day to call on a Miss Arnold, who is staying with Julia Prescott. She is a nice girl. I think you will like her."

" I did not know any one was staying with Julia," said Charlotte. " I was there only yesterday to inquire after uncle Algernon.".

" Oh, Miss Arnold was not there then," said her brother, carelessly. " She only arrived last evening. I chanced to be in the same train with her coming from New York."

" Is she pretty?" asked Miss Wilmott suspiciously.

" Yes, rather. She has a sweet, fair face and a pretty figure. How did that accident happen to my uncle? I thought he was too good a rider to be thrown."

" He was not thrown," answered Charlotte. " His horse fell with him."

" A distinction without a difference," said her brother, with an aggravating smile.

"Oh, no, Ceci. Charlotte is right. There is a great deal of difference," asserted Mrs. Wilmott.

"As for that," said Charlotte, "I have heard Philip say that the best riders are not unfrequently those who are thrown the oftenest."

"That sounds like him," cried Cecil; "but it is a proof of excellence which I should omit, and so far as I know it is one which Philip has not given himself."

"True, Ceci," said his mother, "and yet there is no doubt of Philip's horsemanship; but my brother, too, rides well. It was he who taught Philip, and the accident might have happened to any one."

"I am glad it did not happen to me. Why did he undertake to ride in this very slippery weather?" asked Cecil.

"Because Philip was away," explained Charlotte. "He had gone to Washington on business, and the groom told uncle Algernon that his horse was kicking everything to pieces, for want of exercise in his master's absence."

"I should have let him kick," said Cecil.

"I believe you would," replied Charlotte.

"I forgot to ask you, Ceci," said his mother, "how you left the Pembertons. Was William very much shaken? I fear he must be."

"Well, he could not be expected to be very jolly under the circumstances," answered Cecil, "but he bears up pretty well. They have persuaded him to drive out lately."

"And how is your cousin Emily? Redwood's death must have been a terrible shock to her."

"I thought she seemed very much as usual. She gave me a long rigmarole of a message to you, mother, about something or other, Heaven knows what it was."

"I hope you recollected my message to her about the breakfast caps, my dear?"

"I am afraid I forgot it. I am very bad about messages, you know. I gave her your love. Won't that do?"

"I suppose it will have to do, but I am very sorry about the caps, for she particularly wanted one. They are so appropriate for mourning."

"Oh, nonsense, mamma!" cried Charlotte impatiently. "As if cousin Emily could not get all the caps she wants in New York, without sending here for them!"

The truth was that Miss Emily Pemberton, who was known as a rather sour old maid, was no favorite with Charlotte; and as the uncle William referred to, who had just lost his only son, was worth untold wealth, she thought he could provide his daughter with caps in or out of mourning.

"She could not get this special kind of cap, my dear," said Mrs. Wilmott, with quiet persistency. "There is only one woman who makes them."

"Do not worry about it, mother, dear," said Cecil. "I will write to uncle Will, and confess my sins, and ask him to explain to her. that it was all my fault."

"My dear child, I did not mean that it was a fault at all," said his mother. "I was only thinking about the loss of time. If I write to Emily at once I have no doubt that it will all be right." She rose as she spoke, making some excuse to cross the room, and paused, in passing, beside Cecil's chair.

He put up his hand and patted hers as it rested on his shoulder for a moment, and Charlotte took up the newspaper and began to read. It was easy to see that Cecil was his mother's idol, and Charlotte was a little tired of seeing it, although she was fond of him, too, in her way.

Charlotte was not an ill-natured girl, but a very practical one, to whom all forms of sentiment were highly distasteful. She liked comfort, and handsome dresses, and plenty of money to spend; and it must be confessed that her life was a hard one in that she had none of these things, nor had she the fatal gift of beauty.

Mrs. Wilmott was a widow, who had been left in very moderate circumstances after her husband's death, and had always striven so successfully to put the best foot foremost that few persons, except Charlotte, knew of the existence of the holes in the other shoe.

Charlotte, who was always with her mother, who had no regular hours for leaving the house and returning to it, as Cecil had, and, above all, was not of the same careless, easy-going temperament as her brother, knew all about the holes, just how

many there were, and how large, and how difficult
to patch; and yet, in spite of the trouble she had
in assisting the process of patching, she was as
anxious as her mother to conceal her occupation
even from Cecil, and did, after a different fashion,
quite as much as Mrs. Wilmott to spoil her brother,
for whom the two women seemed to have formed a
plot to bear, or soften, all the troubles of life.

Cecil accepted their devotion very graciously.
He was not exactly selfish, for he was always doing
things for other people; but the things he did it
suited him to do, because he thought them good-
natured, and it was rather a hobby of his to be
good-natured. He was very self-centred, and from
this habit of mind was almost obtuse to much that
passed directly under his eyes.

He did not notice that Charlotte's hands were
red and roughened with the cold, because in the
room in which she slept, in the third story, there
was no fire, and the furnace heat was confined to
the story below, where he had a room, next his
mother's, on pretext that Mrs. Wilmott was timid
about possible house-breakers, while Charlotte, as
every one knew, was strong-minded, and not subject to imaginary fears. It never occurred to him
to suspect the reason why Mrs. Wilmott and Charlotte persistently refused broiled oysters, and breakfasted on cold mutton, although there certainly
were not more oysters than he could enjoy. And
yet, as he went down the street to his office, he
was meditating how to do a kindness which had

been asked of him by the man whose request had been so unwelcome as preferred in the letter which he had received at breakfast.

The profession to which Cecil had chosen to dedicate himself was that of the law. He shared an office with his cousin, Philip Drayton, as they had both been recently admitted to the bar, and it was to break some unpleasant tidings to Philip that Wilmott had been chosen by a madcap of a fellow whom they both knew, both laughed at, and both liked, although he was a constant trouble to his friends, and seldom did them any good in return for the trouble.

This was no other than Charley Hazzard, whose stepfather owned a country-seat near Mr. Drayton's, and who was, of course, intimate with all the family, being the sort of man whom one must know well or not know at all. He was, however, an old friend of Cecil's, and they had been in so many scrapes together that it was not unnatural that he should have called upon Wilmott to help him out of this one.

"I got a letter this morning from Charley Hazzard," said Cecil, plunging *in medias res* as soon as he had said good-morning to his cousin.

Philip looked up a little absently from a paper with which his attention was evidently still occupied.

"Yes?" he said interrogatively. "Oh, good-morning, Cecil. I want to have a talk with you about this deed which Mr. Turner has sent for."

" With all my heart," said Wilmott, " but I must tell you about Hazzard's letter first."

" Well, what about it? Where is Hazzard? "

" He is at Wymbleton. It seems that your old chum, Carey, has just come on from Boston to make him a visit, and he has taken him out to Wymbleton for a little shooting."

" Indeed," said Philip, with growing interest. " I must look up Carey. I knew he expected to be here some time this winter."

" Hazzard wrote to me about a dog of yours. Did you say that he might have one of your dogs at any time he wanted him, to shoot over? " asked Cecil.

" Yes. Larry, my red setter. What is the matter? Is the dog lost? "

" No, but his leg is broken."

" Where? "

" In the woods back of Heronsford."

" What has Hazzard done with him? "

" He left him under Murphy's care, at the house."

" When did it happen? "

" Early yesterday morning. He says he was run over by the dog-cart, and what he feels most badly about is that he had taken the cart without your permission."

" Let me see the letter."

" Charley seems to be very much cut up about it," said Wilmott, reluctantly. " He wants to know whether you think the dog had better be shot."

4

"Shot?" repeated Philip angrily. "What does he want to shoot him for? I should think it was enough to break his leg."

"You had better read the letter," said Wilmott, seeing that he could do nothing farther in the way of interposition.

Philip took the hasty scrawl, in which Mr. Hazzard had narrated the misfortune and the manner of it, as laconically as possible.

"He did not mean to do it, of course," said Cecil.

"When did Charley Hazzard ever mean to do anything that he did do, or mean not to do anything that he didn't?" asked Philip angrily. He got up as he spoke, and began hastily stuffing some papers into the drawers of his table.

"What are you going to do?" asked Cecil.

"I am going down to Heronsford."

"Oh, nonsense, Philip! It's not worth while to do that."

"I think so," said Philip, quietly. He looked at his watch. "I shall just have time to catch the eleven o'clock train," he continued. "Will you see Julia for me, and tell her that I shall probably not be back to dinner?"

"Certainly. I will see her and give her your message," assented Cecil, with alacrity.

Philip crossed the room, and took his coat from a corner closet. Suddenly he paused in the act of putting it on. "There is that deed, Wilmott. Can I depend on you to see that it is prepared?"

"Oh, depend on me to any extent," answered Cecil, installing himself in a comfortable leather arm-chair near the window, and lighting a fresh cigar.

"That deed must be sent off to-day," said Philip.

"All right, I will attend to it."

"There are one or two changes of boundaries to be made," pursued Philip. "I will show you what they are."

"Are not the changes indicated on the plot?" asked Cecil, with an impatient frown.

"Yes, but they are a little intricate," replied Philip, anxiously, taking the deed from the table as he spoke. "I had better point them out."

"You had better go," said Wilmott, "if you have any idea of catching your train."

"You are right," said Philip, looking again at his watch. "I have no time to lose." He replaced the paper on the table reluctantly, with a troubled glance at Cecil, who had taken up the "Times," and seemed lost in its depths. "Good-by, Wilmott."

"Good-by, old fellow," answered Cecil cheerfully from behind the newspaper, while a huge cloud of smoke passed over the top as he spoke. "I hope you will have good luck with your dog."

By and by, having read the city news, dear to the heart of all Philadelphians, and finished his cigar, he rose and stretched himself, and settled down with a very much bored expression to the task Philip had set, of copying the deed. Many were his impatient shrugs and vigorous ejaculations at the disagreeable necessity of going without his luncheon, in order to accomplish it and be able to leave the office early, as he was especially anxious to do ; but at last, at a little after four, he folded it up and addressed it to Theodore Turner, Esq., with an unusually virtuous sensation, and then proceeded to refresh himself with a glass of ale and some biscuit, as the hour was long passed when luncheon could be found in any sort of comfort at the " Lunch Club," of which Mr. Wilmott was a very popular member.

CHAPTER VI.

"Whate'er he did was done with so much ease,
In him alone, 't was natural to please."
DRYDEN.

AT luncheon the day after her arrival, Miss Arnold was introduced to Mr. Drayton, who made a special effort to appear, leaving his chamber for the first time since his accident.

He was a tall man, with slightly aquiline features, and dark hair not yet touched with gray. He rose from a chair near the fire when the girls entered, and as he came forward to greet her Edith stood still with astonishment. He was so much younger than she expected to see him that she looked about her for a moment, doubtful whether this were not the reserved Philip, of whom her friend had spoken; but a glance at Julia's face showed that it could be no other than her guardian.

Edith was impressed with the natural dignity of his bearing, perhaps all the more for the pleasant mixture of ease and courtesy in his manner. He appeared to her young, not only in years, but in a certain sparkle of vitality in his dark eyes and the unimpaired elasticity of his step; and she was provoked with herself that, in rallying from her surprise, she was overcome with an untimely fit of shyness.

She felt her stupidity so much that it was quite a relief when Julia presented her to an old lady, dressed in dark gray silk, with white muslin crossed over the bosom, and a tall white cap. This was Miss Ruthven.

" So she is a Quaker!" said Edith to herself, with some excitement, wondering how Julia had failed to mention so interesting a fact.

" I am very glad to meet thee, my child," said the old lady, extending a delicate, withered hand.

She was small and slight, but there was something stately in the way she held herself and a tone of authority in her voice, not naturally a soft one, which accounted to Edith for the awe with which Julia had spoken of her. Strange to say, her own spirit slightly revived. She felt on her mettle. It was evident that persons outside the family were not taken on trust by Miss Ruthven. They must prove their claim to her regard. Her small gray eyes met Edith's startled ones kindly, it is true, but questioningly. Perhaps she was impressed, as Wilmott had been, by her air of extreme inexperience.

" Didst thou not find it difficult, my dear, to travel so far alone ? " she asked.

" Not very difficult," said Edith, smiling and blushing a little as she spoke. " Not until I reached my journey's end."

" Ah, then it was difficult," said Mr. Drayton, —

"so difficult that you must have been inclined to
cry with Dr. Johnston, 'Would to God it were
impossible!' I am very regretful," he proceeded
more seriously, "of the accident which prevented
me· from meeting you at the station. It was a
mere tumble and a scratch or two, but Julia was
foolishly alarmed about it."

"You know that it was a great shock to you,"
cried Julia.

"Oh, yes, I was a little stunned; but it was not
worth while to send letters and telegrams all over
the country on that account."

"You may say that now, Mr. Drayton," said
Julia earnestly, "but if you could have seen yourself, when you were brought home on Tuesday, you
would have thought my anxiety very natural."

"Happily that is a gift the gods deny us," he
answered. "But I am really very sorry that by my
inconsiderate appearance on that occasion I should
have caused Miss Arnold real annoyance and
placed her in so painful a position."

"I am so glad you are willing to admit your
want of judgment in looking as if you had been
killed," said Julia, demurely. "I will confess in
return that I was unfortunate in writing to Edith
not to come, and taking it for granted that she had
received my letter."

Miss Ruthven looked at Miss Prescott, as she
made this speech, with dignified amazement, but
Mr. Drayton only answered by an amused smile.

"I do not know whether to consider myself fortunate or unfortunate that the letter did not reach me," said Edith. " I am certainly very glad to be here, although I was a little frightened last night."

" It would have been quite impossible for thee not to be frightened," said Miss Ruthven, who had seated herself with her knitting near the window, where Edith had noticed her when she first entered the room.

Miss Arnold fancied that there was a faint shade of approval in her tone, and perceived with satisfaction that she was engaged in the construction of a baby's sock, which made her seem less formidable.

" I hope I did not disturb you by my late arrival," she said, taking heart of grace and sitting down beside the old lady.

" Thy safe arrival would have given me pleasure," replied Miss Ruthven graciously, a placid smile momentarily relaxing the rather stern expression of her features, " but," she added, turning to Miss Prescott, in her more lofty manner, " I was not informed that thy friend had come, Julia, until I learned it from thy guardian a few moments ago, and Philip, who breakfasted with me, was equally ignorant."

" I am sorry," answered Julia carelessly, " that Edith and I felt a little too tired to get up for breakfast."

" We will begin to-morrow morning," said Mr. Drayton pleasantly. " I hope to be able to get up, too, if I meet with no new accident."

Glancing about her after they sat down to table, Miss Arnold noticed that the general aspect of the long dining-room was careless and cheerful. It was in the back-building, as is usual in old-fashioned Philadelphia houses, with another smaller room at one end, which opened out on a veranda. The walls were hung with small pictures, many of them water-colors. There were a few engravings and several plaques of brass or painted porcelain, to say nothing of a cabinet filled with fine old china; one or two easy-chairs, and some small tables covered with books and papers, stood about temptingly near the open fire.

Luncheon was usually an informal meal, and one of which Mr. Drayton himself rarely partook, but on this occasion the repast was served with some ceremony by an aged gray-headed negro, who kept his eye constantly fixed upon his master, ready to obey his slightest gesture, but in no way allowed this fact to interfere with the solemn routine of his duty. When it was over Mr. Drayton returned to his library, a large, lofty room, opening with folding doors into the drawing-room, which was also very large, with a high ceiling, and looked out on the square, in front of the house, through two long windows, between which hung an old-fashioned mirror with a curiously wrought frame, formed by a vine of gilded flowers and leaves.

The two girls betook themselves to the drawing-room, from whence they could see Mr. Drayton seated by the library fire gravely smoking his afternoon cigar. His face was a sad one in repose, and looked almost stern, seen thus in profile, while the smoke of the cigar curled up and faded in the dim vista overhead.

" Will you not play something for mè, Julia ? " asked her friend. " I have not heard you play for so long."

Julia nodded, and softly closed the two massive doors of dark mahogany which separated the rooms.

" Does not Mr. Drayton like music ? " inquired Edith.

" Oh, yes ; when he is well, he is very fond of hearing me play, especially in the evening, but he likes to be quiet when he is in the library, and, not feeling very strong, we might disturb him."

She opened the piano, and ran her fingers softly over the keys until her fancy took a definite shape, and then she wandered into one of Schumann's melodies, with such a clear, light touch that the music hardly went beyond the room they were in.

There was a young man at that moment on the front doorstep, who fancied that he heard it, but then he knew that it was a habit of Miss Prescott's to seek to draw out the lovely possibilities of the piano at about this hour of an afternoon.

Yes, the ladies were at home, the old butler said. " They is jist amusing of theirselves in the front parlor ; " and knowing that Mr. Wilmott was accustomed to the ways of the house, he left him to announce his own coming.

Cecil paused on the threshold of the drawing-

room, half in doubt how best to do so, and took in
the scene before him as an accompaniment to the
softly modulated music. Julia's was a grand piano,
and stood rather awkwardly across one corner of
the room, so that the player could sit with her back
to the window.

There was a sofa in the opposite corner, near the
other window, on which Miss Arnold had seated
herself. She was leaning back a little, her pretty
head resting against a dark purple velvet cushion,
which threw the fine outline of her features into
distinct relief, and made a perfect background for
her fair curly hair and delicate complexion. Her
eyes had grown dreamy as she listened.

The sun gleaming from beneath the heavy window curtain crossed her lap in a long shaft of light,
just where her hands were lying, bringing out the
faint red tints between the fingers, and making a
small sapphire set in a slender ring on one of them
shine like a star, while the rest of the room was
thrown by contrast into deeper shadow.

Presently Wilmott advanced a step or two.
Edith started at the sound, and rose in some confusion before she saw him. Julia only glanced towards him, and recognizing Cecil smiled and nodded
to her visitor, without lifting her hands from the
piano. Mr. Wilmott bowed in return, and then
crossed the room to Edith.

She had resumed her seat, and received him very
quietly, but with a slight restraint in her manner,
caused by her shyness. Perhaps he thought that

she did not show a sufficiently cordial remembrance of his kindness to her, or he may have been himself infected with her want of ease, for after talking a few moments he turned to the piano, where Julia was still playing, but had fallen upon a more stirring air, and was rendering it with much spirit.

"I have a message for you, Julia," he said, when she had ended, leaning over the piano and speaking low, so that Edith did not catch what he was saying, while Julia played on more softly, and listened with the lids of her eyes down, and his eyes followed hers, watching her small brown hands as they coquetted among the keys.

Edith Arnold felt a sudden sense of loneliness and exclusion. She knew it was not intentional, but for the moment she seemed to be entirely forgotten. She was prompted to leave the room, but checked herself with the fear that this would show what she was feeling, which she was particularly anxious not to do.

She gazed out of the window drearily enough, until her attention came really to be distracted by the frolics of some children who were playing in the square opposite.

"Who are you looking at, Edith?" asked Julia's voice at last, as the low conversation and the music ceased together.

Edith did not answer at first. She was standing shaking her head vigorously at some one outside the window. Prompted by curiosity, Miss Prescott left the piano and drew near the window.

" What in the world are you doing? " she cried.

" I am shaking my head at a naughty little boy in the street," said Edith excitedly. " He is threatening to snowball me, and I am afraid he will break the window."

" Where is the little boy? " asked Julia, coming behind her and looking over Edith's shoulder. Mr. Wilmott did not follow her. He took up a book which lay half open on the centre table, and began looking it carelessly over.

At this moment an old fashioned coupé stopped before the house, and the coachman, dismounting, opened the door for an old lady wrapped in a fur mantle.

" Oh, there is Miss Ruthven come back from her afternoon drive," said Julia. " I must go and help her; " and so saying hurried from the room, leaving Miss Arnold and Wilmott together. Cecil continued to turn over the pages of the book he had taken up. Edith remained at the window.

The little boy who had attracted her attention had come across from the square with a small painted wheelbarrow filled with snowballs, and, catching sight of her wistful face, had looked up with a mischievous smile, then, growing bolder, threatened to pelt her; but having now been diverted by two fat little girls walking sedately with their nurse, he had begun to snowball them most unmercifully. Edith disapproved very much of the want of gallantry of this proceeding, but she felt powerless to interfere.

There was a silence after Julia went away, which lasted for some moments. Then Cecil Wilmott closed the book, and sauntered over to where Edith was standing.

"Is that your wonderful little boy?" he asked, seeing that she was still watching an active little fellow in knickerbockers and bright red stockings, who was making off in the direction of the square, apparently bent on replenishing his wasted ammunition.

"He is a very bad little boy," said Edith decidedly.

"I am afraid you are a stern moralist, Miss Arnold."

"I don't know about that," answered Edith, smiling. "I see the faults of people I do not like, very plainly."

"You can hardly have formed a rooted dislike, in this case, to the culprit."

"No, I confess that he is interesting, though wicked."

"Although he threatened to snowball you?"

"I thought him a good little boy until then."

Cecil laughed. "I see you are a bad enemy; are you an equally good friend?"

"I think I am a fairly good friend," said Edith. "Are you?" They sat down on the sofa as she spoke.

"To be frank with you, I am not. I am a very worthless sort of fellow. I always like people either too much or too little."

" Oh ! "

" I see you have been reading ' Ayala's Angel,' Miss Arnold. Is not that your book, on the table, which I was looking over ? "

" It is. How did you know it ? "

" I fancied it was the same you were reading yesterday in the railway train. Are you fond of Trollope ? "

" Very."

" And which do you like best, Ayala or the Angel ? "

" I like Ayala the best."

" Do you not like the Angel ? "

" I think Ayala was too good to him."

" Too good ! How ? In refusing him twice before she accepted him, or in accepting him at all?"

" That was very kind of her, of course," said Edith, smiling ; "but I meant *after* she had accepted him. I do not see why, because the man was ugly, she should have been continually telling him that she adored him."

" Oh ! " said Wilmott, and as his eyes met hers he smiled a smile of the most intense amusement.

Edith blushed hotly and became dumb. The truth was that she had happened to look at Mr. Wilmott in pronouncing the word *ugly*, and it suddenly occurred to her that he was anything but handsome. At no time during their varied experiences of the evening before had she seen him except in a faint light ; but now, as he sat at the other end of the sofa, that from the window fell full upon him, and she saw that his complexion was sallow, his eyes were light and small, and his features irregular.

He certainly was ugly, and he evidently knew it, for his face conveyed the keenest and most cordial enjoyment of her discomfiture ; yet, though in no mood to be charitable, justice compelled her to acknowledge a certain charm in his ugliness. His eyes were not wanting in life and intelligence. His hair, although a dull brown, approaching too nearly the color of his skin, curled in a jaunty sort of way, and in spite of his mouth being large, she thought it attractive on account of the unconscious play of expression of which it was capable, while when it opened it disclosed a row of very white teeth. His smile at this very moment was delightful, although the joke was at his own expense.

" You naturally think that an ugly man should be continually adoring other people," said Cecil.

" I have never thought much about them," she answered dryly.

" Perhaps you never met one before," said Wilmott. He was still so full of mischief that she did not know what he might say next, and was heartily glad that Julia's return to the room at this moment gave a new turn to the conversation.

" What are you two persons laughing about ? " she asked curiously.

" We cannot possibly tell you," said Cecil gravely. " I have bound Miss Arnold to secrecy."

" Then it is a plot ? "

" A very dangerous plot."

CHAPTER VII.

. . . " Men only disagree
Of creatures rational."
MILTON.

PERHAPS there is nothing harder to account for than degrees of intimacy between men. They may be united in the closest ties of relationship or interest, they may be sincerely and strongly attached to one another, they may live together for years under the same roof, and yet not be friends.

The reserve which seems to hedge them round and keep them estranged, in spite of an effort on both sides to draw together, appears often quite mysterious, for one honest man ought to be able to understand another, however different. But searching for the cause, one usually comes upon the unfortunate woman, who has borne the sins of man since the time of the creation. She may be very far removed, this woman, but she is generally in the case, although neither man may be conscious of her influence.

As Mr. Drayton and his son sat talking and sipping their sherry, after dinner, on the day following that of Philip's visit to Heronsford, an observer would have been impressed with the consideration shown by each towards the other; with

5

the great respect of the son for the father, and
the ready acquiescence of the father in all the son's
practical suggestions, although not in those opinions which were based upon theory, for in these
they differed widely, but even these were treated
with forbearance.

Mr. Drayton seemed to wish to be most kind,
and Philip most responsive, and yet the very care
which both took showed the absence of real ease or
warmth of sympathy. In truth, in a certain practical habit of mind, a love of thoroughness and
method, an absence of imagination, Philip resem-
bled his mother too much ever to be entirely congenial to his father, and, unfortunately, Mr. Drayton knew it.

Philip did not. He was, naturally, unaware of
the fact that his mother, who had died when he
was quite a child, had not proved companionable
to his father. This minor misery had been lost
sight of even by those who suspected it, and temporarily by Mr. Drayton himself, in the greater
misfortune of her early death. Her husband had
had a sincere affection for her, and in the midst of
the desolation of the first few years of widowhood
he quite forgot the many lonely hours, the misun-
derstandings, the estrangement, which had grown
between them since their marriage, and remembered his wife only as the handsome, winning girl
whom he had first met when on a journey among
the mountains of New England. He had sought
them for rest and change of air after hard work in

a hot city. In his own estimation he was no longer
a young man even then, for although barely twenty-
three he had outlived what he believed to be the
one passion of his life, having given his early devotion to a very beautiful, very heartless woman,
who had played with it most unmercifully. He did
not think himself likely to fall in love again, nor
could what took place between him and Miss Lyman be described as so precipitate a proceeding.
They were thrown together by circumstances, and
they drifted into a friendship, enhanced by the
bracing air and the pleasant companionship about
them. They talked together, and although their
talk was almost entirely of what they were doing
and seeing, of people and things, it was a refreshment to him from its very simplicity, because he
was weary of his own thoughts. In an evil moment he was prompted to take the fatal step which
bound them both; for it may be seen that such
an acquaintance was not thorough enough to decide
their destiny, and yet on the engagement which
grew from it they were warmly congratulated by
mutual friends.

Miss Lyman belonged to an excellent Boston
family. Her father was wealthy, and made a liberal settlement on her.

Algernon Drayton bore a name which had stood
high in the legal profession for generations, and he
had not failed to do it honor. In Philadelphia,
where this kind of reputation was much valued, he
was therefore highly esteemed, and as he had in-

herited and acquired some means he was able to support his position in a manner which seemed most satisfactory to his bride. But she was unfortunate in bringing some prejudices with her from her native city, and in exciting others in his.

Mrs. Drayton thus failed to become popular. It was said of her that she dressed badly and was conceited; that she had an undue estimation of her own importance, and lacked the consideration for others required by courtesy; that she was over-confident in herself, and had too little confidence in her neighbors. In short, her every fault was noted, while her virtues were unsung; and although Mr. Drayton never heard what was said, he knew that his wife was not liked, and it pained him for her sake, even while he suffered himself from her want of adaptability.

But these troubles were long past. Mr. Drayton had been a widower now for eighteen years. His wife had died of diphtheria after a few days' illness, when Philip was only five years old, and her sudden death had silenced all evil tongues.

It had, in truth, been remembered that she was very good-tempered; that she was loyal to her friends; that she was an excellent housekeeper, and a most energetic member of such philanthropic societies as succeeded in engaging her interest. It was, perhaps, never understood how, coming from Boston, she failed to be intellectual, but in this respect she was set down as one of the exceptions that proved the rule.

Philip only remembered his mother as a shadowy presence in his childhood, more felt than seen, but it is quite certain that he missed her. What motherless child does not?

He was a sturdy little chap, and his father was very fond of him in an abstract way, but his fondness was not quite personal in the sense that he felt more tenderly towards the boy when they were separated than when they were together. For the rest, Algernon Drayton's heart was an exquisitely sensitive piece of mechanism, which its owner had long given up the hope of understanding; but its intricate action was not impeded by this, and although he did not let it govern him he did not attempt to govern it. The fact of Philip's existence, as his son and heir, was a constant stay and comfort, of which he was quite conscious, but the fact was all sufficient. He did not require his son's presence, or depend on his society, nor had he ever made much attempt at parental guidance of his early thoughts and aspirations, except such moral suasion as might result from the example which he himself set of an upright, honorable career.

Philip admired his father all the more, perhaps, for the difference between them. He considered him quite unprejudicedly the cleverest man he had ever known, and it gave him sincere pleasure to hear him talk, especially when there were others present to lead him to do so; for Philip was perfectly aware that he himself had not that happy faculty.

In the matter of self-confidence Philip certainly
did not resemble his mother. He thought himself,
indeed, rather a stupid fellow. He knew he could
learn things, if he set himself to do so, but that
was because he had a strong will and great powers
of application.

He felt quite sure that he would never originate
anything, and yet in spite of his keen admiration
for his father he held, as has been said, opinions
which were widely different. He did not consider
himself responsible for these opinions. They seemed
to him necessities, because they were the result of
careful reasoning, and could be logically explained
whenever there was time enough to explain them.

Mr. Drayton had never found time to listen to
the explanation. He thought Philip's opinions as
uninteresting, from an intellectual point of view, as
poor Philip himself, but others who knew him were
more appreciative. His judgment was much valued
by other men, and his thoroughness and consis-
tency gained their respect as much as his manli-
ness, which was very pleasantly prominent in all
he did and left undone.

Such were the father and son. Their talk, after
the ladies had left them, had been of a famous case
which had at one time occupied the attention of
the good citizens of their town. It was nearly forgotten by the public now, but some chance allu-
sion had brought it up, and the younger and the
older lawyer had instinctively taken sides against
each other.

They both remembered the case quite well, for it was one in which the power of the law had been enlisted against the prerogative of the church.

A certain church — or rather the bells of a certain church — had been indicted as a nuisance, and half the town was filled with indignation, while the other half sympathized with the indicters, the unfortunate residents within too close proximity to the chimes, of which the reiterated ringing was, as they averred, so distressing to their nerves and trying to their tempers that they found neither peace by day nor sleep by night.

Mr. Drayton had always felt a sincere veneration for the Church, and was rather a rare instance of a man the breadth of whose views made him more firm on those points where he had formed conclusions. Whether there might not be a form of worship evolved for the acceptance of future generations, which should be less trammeled with objections to the thinking mind than that of the Church of England, he was not prepared to say, but for the present he accepted it, and was jealous of every fragment of traditionary dignity which belonged to it.

He cited the many instances of persistently ringing bells in the cathedral towns of England, and declared that if it had been the discordant whistle of locomotives emanating from some engine depot, protected by one of the great railway companies, instead of the tintinnabulation of church bells, which the rebellious neighborhood had had to complain of, they would have found little sympathy for their outcry, and no redress for their injury.

Philip was not so stout a Churchman as his father, but it was on no theory of disrespect to the Church, as he strove to explain, only on that of personal liberty, that he maintained the right of the outraged neighbors to their protest. He said that the court might grant their suit or not, as it saw fit, but there was no reason why they should submit in silence to hourly discomfort and annoyance. They certainly had a right to object, and their objections should be listened to.

" On the same ground," answered his father, " all the servants in a household might indict their mistress' baby for a nuisance, because it cried at night."

" Oh, no," returned Philip, " for their complaining of it would not make it cease to cry."

" But they would have a right to protest," said Mr. Drayton sarcastically. " Should they bear such inconvenience in silence? "

" The servants could leave the situation if they did not like the noise," replied Philip gravely.

" That is exactly what the inhabitants of the houses near the church might have done, if they were seriously inconvenienced," said his father.

"They would be doubly injured in that case," answered Philip, " for the value of their property would be depreciated if they left for such a cause."

" My dear fellow, the servants' characters would go with them, I assure you, if they left for such a

cause. The mother of the baby would see to that.
Do you suppose she would not tell every one that
she believed their minds were deranged and they
had no hearts? "

" Ah! I see, sir, that you are joking."

It was quite natural to Mr. Drayton to give a
humorous turn to an argument which seemed in
danger of becoming tedious, but Philip always continued to argue seriously after his father had ceased
to do so, and felt rather discomfited when he discovered that he had been wasting his force.

It was no deliberate device on the part of Mr.
Drayton. He did not intend to end the discussion, only to make it more amusing, and expected
Philip to catch the spirit of fun as he himself
would have done, but Philip was too intensely in
earnest. His father's lightness of tone annoyed
him, not for his own sake, but for the sake of the
subject, in which for the time being he had become
absorbed ; and when Mr. Drayton found that they
were thus at cross-purposes, he would grow very
weary. He often was weary in Philip's society.

" You must not misunderstand me, my dear boy,"
he said now, in a tone which itself deprecated any
intention of wounding his son's feelings ; but the
spirit of mischief got the better of him, and he
added, " The truth is that I was not engaged in
the case, and that accounts entirely for my non-ap-
proval of the indictment."

" Not to me, sir," rejoined Philip stoutly, " or
to any one who knows you."

CHAPTER VIII.

" For, boy, however we do praise ourselves,
Our fancies are more giddy and unfirm,
More longing, wavering, sooner lost and won,
Than women's are."

SHAKESPEARE.

As the next day was very fine, with a touch of that softness in the air too apt to degenerate into dampness in the climate of the Quaker City, a drive was planned to show Miss Arnold the Park.

Mr. Drayton, entering the library, found all the party assembled except Miss Ruthven. Philip had returned early from his office, and brought with him his friend Dr. Carey, of Boston, who was standing on the hearth-rug talking to Julia. She looked full of fun and spirit and was ready equipped for her drive.

" Philip said that he thought of taking Miss Arnold to the Park," said Dr. Carey, " but I have not the faintest idea who Miss Arnold is."

" She happens to be my most intimate friend, but for an introduction I must refer you to Philip, who is talking to her in the other room," replied Julia. " Are you sure you are warm enough, Mr. Drayton?" she asked, turning to her guardian.

" I am sure I am a great deal too warm, which I suppose is as it should be," he answered resignedly.

" And you know you promised to go in the close carriage," said Julia. " It is a great deal safer, and I am going with you."

" I am sure it will not be at all safe for Miss Ruthven to drive in an open carriage at this season of the year," remarked Dr. Carey gravely. " You had better let her take your place with Mr. Drayton, and come in the T cart with us."

Julia smiled, but shook her head. " I am afraid you need Miss Ruthven to keep you in order."

" I wish you would come with us," said Dr. Carey.

" So she will," said Mr. Drayton. " She only wants to be persuaded a little."

" No, I want to enjoy my drive."

" Perhaps I am the person who would be unfortunate enough to interfere with your enjoyment," returned Dr. Carey stiffly.

" How can you, if I am not in the same carriage with you ? "

" If I were you, Carey, I should pay her back by being exceedingly disagreeable all the afternoon," said Mr. Drayton.

" It may not be easy for Dr. Carey to make himself disagreeable," remarked Julia.

Mr. Drayton began to laugh.

" If that is a hit at me," he said, " I think it is time this party were in motion. Where is Philip ? Why do not you young people get off ? "

" Shall I look up Philip ? " suggested Dr. Carey. " I believe he is in the drawing-room."

"Edith is there, too," said Julia. "They will be ready to start in a moment. They are only waiting for Miss Ruthven."

"Pray who do you consider young people, besides Philip's great-aunt, my dear?"

"I think you are rather inclined to be juvenile," replied Julia; and then they both laughed, as they often did, at nothing.

"Seriously," said Mr. Drayton, "I do not intend to let you go with me, so you may make up your mind to be stupid."

"Who are you going to take?" asked Julia, in a tone of genuine disappointment.

"Suppose that I prefer Miss Arnold's company?"

"But you don't."

"I may prefer it, but I am too generous to monopolize her. I shall ask aunt Margaretta to go with me. That will be next best."

"Ah! I see what you mean," said Julia, linking her arm lovingly through his, "but I would really rather go with you."

"Stupid child!" cried Mr. Drayton. "It is kinder that you should go with your friend," he added more gravely. "She will enjoy her drive more, and it is better for you to be with companions of your own age." He stooped as he spoke, and kissed her gently on the forehead.

This little scene was not noticed by Dr. Carey, who was talking to Edith Arnold in the drawing-room, between which and the library the folding doors were open. Edith had found her old place by the front window, for everything that happened was a pleasure to her just now, from its novelty, and she was brimful of expectancy at the mere prospect of the drive. The carriage, for which she was looking with some eagerness, had not yet appeared, and Philip had gone to inquire into the cause of the delay.

Meanwhile, Lawrence Carey had been introduced to her, and was making himself amiably stupid, as we all feel it our duty to do on such occasions. He was struck, as Cecil Wilmott had been, with the fact that she was very pretty.

"Is this your first visit to Philadelphia, Miss Arnold?" he asked.

"Yes," said Edith. "It is my first, but I hope it may not be my last. I think it such a delightful place!"

"You must find it quiet, though, after New York," Dr. Carey remarked.

Edith smiled to herself. Philip Drayton had introduced her to his friend as "Miss Arnold, from New York."

"I do find it quiet," she answered wickedly, "but perhaps I enjoy it all the more for that." She wanted to hear what he would say next.

"You like the contrast," rejoined Dr. Carey sympathetically. "I have heard that there is, a great deal going on in New York this winter."

Edith laughed outright. It was not much of a joke, but it seemed to her infinitely funny that the visit to Philadelphia, which was by far the greatest event of her hitherto uneventful life, should be looked on in this light.

"Yes, I like the contrast," she said, with a complacent little nod of her head.

Just then Miss Ruthven appeared, followed by Philip, and the party began to move. Mr. Drayton helped his aunt into the coupé first, and then asked her to wait until he had seen the other ladies seated in the open carriage.

"Where shall Edith sit?" asked Miss Prescott.

"I think she will have the best view in front," said Mr. Drayton.

"Will you not sit beside me, Miss Arnold?" asked Philip, who was drawing on a pair of dog-skin gloves, and was evidently to drive.

"I will, with pleasure," she answered, smiling. It seemed to her that any seat in such a pretty carriage would be delightful. She looked at Philip as she answered. They had just stepped out upon the pavement, and the glow of the afternoon sunshine fell warmly upon his face, which was full of strength and energy.

His hair was straight hair, thick and dark; his eyes gray. His skin seemed to have been browned by exposure. His nose and mouth were well shaped, and the more strongly marked for the absence of beard, whiskers, or mustache. He returned her glance in an open, manly way which prejudiced Edith in his favor.

"Then, Julia, you must get in first," said Mr.

Drayton, helping her into the back seat; and when
the others were ready Dr. Carey took the seat beside her with evident satisfaction. The horses were
so impatient that the groom could scarcely hold
them, but once off they became quite amenable to
control, evidently recognizing Philip's hand as that
of their master. In spite of the spirited horses,
however, the sunshine, and the pleasant companionship, Miss Arnold was not very favorably impressed with the drive until they entered the pre-
cincts of the Park, and rounded the hill by ven-
erable Fairmont, when she was delighted with the
varied, animated scene which opened out before
her. They were not long in gaining a road beside
the river, on which they bowled along among a
crowd of other dashing vehicles, past trees and
pretty boat-houses, to where their way was cut for
them out of a solid mass of rock, which formed a
rugged archway overhead, and the road curved
close to the water's edge. Here Philip stopped
for a moment that they might enjoy the view of
the blue river winding away in the distance, with a
high wooded bank seen all in shadow opposite, and
a pale winter sky above flecked with cirrous clouds.

"Oh, how charming this is!" cried Edith. "The
natural scenery is so beautiful! Where did you
get such a wonderful park?"

"Do you really like it?" asked Philip.

"Of course I like it. Is the other side of the
river as beautiful as this?" she asked.

"Not quite," he answered. "It is different, but

many of the prettiest parts on either side cannot be seen from the carriage road. One can only approach them through the bridle paths. I know them well, I ride so often."

"Central Park is a nice place for riding," said Dr. Carey. "Are you fond of riding, Miss Arnold?"

"Very fond."

"Then you will perhaps like to ride with me some day, if we can find you a good horse?" asked Philip.

"I should, indeed!" cried Edith. "I think it the most delightful thing in the world to ride a spirited horse through a pretty country, — although I have never ridden in Central Park," she added, with a glance at Dr. Carey.

"It is very pleasant to ask you to do anything," said Philip.

"Why?"

"You respond so heartily."

"That is because you ask me to do such pleasant things."

"I can see that you think them pleasant," he admitted. "It is the sincerity of your manner which is so satisfactory. I think you would say just as frankly that you did not like a thing, if one asked you to do what was not to your taste."

"But it would not be polite to express myself quite so strongly in that case, would it?"

"I don't know," said Philip. "I am not much of a judge of politeness. I hate it."

" What ! "

" I suppose that shocks you very much."

" No, it surprises me. Do you not like to be treated with civility ? "

" Of course, but that is another thing. I hate people to be full of airs and compliments, or else so stuck up and formal that there is no knowing what they really think about anything."

Edith laughed. " I dislike that kind of person, too," she admitted ; " but as for being full of airs and compliments, I do not know that I object to them so much."

" Do you mean that you like people who flatter you ? " asked Philip, in a grieved tone.

" Oh, no," she answered, blushing. "Flattery is different, and there are all sorts of ways of complimenting, too, I suppose ; but a compliment may be given in an honest manner, which makes it pleasant to receive, I think."

Philip looked thoughtful.

" It had not occurred to me to make that distinction, but I do not know but that you may be right," he said.

" It is rather windy here, Philip," remarked Julia, drawing her fur-lined cloak more closely about her.

" It is a trifle bleak," said Lawrence Carey. " Those fellows, by the bye, must be having a rather chilly time of it in that wherry." He indicated, as he spoke, two oarsmen, with bare arms and bodies stripped to the waist save for their boating-shirts, who were pulling rapidly by, with long, swift strokes.

" They are working so hard," replied Philip. " they probably scarcely feel the cold. By Jove ! " he exclaimed presently, " do you see who the stroke is ? "

" To be sure ! " cried Dr. Carey. " It is Charley Hazzard ! "

Edith looked after the boat, and caught an indistinct impression of a handsome head, with dark curly hair closely clipped and rather a massive forehead. Both the rowers had gained a brilliant color from the exercise. She had somehow managed to contract a dislike of what she heard about Mr. Hazzard, and this view of him surprised her. It was different from what she expected, although what she did expect it would have been difficult to say.

" What a mad fellow he is ! " said Philip.

" He is a very good fellow," said Miss Prescott.

" Oh ! I forgot that you always take up the cudgels for him," returned Philip.

" I never take them up first," rejoined the young lady.

" I think you do. I had no idea of attacking him."

" Nor I of defending him. I was simply doing him justice."

" So was I ! " said Philip, at which Edith laughed, and the laugh was so contagious that Julia joined in spite of herself. They were now climbing a hill, partly covered by a wood. The carriage passed between tall trees, the branches of which nearly met overhead, and emerged from thence upon a broad level road at the top. As it did so they came in sight of the coupé, which had distanced them while they enjoyed the view, like the tortoise in his race with the hare.

"I hope it will not tire your father, Philip," said Julia seriously.

"I believe you would really rather have gone in the other carriage," said Dr. Carey.

"It seems hard for you to believe that," answered Miss Prescott serenely.

At which Dr. Carey was mute with surprise. He glanced uneasily at his companion to see whether she really intended to be rude, and perceived that she was smiling the most amiable of smiles.

"I hope you brought your flute with you, Dr. Carey," she remarked presently.

"My flute?" he repeated.

"Yes. I remember how beautifully you played it on that Class Day evening which I spent in Philip's room. Do you not recollect? Mrs. Davering went with me on to Class Day, and we took tea with you, and you and Philip showed us some wonderful programmes of the Hasty Pudding, and photographs of some of the fellows dressed as heroines for the different plays."

"Certainly I recollect," answered Dr. Carey. "It was a very pleasant evening — for us; but I do not remember playing on the flute."

"Oh, yes, you did," said Julia. "Philip insisted upon it, and Mrs. Davering and I sat in one of those deep, deliciously cushioned window-seats and listened, and it was a moonlight night. Surely you have not forgotten about the flute?"

"Ah, no; I remember now," said Lawrence Carey, blushing a little at the recollection. "I believe I did play for you. It was in old Holworthy, before we changed our room."

"But do you never play on the flute now?"

"No, never. I do not know what has become of my flute."

"I should think you would sometimes wish yourself back at college," said Miss Prescott. "Life there seemed so happy."

"Most men like it," he answered; "but I think I am rather glad that it is over. I can hardly imagine wanting to live again any part of my life. It is such an unreasonable thing to wish!"

"So it is," assented Julia; "but do you never want anything which is unreasonable?"

"I should be quite content," replied Dr. Carey, "if I could have all the things which I have a reasonable right to expect."

"I think that you are very fortunate. The mere fact that I have a reasonable right to expect a thing often prevents me from caring about it."

"But you would be very sorry not to have it, for all that," said Lawrence Carey.

"Do you think that I should? I am not certain. I am not very tenacious of my rights."

" Few women are."

" I thought that it was very much the fashion in Boston for women to insist upon their rights," said Julia.

" Not as much as it is supposed elsewhere," replied Dr. Carey, " among the women one meets in society; but granting that they are more anxious to make good their claims than they once were, it is the rights of women in general, not any particular woman's rights, which they advocate. Individually they will almost all of them allow themselves, if you will pardon the coarseness of the expression, to be bullied to any extent."

" It is rather a rough use of words," said Julia, " and I for one should not allow myself to be bullied. That is a very different thing from yielding one's rights."

" You lose them, all the same."

" Ah, yes, but in one case you keep your self-respect."

" I prefer to keep both."

" If you are so determined to have your due," said Miss Prescott, " it would be very awkward to make a mistake about it."

" How do you mean ? What kind of a mistake could one make ? " asked Dr. Carey blandly.

" Might it not be possible to fancy it a little larger than it was ? " she responded significantly.

" Ah ! in that case," said Lawrence Carey coolly, " one would be obliged to make good one's claim."

" How could that be done without the where-
withal ? "

" If one had claimed more than one deserved,"
said Carey, " one could simply set to work to deserve what one had claimed."

" Ah! I see," cried Julia ; " and if one failed ? ".

" I can only refer you to Lady Macbeth for
comfort in that contingency."

" But I am not talking of myself," said Julia,
with a light laugh. " I would always rather claim
less than more than my desert, for I should not
enjoy making good my claim, as you call it. My
experience of that process is that it generally involves the sacrifice of the rights of some one else,
as in the case of Macbeth for instance."

" He did deserve what he claimed, only chance
deprived him of it," said Dr. Carey ; " but the stakes
are not so high as his were, usually. Unless for a
kingdom it would hardly pay to commit murder."

" Who talks of committing murder ? " inquired
Philip.

" Who, indeed ? " asked Julia. " Dr. Carey and
I are just resolving to resist the temptation."

Every one laughed, and the conversation became
general.

They had made the round of the Park, and were
returning from their drive a little early by the
same road, Edith having begged particularly to
have another glimpse of the river ; when she noticed a figure a long way off which she fancied
that she recognized, and on nearer view it proved

to be Cecil Wilmott, walking towards them on the
foot-path beside the road.

" I hoped I should meet you," he said, as Philip
drew up in response to an imperative sign to stop
and parley. " I found Charley Hazzard, at the
boat-house below here, about half an hour ago, with
a sprained ankle. He slipped and twisted it as he
was helping Freeman to carry up the boat they had
been rowing in, and is in a great deal of pain. I
heard you were out driving, and that Dr. Carey
was with you, so I took the chance of intercepting him, as Hazzard is sorely in need of his professional aid."

" Thank you, Wilmott, for coming for me," said
Dr. Carey gravely. " I almost wish I had stayed
with Hazzard," he added half to himself, as he
jumped out of the carriage.

" It is too bad about Charley," said Philip, " but
I don't see how you could have prevented the accident, although one always feels as if he ought to
have some one with him to look after him. We are
sorry to lose your company, old fellow."

" I am sorry, too, but will stay, of course, and
help to get Charley safely home."

At this moment Mr. Freeman drove up with a
cab which he had gone to summon for his disabled
comrade, and Philip turning to Cecil suggested that
he should take Dr. Carey's seat in the carriage, so
that they were once more off, at a rapid rate.

" Is Miss Arnold to make you a long visit? "
Cecil asked of Julia presently, in a low voice.

"I hope so.   Why?"

"I hope so, too."

"I am glad you like her," said Julia. "I do
not see myself how any one can help it, but then
women and men do not always have the same
favorites."

"My sister was sorry not to see her yesterday."

"I was very sorry to miss Charlotte; and that
reminds me that Mr. Drayton wants you both to
dine with us to-morrow.   I sent a note to Charlotte
this morning."

"So she told me."

"I hope you have no other engagement?"

"I think not.   Not if you are sure you want me.
If I come, will you put me beside Miss Arnold?"

"Of course I will, if you would like it," said
Julia, kindly.

They were passing a colossal bronze image of
President Lincoln in a sitting attitude, which bore
an unfortunate resemblance to that of a negro min-
strel.   He looked very solemnly grotesque in the
gathering twilight, with his long plume pen extended above their heads like a warning finger.

Here the river road was crossed by another,
that turned inward and passed round a hill which
Philip was carefully explaining to Miss Arnold
had once comprised the limits of the Park, and
they thus came in sight of two persons riding rapidly along the converging road, to meet them.   The
lady, who was a little in advance of her cavalier,
was evidently very lively and unmistakably hand-

some. She had a brilliant complexion, flashing dark eyes, and a beautifully rounded figure.

As the carriage came nearer she perceived its inmates, and began to smile, displaying two lovely dimples, and bestowing a mischievous little nod on Cecil Wilmott as she passed.

"Oh! who is that?" cried Edith, turning impulsively to Cecil, who blushed a little as he answered,

"That is Mrs. Percy."

"An old flame of yours, Wilmott, is she not?" asked Philip.

"Ah, yes," said Cecil indifferently, "very old. I knew her before she was married, and now she is a widow."

"How pretty she is!" exclaimed Edith. "She does not seem very sad for a widow."

CHAPTER IX.

"One science only will one genius fit;
So vast is art, so narrow human wit."
                                    POPE.

It chanced that Miss Arnold, happening to be dressed for dinner, on the following Friday, a little before dinner-time, found her way to the library, which was usually unoccupied at this hour, intending to await Julia's appearance before venturing to the drawing-room. On opening the door, however, she was startled to find Mr. Drayton and Philip in close conversation. She was about to close it hastily and withdraw, when Mr. Drayton, catching sight of her, called out to her to enter.

"Come in, my dear, I beg of you," he said, with a parental air, which pleased her, as it seemed to claim her as belonging to the household.

"I am afraid I shall disturb you," she answered, still hesitating.

"Not at all," replied Mr. Drayton, drawing a chair in front of the fire for her as he spoke. "Philip was telling me about some improvements which he is ordering at Heronsford, — that was all; and I was simply wasting the time in which I should be dressing for dinner."

"I beg your pardon, sir, for delaying you," said Philip quickly.

"I hardly know whether to pardon you or not," answered his father, laying his hand affectionately on his shoulder. "A young fellow like you, who travels home before me as though walking for a wager, puts on his dress-coat in no time, and meets me as I enter my house, stupid and tired, with a long and interesting letter from a carpenter and builder, every detail of which he is eager to sift. Do you think that such an offense as that should be permitted or forgiven, Miss Arnold, on the first day of my return to the duties of my profession?"

He looked anything but stupid or tired, but quite eager and boyish, Edith thought, as he stood beside his son upon the hearth - rug. Glancing from him to Philip, she was surprised by the look of real pain in the face of the latter. It seemed so disproportioned to the occasion.

"Truly it should not," said Philip seriously.

"But perhaps the letter from the carpenter was very important," suggested Edith shyly, with an appealing look at Mr. Drayton.

"Of course it was very important," he answered good-humoredly, "and so is my being ready to receive my guests. Therefore, if you young people will excuse me, I will be off to my toilet."

Philip turned toward the fire when his father was gone, and stood silent for a moment, with his back to Edith; then seeming suddenly to realize that this was not very civil, he drew a chair beside her and sat down. She had taken a magazine from the table and opened it, not wishing to appear to notice him too critically. It chanced to be a number of the "Century," beginning with a humorous paper describing the adventures of an erratic band of artists styling themselves the "Tile Club." She glanced up to see him still looking despondently into the fire.

"Are you fond of decorative art, Mr. Drayton?" she asked, not choosing her topic, in her desire to change the current of his thoughts.

"I am, indeed," said Philip, "but it is as an artisan."

"What do you mean by that?"

"I mean that I look at it, perhaps, too much from its practical side."

"Then you must be an artist yourself?"

"Hardly. I am a painter, a carver, an experimenter."

"I did not know that," she said. In truth she was very much surprised.

"I know you did not, but if I were an artist I think you might have guessed it."

"Why?"

"Because there is something in the look of a man who has devoted himself to art which I think is unmistakable. Just think for a moment of all the artists you have ever known. Have they not looked like artists?"

"They are not always very clean," said Edith reflectively; and then, suiting her humor to the more serious tone of her companion, answered demurely, "I think they have."

"Why do not you?" she asked presently, with an amused smile.

"Because I have only turned to the arts I practice as pleasant occupations. I have taken them up as a diversion from my more prosaic profession."

"I thought you loved your profession."

"Not as I ought to do."

Edith hesitated a moment. "If you love art better, may you not have mistaken your profession?" she asked.

"I have just told you that I am a mere laborer in art," he said impatiently. "Excuse me," he added suddenly, with a change of tone. "I did not mean to speak like that, but my choice of a profession has always been a sore point with me."

"Then there was a reason why you were not what you would like to have been?" she asked quickly.

It was Philip's turn to smile at her earnestness.

"Several," he said. "Are you fond of drawing?" he asked, after a pause, by way of carrying the war into the enemy's country.

"I? Oh, no, I know nothing about it, but I always feel at home with people who do, because I have a sister who is quite an artist."

"Have you, indeed?" said Philip, in a tone of warm interest. "What does she like best to paint?"

"She is fondest of figures — portraits, but she paints landscapes too."

"Has she ever painted a picture of you?"

" Why do you ask ? " she answered, with a faint
blush. " I believe she made a portrait of me once,
sitting on the steps of our piazza."

" Is it a good picture ? "

" It would have been if it had happened to be of
somebody else. The view of Long Island Sound
in the distance is lovely."

" Why if it had been of somebody else? Is it
not a good likeness ? "

" My mother thinks so, but I do not like it. It
looks sentimental, which I am not, and the dress is
ugly. Altogether, I think I spoil it."

" I should like to see it, and judge for myself."

" You must come to New Rochelle," she answered
playfully.

" Perhaps I shall come ; do not forget that you
asked me. Meanwhile, would you care some day to
see a few things which I have gotten together in a
sort of sanctum of mine at Heronsford ? "

" I should like to see them of all things. You
will not forget either ? " she asked, glancing at him
brightly.

" No, I will not forget," he said, folding a large
piece of yellowish-white paper, as he spoke, which
had been lying outspread on the table.

Her eye was caught by a little sketch in pen and
ink upon the border, representing a picturesque
house, surrounded by trees.

" Is that a picture of your country seat ? " she
asked.

" Yes, that is Heronsford."

" How pretty it is ! "

" Do you really think so? I am very glad."

" I should think the house must be lovely, is it not ? "

" Perhaps I am hardly a fair judge," he answered. " It is the first I ever planned, and I am rather foolishly fond of the whole place."

" Do you mean that you made the plan yourself ? " she asked in surprise.

" Yes. I made it, and my father was good enough to allow me to carry it out."

" Oh, will you not let me see the plan ? "

" Certainly," he answered, flushing with pleasure. " If you will come here I will explain it to you." He spread out the paper once more, and made room for her at the table as he spoke, standing behind her chair, and pointing out with a pencil " the ground floor — the second story — and here is the room of which I told you," he said.

" Your little den ? "

" My little den."

" I like the inside of the house, too," said Edith.

" It has its defects of course," said Philip, with an attempt to speak impartially, " although at one time I thought it perfection."

" Was that long ago ? "

" Not very. It has only been built two years. That was when I hoped it would serve as an opening to future orders," he said, with a smile and a sigh.

" Ah, I know now what you would rather have been," said Edith, " an architect, and I see what you meant about art. Of course you only care for it in its relation to architecture."

" That is quite true," said Philip.

" What a pity that you could not have been what you wanted to be," she said earnestly.

Philip looked at her keenly. " Do you really think it to be regretted ? " he asked, and his face was quite a study for its complexity of expression.

" Of course I do."

" But many persons would think the legal profession much higher."

Edith hesitated for a moment. Her sympathies were awakened by Philip's manner more than by anything which he had said, but she wished to be honest. " I can understand their thinking that," she said, " but I meant that it was a pity to give up what you most cared for." She noticed .that his face fell. " Do you not think that architecture could be made a great deal higher than it is ? " she asked.

" That is exactly the ambition that I had," cried Philip. He was radiant. She could not have said anything to please him more.

" And why did you give it up ? "

" It was my father's wish. He did not think as I did, but desired, not unnaturally, to have his son follow him in the profession he most honored."

" But he must have encouraged your taste if he allowed you to build this house."

" He knew that I studied architecture abroad. He had recommended it to me himself as an interesting subject, a means of general cultivation, and so he was quite willing to indulge my fancy in the house at Heronsford; but when I suggested taking up architecture seriously as a profession, he looked upon it as a mere boyish whim."

" I don't see why he should have," said Edith impulsively.

" He was convinced, to do him justice." Philip answered, " that if I did not study law I should regret it all my life, — as he would have done himself, — and believed he was acting most kindly. Curiously enough," he added, half to himself, " it is the only instance in which he has ever attempted to influence me in thought or action. But there is Rodgers to call us to dinner, and you must be heartily tired of hearing me talk about myself."

The guests whom they found assembled were Mr. and Mrs. Davering, Miss and Mr. Wilmott, and Dr. Lawrence Carey. Miss Ruthven was helping Julia to do the honors of the house, in the absence of her nephew, who had not yet made his appearance. They welcomed the advent of Philip and Edith with no small satisfaction.

" I could not think where you were," whispered Julia. " Come here and let me introduce you to my friend Mrs. Davering." And then followed several other introductions, and Mr. Drayton coming in a moment afterwards, dinner was announced.

7

CHAPTER X.

" Where be your gibes now? your gambols? your songs? your flashes of merriment, that were wont to set the table on a roar ? " — SHAKESPEARE.

IT is a mistake for the lady of the house, at a dinner party, to place a silent man on her right hand, even though in so doing she may be actuated by the most disinterested of motives; and the better hostess she is the more of a mistake she makes, for the unresponsive person acts as a sort of pad, through which whatever effect her own efforts to enliven the rest of the company might have is deadened. Miss Prescott realized this a little too late to profit by the knowledge, her guests being seated and dinner begun. Her unremunerative neighbor happened to be Mr. Davering, and this was all the more aggravating that his position at table had been a subject of grave doubt.

He was a light-bearded, sleepy-looking man, with mild blue eyes, and what might be described as a stylish slouch; his profile would have been handsome, but that it in some unaccountable way suggested the head of a sheep. When he was amused by anything he laughed very hard, and showed a row of very strong white teeth. When he was angry, which happened seldom, he went away and sulked ; but most of the time he was amicably un-

conscious of what was going on about him, not because his thoughts were otherwise engaged, but
because there was a thick skin, as it were, over his
powers of perception which things must be very
pointed to penetrate. It had first been suggested
that he should take in Charlotte Wilmott, and sit
on Julia's left. Perhaps it was thought that there
was some congeniality of spirit between Charlotte
and himself, but it had been realized that in this
case, Miss Wilmott and her brother would be
brought side by side, and Miss Ruthven would be
obliged to go in with her grand-nephew, which was
hardly in accordance with the fitness of things, although there could be little doubt that the old lady
preferred Philip to any of the rest of the company.

Accordingly Julia had pronounced that Mr.
Davering must take down Miss Ruthven, and that
Philip would have to take Charlotte Wilmott, and
place her beside Mr. Drayton. -Her uncle, with
whom Charlotte was not a great favorite, made a
mental wry face when he saw this arrangement,
but swallowed it, as he did his raw oysters, in submissive silence, deferring to justice in Julia's *dicta*.
She certainly had not done better for herself, for
although Dr. Carey, who had taken her to dinner,
was a clever man, she had placed beside him Mrs.
Davering, much too energetic a person to allow
him to converse with any one else for more than
five minutes at a time. Julia had intentionally
given this lady a central position, for she knew
that she loved to command the conversation as far

in all directions as her faculties permitted, and that on the whole her effect upon a dinner was beneficial.

Cecil Wilmott had found himself between Mrs. Davering and the young lady to whom the dinner was given, in the close vicinity of his host, and the happy necessity of lending an ear to Mr. Drayton gave him an excellent opportunity of observing his nearer neighbor.

Miss Arnold was very simply dressed this evening in a pale blue Roman silk, the scarf-like trimming of which lent here and there a touch of brighter coloring. The faint shade of blue was becoming, and it was one of those dresses which are always in fashion; a fortunate fact for Edith, since it had belonged to her mother before it had been "made over" for herself. She looked younger than ever, a mere child, Cecil thought, as she sat, with her eyes cast down, listening to Mr. Drayton, and he wondered what it was about her which so attracted him. Whatever it was he could see that other people felt the charm. It was evident that Mr. Drayton really liked her. Cecil had seldom seen him take so much trouble for a young girl, and as for Philip, his eyes were almost constantly turned in this direction. Wilmott was not slow to seize the first moment when his uncle turned to say something polite to Charlotte to address Edith.

"Did you enjoy your drive yesterday?" he asked.

"Very much."

" Were you not rather surprised to meet me ? "

" I think I was," said Edith doubtfully.

" You think you were ? "

" Yes. I mean that that seemed a very unlikely place for you to be."

" And yet you are not sure that you were surprised to see me ? "

" No, not altogether, because I have almost always seen you in places where I did not expect you to be," said Edith, looking at him seriously ; and then seeing that he had begun to laugh she colored, as she had a way of doing when his eyes met hers.

" Shall I tell you a secret ? " asked Cecil.

" Must I keep it ? "

" That shall be as you please. It is that I walked all the way out to the Park hoping that I should see you."

She started a little. " Did you really ? " she exclaimed, with a look of simple wonder.

Cecil smiled. " Were you glad to see me ? " he asked, in a low voice.

Her manner suddenly changed. She dropped her eyelids and raised her head a little.

" I am sure we were all glad to see you," she answered. " Will you not tell me, by the bye, who that gentleman is, on Julia's right ? I think he was not presented to me."

" That is Mr. Davering," said Cecil, speaking in a guarded tone. " He is the husband of the lady on my other side, so be careful what you say."

"There is not much to say about him," replied
Edith, "except that he seems to enjoy his dinner."

"He does not say much himself, certainly," assented Cecil. "He is one of those men who, if he
does not feel in a humor for conversation, sees no
reason why he should talk. Now it is different
with my neighbor. You see how persistently she is
drawing out Philip Drayton, not because she cares
a rap what he is saying, but because she likes to
make conversation general, and to hear the sound
of her own voice in return."

"Mrs. Davering is a great friend of Julia's,"
said Miss Arnold. "I have never seen her before."

"What is the proper day to visit Girard College,
Cecil?" asked Mr. Drayton. "Charlotte is asking me, and I confess I have forgotten, if I ever
knew."

"I was saying, Cecil," said Miss Wilmott, speaking deprecatingly to her brother across the table,
"that I should be so glad if Miss Arnold would
lunch with us some day, and we could take her afterwards to see the College. You know it has always been considered one of the sights, and there
are several others which we might see at the same
time."

"Such as the Eastern Penitentiary?" asked
Wilmott, wickedly. "I have no objection, if Miss
Arnold would like to go."

"I should like to go very much," said Edith,
disregarding his tone of mockery.

"Then I will speak to Julia about it," said Miss Charlotte Wilmott, with an important air, "and Cecil must find out which day it is that visitors are admitted."

She was evidently greatly pleased, and Edith felt a touch of kindly compassion for the unattractive girl whose pleasures, as she guessed, were not frequent.

"I must tell you the last achievement of Oscar Wilde," said Mrs. Davering, turning to Cecil with an air of confident possession. She had been the round of the table and was in a happy mood. Only her husband had escaped unchallenged, and he seemed quite to revel in his immunity. Julia had tried every conceivable topic with him and had given up in despair. She was not sorry, therefore, to find that Mrs. Davering had left Dr. Carey once more at liberty.

"How is Mr. Hazzard to-day?" she asked. "My uncle was so sorry that his accident would prevent us from seeing him."

"Oh, he is better. He is really doing very well, only he must be quiet, and that you know is especially difficult for him."

"It is very fortunate that you happen to be with him to take care of him."

"He says he is glad to have me, and is always urging me to prolong my visit, but what possible good I do him, I fail to see. He is a very bad patient, and as a friend, one of the hardest men to amuse I ever saw. He hates to be read aloud to,

and does not care a snap about any of the ordinary
games which I have ever heard of being used to
divert invalids."

" He likes to talk, I suppose."

"Yes, he likes to talk and smoke, and is very
fond of poker, but one cannot play poker forever."

"Why do you not send for your flute?" exclaimed Julia. " It would be just the thing!"

Dr. Carey laughed. "That flute seems to have
made an unfortunate impression on your mind,
Miss Prescott. To be frank with you, I fancy that
if I did send for it, Mr. Hazzard would cease to
urge my neglecting my lucrative practice at home.
How very charmingly, by the bye, your little New
York friend looks this evening."

" Miss Arnold? Yes, she does look very lovely,
does she not?" said Julia, glancing down the table.
"And Mr. Drayton, too, looks wonderfully well,"
she added, proudly. "I do not think any one would
guess that he had been ill so lately."

" Are you speaking of Mr. Drayton?" asked
Mrs. Davering, catching the last words. "I was
saying just now to Mr. Wilmott, that I had never
seen him looking better, but then he is really a
comparatively young man, as I happen to know.
He and Buchanan were classmates, and I believe
Mr. Drayton is barely forty-eight. It is really
rather hard on him to have such a sedate-looking
person as Philip to present as his son, for of the
two, I sometimes think that Mr. Drayton looks the
younger."

Julia laughed. "Philip is certainly rather graver looking than his years," she said. "I can hardly believe that he is only four years older than I am."

"Nor I," said Dr. Carey, looking steadily away from Miss Prescott as he spoke, by way of rendering the remark impersonal. "Philip was always a little old for his age," he added, "even at college."

"Speaking of college," cried Mrs. Davering, "you must tell me all about the Greek play at Harvard. What was it like? Could one really sit through it with any comfort, or were you bored to death?"

"I individually was not," said Lawrence Carey, and being further questioned by the lady, gave quite a fine description of the manner in which the Œdipus of Æschylus had been brought out by students and graduates in Cambridge that winter. They thus all three talked on until the last course had been served, for Mrs. Davering perceived with uneasiness, that Dr. Carey was inclined to admire Miss Prescott, and it was her object to prevent the conversation from relapsing into a *tête-à-tête* between them.

It seemed to her a hard stroke of fortune, which had not only rendered her own son unfit for the combat, but detained this dangerous Bostonian on the scene just at a moment when Charley's loss was his gain. That Charley himself should be the only person to blame for the whole situation was natural, his mother admitted to herself, but all the more aggravating.

When the ices appeared it occurred to her that she would like to hear Mr. Drayton's opinion of the last attempted assassination of the queen, not an old topic then, as now, but one which had been very thoroughly canvassed. Julia had suggested it in desperation to Mr. Davering *à propos des bottes,* and that worthy gentleman had disposed of the whole matter in the one word " outrageous."

His wife's mind was not so easily set at rest. She felt sure that Mr. Drayton could throw new light upon the motives of the assassin.

" Did he think he had been a nihilist, or an Irish leaguer ? " she asked, with interest, " or did he believe that story about the man's being hungry ? What possible good could Queen Victoria's life be to a hungry man ? He had better have stolen her dinner."

" My dear lady, all is quite well known about the fellow," said her host, proceeding to give a short account of MacLean.

" Do you know, I felt very sorry for that man," said Miss Arnold, in a tone which only reached one of her neighbors.

" Why did you feel sorry for him ? " asked Cecil.

" Because, as Mrs. Davering says, there was nothing to be gained by what he did, and I think he must have been so terribly at odds with all the world, before he was driven to such an act of madness."

" Do you not think it was rather cowardly to attempt the life of a woman ? "

" Of course, such attempts are always cowardly,
when considered, whether on the life of a man or
a woman, but I do not believe that this poor wretch
gave himself time to consider, or that he thought
of the queen as a woman, but only as a queen."

She did not notice that Mrs. Davering and Mr.
Drayton had paused to listen to what she was saying.

" You would make an able advocate, Miss Arnold," said Mr. Drayton. " I never heard a bad
cause better defended."

" Would you consider that you had done very
well for your cause," she asked shyly, " if when
you ended people still thought it bad ? "

" I will answer you like the clown in ' Hamlet,' "
he said, mischievously. " ' The gallows does well
for those who do ill.' "

" That reminds me, Mr. Drayton, of what a
friend of mine was telling me the other day about
your acting. She said she remembered seeing you
act Malvolio in ' Twelfth Night,' in some private
theatricals, a great many years ago, and that it
was inimitable."

" Your friend must be a very old lady," said Mr.
Drayton, " but pray do not tell her that I said so."

" Oh, she is quite beyond caring what people
say about her age," said Mrs. Davering, " provided
they defer to her opinion, which they almost always do."

" I wonder if I do not know about whom you are talking ? " asked Cecil.

" I fancy you do," said Mrs. Davering, laughing. " I went to consult your mother with regard to some private theatricals which I was thinking of getting up myself. You know she has so much judgment about everything, and she advised me by all means to try to persuade your uncle to help me."

" I should never have suspected my sister of that," said Mr. Drayton ; and just then Julia gave the sign and they all rose from dinner.

" You were very silent during dinner," said Edith softly to Philip, who was holding the door open for the ladies to pass out of the room.

He smiled at her kindly. " Did I seem silent ? " he asked. " I was really trying to talk."

"DEAREST GERTRUDE " (wrote Miss Arnold that night, in a burst of sisterly enthusiasm) — " if you could but have seen Julia this evening, there would be one more beautiful picture in the world ! Whereas, now, it only lives in my memory. Imagine her in an écru - colored brocade, with any amount of soft, creamy lace about the throat, front, sleeves, etc., and you will confess that it was just the contrast to bring out the brown tints of her complexion and the magnificent depths of her dark eyes. She is such a spirited-looking girl, so full of fire and repartee, and so perfectly at her ease in society, that I confess, in this last respect, I envied her.

" For my part, it was so new a sensation to be at
a dinner party, that I felt as if nothing that I could
think of was important enough to be worth mentioning on such an occasion, especially to Mr. Drayton. Was it not very nice of him to take me in to
dinner? He talked delightfully, but I was dumb.
Mrs. Davering, Julia's great friend, seemed to find
plenty to say to him, yet I may as well acknowledge
at once that I do not like Mrs. Davering. She is
what is called a fine looking woman; but there is
something about her, a sort of observant imperti-
nence in the expression of her eyes, which makes
me sure that I never shall like her. It is ungrateful perhaps, for she asked us both to receive with
her on New Year's day, and Julia says that she
has offered to take me to the Assembly, which is
certainly very kind."

Later she wrote : " I had almost forgotten to
tell you about Dr. Carey. He is from Boston,
and I rather expected to find him a 'little tin God
on wheels,' but he is not. I think him decidedly
odd, but agreeable. Fancy a tall, thin, angular person, who stoops a little and wears eyeglasses, with
black hair and a brown moustache, rather thick
and long, and a face full of intelligence, although
the nose is a trifle long for beauty. I wish he did
not use quite so much slang, but he has a great
deal of general information, and talks unassum-
ingly, as if he expected, of course, to find other people as well posted as himself. I like that, for even
if I do not know a great deal about a subject, I

would rather confess my ignorance than have it presupposed. Would not you? Perhaps I am inclined to think well of Dr. Carey at any rate, for he is a great friend of Mr. Philip Drayton, whose judgment I feel almost sure is good in the choice of his friends. I had a long talk with him to-day, and such a pleasant one! He has the same way which Dr. Carey has, of becoming interested in his subject for its own sake, whereas Mr Wilmott seems to care much more who says a thing than what is said."

Here the young lady, who had apparently gone rambling on with her letter quite unrestrainedly, seemed suddenly to have checked the flow of her pen.

CHAPTER XI.

" Much like a subtile spider which doth sit
In middle of her web, which spreadeth wide,
If aught do touch the utmost thread of it
She feels it instantly on every side."

SIR JOHN DAVIES.

NEW YEAR'S DAY proved to be very raw and disagreeable.

Mrs. Davering had intended to receive in what she called "the old-fashioned style," no effect being striven after, except that of making the aspect of things ideally homelike; but the cheerlessness of the day led her to change her plan, and when Edith and Julia arrived, at a little after twelve, they found the blinds closed and all the gas lighted, as for an evening entertainment.

Miss Charlotte Wilmott was there before them, and there were three or four other young ladies, to whom the honor had been extended of casting their fortunes for the day with those of Mrs. Davering.

The reception rooms in her house were very large and luxurious, with numerous sofas and divans and several curtained alcoves tempting to quiet chats, and they opened from one another in unexpected ways, which lent an added charm of mystery, Edith thought. The reader has already been introduced to the largest of the rooms and may feel a moment's passing interest in the unfortunate scion of the house, who was reclining in a smaller one which was temporarily shut off from the others, and had been devoted to his special use since his accident.

His ankle was slowly improving, much more slowly than seemed to him in any way just or bearable, and his constant attempts to use it before it was ready for use resulted in fresh delay.

While the young ladies were taking off their cloaks in the dressing-room, Mrs. Davering drew Julia aside.

" I should like you to see Charles for a moment," she said. " He is so tired of his confinement."

" Poor fellow ! I should like to see him."

" Oh ! how do you do, Miss Prescott? Upon my honor this is very kind," cried Mr. Hazzard, as Julia entered with his mother.

" If you get up, Charles," said Mrs. Davering severely, " I shall take Miss Prescott away at once."

" I won't indeed, mother. I had no idea of getting up, except to shake hands," he answered with submission.

" Mahomet will come to the mountain," said Julia, laughing as she approached.

" Will you excuse my leaving you for one moment, Julia? " said Mrs. Davering. " I want to see what the other girls are about."

Julia, who had seated herself in a basket chair

beside Mr. Hazzard's sofa, looked gravely at his mother, with an expression of slight surprise.

" I will excuse you for a moment, certainly," she said.

" I will return in two seconds," said Mrs. Davering hurriedly, coloring a little, and avoiding Julia's direct gaze, as she left the room.

" It is awfully good of you to come and cheer me up," said Charley, with a grateful look, after she was gone.

" Yes, I think it is," said Julia, in a tone of conscious virtue.

" I heard you were driving in the Park the very day it happened."

" So we were, and we saw you and Mr. Freeman in the wherry. What induced you to go out on such a cold day ? "

" It was n't so cold in the morning, and we wanted exercise, you know ; besides, don't you remember what I told you about the importance of practice ? "

" Distinctly. ' 'T is in my memory locked, and thou thyself shalt keep the key of it,' " said Julia, with a wave of her hand.

" That sounds very well," said Charley phlegmatically, " and it seems to me I have heard it before, but I don't see what it has to do with training."

" Everything," said Julia. " It is the result of training upon me."

" I 'll tell you what it is !" exclaimed Mr. Hazzard, as though struck with a brilliant idea. " Did not my mother say that you had a young lady from New York staying with you?"

" Yes, I fancy so. I have one certainly. Is that *it?* "

" No ; but I was thinking that as soon as I am a little better of this stupid trouble with my ankle I might take you both to row. Do you think she would like it?"

" She might when the weather is warmer."

" Should you?"

" *It* seems to me delightful."

" Really?"

" I really think you are very kind to suggest it; and here comes Mrs. Davering."

" Then we, will go some time," said Charley, with a gratified expression.

" Yes; some time towards spring."

" Where is ▓▓▓ that you will go, Charley?" asked his mother playfully.

" Nowhere at present," said Julia. " I think Mr. Hazzard is going to be very good now, and take care of his injured ankle, in order to do what he pleases in the future."

She spoke kindly and looked persuasively at the young man, as one might do at a child which was blind to its true interest. Not unfrequently people fell into this tone with him, but he was not a child in all his feelings, and the kind look did some damage, of which its bestower was quite unconscious.

Edith meanwhile had been taken in hand by Charlotte Wilmott, and introduced to the other young ladies with whom they were to receive. She was much surprised to find that three out of five of them were named Davering, and yet the three did not appear to be sisters, but rather distantly related, if at all.

When she expressed her astonishment to Julia, as she found an opportunity of doing later, Miss Prescott explained that among the most influential families in Philadelphia there were one or two names which were very conspicuous, and that generation after generation having succeeded each other in these families, the present representatives were, naturally, not so nearly allied as their ancestors had been.

"But I should think that in that case they would have no reason to lead them to seek each other's society," said Edith. "Does Mrs. Davering feel obliged to invite all her husband's third and fourth cousins to receive with her?"

"Certainly not. They seek each other's society from choice, not necessity, having a confident belief that there is none pleasanter," said Julia, with an amused smile.

Little as Edith liked Mrs. Davering, she was forced to acknowledge that her rooms were furnished with exquisite taste, and in matters of this kind she was a better critique than it might be presumed that a young lady of her opportunities would be. She was not so good a judge, perhaps, but equally observant, of the generalship which her hostess displayed in the disposal of her forces so as best to sustain the coming attack.

She had chosen one of the Misses Davering, the prettiest, to pour out coffee, which was served on a little table in the room adjoining the larger one, in which she herself remained. Opposite to this young lady, at the same table, Miss Charlotte Wilmott had been requested to preside over a pot of chocolate.

There were still two of the Daverings left in the main body, so to speak, besides Miss Arnold, Miss Prescott, and a Miss Louisa Mortimer, who struck Edith as rather a wishy-washy kind of person, not unlike the heroine of an old-fashioned novel, and whom she was sorry to find near her on a distant sofa, Mrs. Davering having decoyed them thither to look at some photographs, and basely deserted.

Edith's companion was pale, with straight light hair and watery-looking eyes. She had an extremely small waist, was dressed in *gen d'arme* blue, a color which Edith happened particularly to dislike, and began to talk about the weather in a monotonous tone, which was quite depressing. Edith looked about her in all directions for some means of escape.

She saw that Mrs. Davering, after detailing Miss Isabella and Miss Mildred Davering to seats on the centre divan, had evidently decided to retain Julia close to her own person, in the part of the room nearest the door, and she resolved that she would find her way to Julia's side as soon as possible; but the room was so large that she felt shy about crossing it, and she was soon prevented from carrying out her intention by the arrival of the first visitors. They were heralded by a cold draft of wind from the front door, which preceded them even to the drawing-room. They made some noise, too, coming upstairs, which was explained when they appeared, for there were four of them hurrying forward in hot haste. They had taken a carriage for the day, and were anxious to make as many visits as possible. Mrs. Davering surprised Edith by bringing over two of these first-comers to introduce to her and Miss Mortimer. They were very young gentlemen, and a good deal frightened lest they should get out of conversation. Edith felt sorry for them, they wriggled about and talked so fast, and was just beginning to say something herself, in order to give them a moment's rest, when they suddenly declared that they must go, and forthwith departed as they had come.

The next arrival proved to be that of a middle-aged bachelor, from the country. He was stout and rather red in the face. He insisted upon being introduced to each one of the young ladies in turn, made gallant speeches to all of them, and hailed the suggestion that he should take a cup of coffee or chocolate with delight, choosing the chocolate and following it up with the coffee.

Miss Arnold was not able to pursue his achieve-ments further, although they interested her on account of their thoroughness. Her attention was again required by her hostess, who had come to present to her a delicate little man with eyeglasses and red whiskers. He had just appeared, accompanied by a tall, elegant looking person, of whom he apparently stood in great awe. Indeed, his august companion seemed to look down upon him from a lofty eminence of supreme fashion, to which the smaller gentleman could not pretend. The name of the latter proved to be Foxall, and Edith rather liked him. In fact, they got on so well that she was quite sorry when, one or two other visitors having entered, his grand associate took it into his head to be introduced to her, and broke up the conversation.

This stylish person was a Mr. Drum Kettleby. In Philadelphia, where origin was a matter of interest, he was said to be of a New York family, but when he went to New York, as he very often did, or among the persons whom he met at summer watering-places, he was only known as " Mr. Drum Kettleby, from Philadelphia."

This simple appellation was, however, no mean distinction, for it was acknowledged to designate an eminently successful society man, whose value and desirability in the world of fashion seemed somehow to be estimated by an inverse ratio of his value and desirability elsewhere.

No one knew how he had gained his preëminence, for he had neither fortune nor family ; but it was remembered that he had first been intro-

duced by one of the Capulets, a chance friendship
with whom had given him the *entré* of people's
houses. He had done everything else for himself,
and, strange to say, the manner in which he had
done it had been by doing nothing. He had simply let himself alone, accepting affably the hands
held out to him, but being especially careful not to
move a finger for his own advancement.

No one could ever say that Mr. Drum Kettleby
was pushing, or that he was anxious to please. It
may not have been in his nature to be either. It
may have been only a part of his art not to seem
to be, but as the fame of Raphael to that of Peru-
gino, or of Leonardo da Vinci to Verrocchio, had
been his strides in the favor of society, compared to
those of his master. The Capulet, who had become
engaged to be married, was actually *nowhere*, and
Mr. Drum Kettleby was everywhere.

Considering all this, or perhaps because she did
not know it, Miss Arnold found his conversation
uncommonly slow, and she was all the more glad
to see Cecil Wilmott enter the room, which was
now beginning to fill with black coats. Cecil came
in with Dr. Carey, and she saw him cast a hasty
glance about him as he advanced to greet his hostess.

Whether his eye had fallen on her in her distant
corner she could not tell, but his presence lent a
certain interest and excitement to her efforts to entertain Mr. Drum Kettleby which her previous
manner towards that gentleman had rather lacked.

She noticed that after paying their respects to Mrs. Davering, Cecil Wilmott and Dr. Carey passed through a curtained doorway from the larger drawing-room to a smaller one beyond, and as from where she sat she commanded a complete view of this room and of the library which opened from it in a long vista, she could plainly distinguish Cecil's slight figure as he stood talking with the pretty Miss Davering, whom he had evidently persuaded to give him a cup of coffee.

The group round the little tea-table formed an attractive picture in the middle distance, Edith thought, and she suddenly experienced a feeling of regret that Mrs. Davering had not assigned to her the pleasing task of pouring out the coffee. From these thoughts she suddenly awoke to the gracious attention which her distinguished visitor was bestowing on her. Since she had ceased to know exactly what she was saying, and had begun to talk merely for the sake of seeming to be talking, Mr. Drum Kettleby had pricked up his ears, metaphorically speaking, and was smiling in a manner which he evidently intended to be encouraging.

She did not yet know enough of society to understand why he was pleased with her; but later she discovered that the kind of conversation with which she was then favoring him was that to which he was most accustomed, and that nothing confused Mr. Drum Kettleby so much as the display of any keen interest in a subject, or to be asked his opinion of anything.

Being at her wits' end to think what further to say to him, she proposed to introduce him to Miss Louisa Mortimer, and suited the action to the word.

Since the departure of the first visitors Miss Mortimer had sat somewhat apart, apparently absorbed in the portfolio of photographs, so that Edith was obliged to rise to perform the introduction, and as she stood talking with her back toward the rest of the room, she suddenly heard Cecil's voice at her elbow.

"How do you do, Miss Arnold? I have been trying in vain to get to you. Will you not come and sit down with me? I am commissioned this moment by Charlotte to arrange a time, if possible, when your numerous engagements will allow you to lunch with us, and go to visit the sights of the town."

"What are the sights of the town?" asked Edith.

"Come back to your sofa, and I will tell you all about them," said Cecil.

As Miss Mortimer moved away just then with Mr. Drum Kettleby, Edith yielded to his request.

"How did you know that I had been sitting here before?" she asked.

"I saw you when I first came in. You were talking to Drum Kettleby. I think you have made quite an impression upon him. He seemed to be very attentive."

"What nonsense!"

"He did, indeed. I had intended to make a

good many visits to-day," he said presently, "but
the weather is so bad, that I am strongly inclined
to give up, and stay where I am."

"Here?"

"Here, exactly. I rather like it," replied Wilmott.

Edith laughed. "I meant at Mrs. Davering's
house," she said.

"I know what you meant," he answered, "and
what I mean. The only load on my conscience is
Lawrence Carey. I don't know whether I ought
to go anywhere else on his account. Philip had
promised to take him about to-day, and was unexpectedly prevented."

"Do you think Dr. Carey wants to go elsewhere?"

"I am not sure that he does," said Cecil. "I
see that he has found Julia, and seems to be very
comfortable."

"They look as if they were having a pleasant
talk," said Miss Arnold, following the direction of
his eyes to the recess of the bay window, where
Miss Prescott and Dr. Carey had found a seat.
It was the same one which Julia had occupied on
the night of the ball, but Mrs. Davering was much
too wise a woman to leave her so long undisturbed,
with her present companion.

"Our hostess is going to make mince meat out
of that arrangement," said Cecil, with an amused
smile, as they saw Mrs. Davering bearing down
upon the unconscious pair, with Mr. William Free-

man, the companion of her son's unfortunate boating excursion. "Carey will soon be adrift."

"Why could not Mr. Philip Drayton come to look after his friend?" asked Edith.

"He had to go to Heronsford again," said Cecil. "Some stupid mistake had occurred about the improvements which he is making there. It was hard luck certainly, instead of coming to wish you a happy New Year."

"Do you know that nobody yet has wished me a happy New Year? That funny little Mr. Foxall told me that he had made a firm resolution, before he left home this morning, not to wish it to *any one.*"

Cecil laughed. "I have no doubt he thinks it a very wicked expression," he said.

"Oh, no," said Edith. "He told me his objection. He has a great dread of saying exactly what every one else says."

"And with reason," said Wilmott. "May I wish you a happy New Year?" He held out his hand for hers.

Edith hesitated, before she took it.

"I wish you many happy years," said Cecil.

"Thank you," she answered, drawing her hand from his, with a half smile at his earnestness.

"For myself, I wish I could believe that when the next New Year's day comes you will remember this one," he continued more lightly.

"Why not?" she asked. "A year is not long to remember."

"But you may be thinking of other things."

"I suppose I shall, of course," said Edith, practically, "but the association of ideas might recall the day very naturally, I should think."

"Shall I be a pleasant association with it?" asked Cecil, taking her fan, which happened to be near him, as he spoke.

Edith could hardly help laughing at the discrepancy between his words and manner, which was rather playful than sentimental throughout; but it had a charm for her, in spite of her amusement.

"I think all the associations of the day will be pleasant," she answered demurely.

"They will for me," said Wilmott. "Where did you get this artistic fan, Miss Arnold?"

"Do you think it pretty?" she asked, with a childlike, eager air, which she had when she was interested.

"I think it is beautiful."

"I am so glad. It was painted by my sister, and is her own design. Wait, I will show you the story;" she took it from him impulsively, as she spoke. "See here," she continued, holding it with one hand and pointing with the small, gloved finger of the other to the pictures which were delicately sketched in water colors on the ivory slats of the fan. "This first scene represents a court fool, who has followed a fair lady into the woods, where she wishes to wander, being inclined to be a little pensive, you know, and the fool is to warn her of any danger, which might approach. You see she has seated herself beneath the shade of a tree, and has fallen asleep, and meanwhile he watches her, and grows very sad — because — because " — repeated Edith, suddenly pausing, and looking rather shy.

" Because what ? " asked Cecil.

" Oh, because he is in love with her, of course," said Edith, in a tone of great impatience. These things were so taken for granted in fairy stories that it had not occurred to her that they might be awkward to explain, in a drawing-room, where the most natural ideas seem suddenly conventionalized.

" In love, is he ? " asked Cecil. " Poor fool! Let me have another look at him. And what does this next picture represent? It appears to be a change of subject."

" Why, that is a knight returning from the war," said Miss Arnold. " Is not his armor well painted, and his horse ? They must have been so hard to do."

" Yes, it is a very pretty picture," answered Cecil. " But what has the knight to do with the lady? Is he in love with her, too ? "

" I suppose he is, for she has been hoping that he would come home — and — he has come."

" Ah, I see ; and here are the knight and the lady together," said Cecil, who had taken the fan from her again.

" Yes," replied Edith ; " and there, on the other side, is the fool, alone."

" Poor fellow," said Cecil ; " he looks very disconsolate. He has taken to a willow tree, has he not ? "

" Yes ; the verse describes him as throwing himself down beneath a willow tree," she answered.

" The verse ? Is there a poem about it ? "

" Oh, no, not a poem. There are a few verses which a friend of ours once wrote, in imitation of an old ballad. They are not much in themselves, but suggested to my sister the idea of the pictures on the fan."

" Have you got the verses ? " asked Wilmott. "I should like to read them."

" I have them, but only in a scrap-book, with a number of other odds and ends. I could copy them, if you really care to see them, though." ·

" Of course I do. Why should you doubt it ? "

" Perhaps you only say so because you think it will please me."

" I think it does please you," said Cecil, " but I can't imagine why. It is so natural that I should want to see the verses, after looking at the fan, that I shall think you very kind if you take the trouble to copy them for me."

At this moment Julia approached, accompanied by Dr. Carey. He had refused to be driven away by Mrs. Davering, but the conversation of three which had followed upon the introduction of Mr. Freeman appeared not to have been very satisfactory.

" Dr. Carey is actually so rash as to believe that he has made all his New Year's calls, Cecil," said

Julia. " Now, I am quite sure that this is impossible."

" I don't think we had anywhere else to go, Wilmott, had we ? " asked Dr. Carey, carelessly.

" I think not," replied Cecil. " Nowhere of any account."

" I do not believe that Dr. Carey has been to half the places he ought to have been taken to," persisted Julia. " In Philip's absence, I really feel responsible for him."

" If you wish me to go," said Lawrence Carey, · in a nettled tone, " I can do so, of course." A gleam of amusement shot from Julia's eyes. It was very unusual for him to display so much feeling, of any kind, and his doing so could only be accounted for by the fact that, besides the contrariety of circumstances, Miss Prescott had been in a most provoking mood all the afternoon.

" How unjust you are ! " she said now, in an injured tone. " It would not be necessary for me to talk to you, if you stayed. I wish you could believe me disinterested."

" We certainly shall not believe you in earnest, in wishing to drive us forth on this inclement day," said Cecil, coming to the rescue, but Julia was in a dangerous humor.

" I was only going to suggest a few visits," she said. " There is your friend Mrs. Percy, Cecil, who lives so near. You surely will not think of omitting your New Year's visit there, and as a stranger Dr. Carey ought to meet her. I have been

telling him about her. Mrs. Percy is considered
one of our beauties," she continued, turning to the
Bostonian, " and Mr. Wilmott can tell you that as
long as he has known her, — and that is a long
while, — and as well as he has known her, although
he has known her very well, she has always been
the same.   Has she not, Cecil ?   She is said to be
as charming now as she was ten years ago."

It is doubtful whether Cecil Wilmott would not
have left Dr. Carey to fight his own battle, if he
had known what he was about to elicit.   To his
surprise, it was Miss Arnold who answered.

" If Mrs. Percy looks as lovely always as she
did when I saw her the other day in the Park, I
should think that might be true for ten years to
come," she said ; " but for all that I do not see why
Dr. Carey should go to see her, Julia, unless he
cares to do so.   And I am very hungry, besides, and
would give the world for a sandwich and a cup of
coffee."

Both gentlemen started forward to supply her
wants, but as Dr. Carey was a little in advance
Cecil turned back and stood beside her a moment,
as though waiting for her to look up.   Edith did
so at last, with an air of surprise, and smiled a
little, for, as her eyes met his, she thought she understood him.

" You were very kind," he murmured, and then
he passed on to Julia, who had seated herself on
the sofa beside her friend, but did not look repen-
tant.   " You must let me get you something, too,

Miss Prescott," he said, with mock formality. " I am sure you require refreshment," and rather to the disgust of Dr. Carey he devoted himself to Julia for the rest of their visit.

9

CHAPTER XII.

" O Memory, thou art but a sigh
    For friendships dead and loves forgot,
And many a cold and altered eye
    That once did say Forget me not."
                                    AYTOUN.

EDITH complained of a headache that evening, and retired early; but after reaching her room she felt restless and adverse to repose. She took down her hair slowly, looking lingeringly at her reflection in the mirror, from time to time, in a dreamy sort of way. Then she put on a long white flannel dressing-gown, which fell about her in soft folds, and lighting a lamp, that stood on a little red-covered table beside the fire, opened a worn morocco scrap-book, and began to copy the verses promised to Cecil Wilmott.

As she turned the pages of the scrap-book her attention was attracted by a flat leather pocket on the inside of one of the covers, which she had quite forgotten. Unclosing this she saw a thin old letter, which she drew from its hiding-place, and was surprised to perceive that it was addressed to Julia Prescott, in a handwriting which she did not know. The envelope had been cut across the top in order to get at the contents, and as she held it Edith noticed that it contained a photograph.

Her curiosity was a good deal excited as to whose it could be, but she remembered that she had no right to look, and thrusting the letter hastily into a square envelope, which lay on the table beside some note-paper, wrote a few words in pencil, which she inclosed with it, and rang the bell.

" Is Miss Prescott still down stairs ? " she asked of the maid who answered her ring.

" Yes, miss. She is in the library."

" Give her this from me, please."

The maid disappeared.

Edith's chamber was a large one in the fourth story of the house. The furniture was fine old carved mahogany, with claw feet and brass handles to the drawers, which shone in the light of a wood fire ; and only the fanciful French curtains of the windows, a creton-covered arm-chair of the present day, and a few bits of modern adornment here and there upon the walls were out of keeping with the revolutionary period of which the huge four-posted bedstead reminded the little lady, who at last lay down in it to dream out her dream, and awake again to the realities of life.

It seemed to her, long afterwards, in looking back upon her first visit to Philadelphia, that it had been made up of odd contrasts like this, — of old historic memories, crossed by light tokens of the frivolous, ever-interesting present. It was as if she had stepped at once into a knowledge of by-gone times and of her own.

The group which Edith had left behind her in

the library hardly seemed disturbed by her defection, although its members had grown to look upon her as one of themselves. It consisted of three persons, as Philip Drayton had gone again to Washington on business. Julia had seated herself near Mr. Drayton at the table, and they were both absorbed in reading. Perhaps Miss Ruthven, who had grown fond of Edith, rather missed the gentle chit-chat in which they usually indulged of an evening, especially as Philip, her great crony, was away. She soon grew sleepy, without any one to talk to, and proposed going to bed.

"Art thou not coming, Julia?"

"Yes, Miss Ruthven, in a little while."

The other two read on in silence for some time after she was gone, until Julia came to the end of her magazine article, and softly laid the pamphlet down. She sat for a few moments watching Mr. Drayton, thinking how long it was since they had spent an evening thus quietly in each other's company, and how much she enjoyed the sense of community with him which always came to her at times like this.

"What are you reading?" she asked at last.

"I am reading Taine's 'Voyage en Italie,'" said Mr. Drayton, without lifting his eyes from his book.

"I fancied that you had read it."

"So I have, — fifteen years ago."

"I thought I had heard you speak of it. Why do you read it again?"

" Why, indeed ? I remember it quite well, but the truth is, Monsieur Taine is a delightful companion to me ; and then I may have to go to Italy this spring."

" I did not know you thought of it."

" Only as the dimmest of possibilities. I am likely to be engaged in a case which may take me to London, and once there might think it wise to go on the Continent for a few weeks. It would enable me to do some business more thoroughly, which must otherwise be done by letter."

" Something connected with *me?*" asked Julia.

" Something connected with your coming of age."

" Then you will take me' with you ?"

" We will see, dear. It is all uncertain."

" I, too, have felt the charm of Taine's style," said Julia, resuming the former subject.

" Every one has who is capable of appreciating it," answered her guardian.

" I am not sure that I should care to re-read his book, though, merely for the sake of his society," said Julia, smiling.

" I do not suppose many persons would," rejoined Mr. Drayton. " It is sad to think that so much talent may be so soon forgotten."

" I should not think any writer of the day was more widely known," said Julia.

" True, and yet it seems as if the first effect both of this book and the ' English Literature ' were passing away without leaving a very decided mark behind. Unfortunately, they contain nothing original except the author's way of looking at things, and that hardly belongs more to himself than to his century."

" I should have said that there was a great deal of thought in them."

" So there is. They may almost be said to represent contemporary thought and feeling, just as they reflect contemporary doubt; and this, besides their beauty of expression, constitutes their chief attraction to contemporaries like myself, but I am not sure that they will continue to be read when the time is past."

" I should think that the more completely they embodied the spirit of the century in which they were written, the more valuable they would be hereafter as a picture of the time," said Julia.

" To students of history, yes," replied Mr. Drayton ; " but they are not, I think, books to be re-read hereafter for the ideas which they contain, because these ideas will be superseded by fresh ones."

" The fact that they are fresh now ought to make them keep longer than if they were stale," remarked Julia.

Mr. Drayton laughed. " That sounds unanswerable," he said, " but I am not sure that it is true. There is so infinitely little added to the great stock of human knowledge in each generation, and it has to be picked out of so much rubbish, that the rubbish of twenty-five or thirty years ago, like the fashion of the period in dress, often seems to us more

jejune than do the exploded theories of the time of
Queen Elizabeth."

" Surely Monsieur Taine's criticism and experiences are not rubbish," said Julia ; " or if so, they
are such sparkling rubbish that I should be more
apt to compare them to gold-dust."

" I accept the correction," said Mr. Drayton.
" Let us think of them as gold-dust, which has
been sifted from the sands of time ; precious, brilliant, volatile, but not cohesive, suited to no end on
which to build a lasting reputation."

" Might they not be smelted over again, and
fashioned to some future end ? "

" They certainly might, and very possibly may ;
but if so, it will be the work of genius, and they
will no longer belong to Monsieur Taine. Analyzed,
without undergoing any such change, their absence
of defect is a negative quality, and I am inclined
to think that the nice taste and fine power of distinction which are left, whether they find expression in art or literature, or even in scientific research, will only be successful to the author's own
standard, and are only likely to be admired by his
own generation. It even seems just that it should
be so, as a proof of the old saying, ' Little venture,
little win.' "

" But what should a man strive to fulfill," asked
Julia, "if not his own standard ? What other
standard can he have ? "

" My dear," said her guardian, " he should have
an ideal. If he have not, he is a mere clog."

"That is, you require him to have an ideal standard. You are not satisfied with his striving to do well what he undertakes?"

"*He* should not be satisfied with it, lest it lead him to undertake only what he is sure of doing well, if he wish to become immortal — even on earth."

"But if he be a commonplace person," persisted Julia, "what is the use of his struggling forever after the unattainable?"

"Did he do that, he would probably not be a commonplace person; but we did not begin to talk about commonplace persons, but about men of exceptional talent, and we were not speaking of the satisfaction which they might find in their own lives, — that is, I suppose, the meaning of the word 'use' as you employ it, rather of the durability of their effect on mankind."

"That is quite true," said Julia, with a puzzled expression, "but I cannot help feeling as if things which are done well ought to have a more lasting effect than things which are merely attempted."

"It depends entirely upon the magnitude of the attempt."

"But you surely do not object to an artist, for instance, who succeeds in his endeavor, that therefore he cannot be great?"

"I say that unless he have a great endeavor he cannot be great, and the mightier the ambition the less hope of fulfilling it."

"Yet there must be a certain proportion of suc-

cess," protested Julia. " He should be able at least
to make us see what he has attempted."

" He certainly should, or he has failed, and the
world has no use for him. What the world wants,
however, is not a perfect painter, like Andrea del
Sarto, but the strength and grandeur of a Michael
Angelo, whose struggle after sublimity is forever
recorded in his clumsy marbles. It does not treasure the memory of a Leigh Hunt, but it does that
of a Thackeray, less for his fine insight into motives than for his large contempt for what is mean
and petty, his faith in the true and beautiful always peeping out between his sarcasms, and the sad
requiem which he is too often singing over pros-
trate human nature."

" I think the world is more in sympathy with
science just now than with art of any kind," said
Julia.

" I think so, too," rejoined Mr. Drayton, " and it
has substituted speculation for religion. But if
it must suffer all its old hopes and feelings to be
knocked on the head, let it not be done by Mr.
Herbert Spencer, with his deftly spun web of inquiry and careful avoidance of conclusions, but give
us a Darwin to do it, who will venture to offer a
new theory, on which the startled world may at least
rebuild when he destroys its ancient edifice."

" Philip would tell you that you do Herbert
Spencer great injustice. He says that he is not
afraid of conclusions, only very slow in reaching
them because he is afraid of making mistakes."

"Oh, if Philip were here I should be wary of mentioning the name of his paragon," said Mr. Drayton, smiling. "But do me the justice to remember that I did not say that he was afraid of conclusions, only that he avoided them. He certainly is not afraid of leading other people to form conclusions, or, if he is, he must quake in his shoes at the amount of unbelief which he has scattered broadcast."

"Philip makes a distinction between unbelief and doubt."

"You may call it what you please. I only know that Mr. Spencer shuts the door upon divine truth," replied Mr. Drayton hotly.

"I heard Philip declaring the other day," continued Julia, with provoking coolness, "that Mr. Spencer was no atheist, only an agnostic."

"I remember, too," said Mr. Drayton dryly, "he remarked at the same time that Mr. Spencer was seeking to find divine truth by the *process of exclusion.* I recall the expression quite distinctly." He smiled in spite of himself as his eyes met Julia's, at which she laughed from sympathy.

"Was that not too delightful?" she asked. "It ought to have been recorded."

At this moment her maid entered.

"Here is a note, Miss Julia," she said, "which Miss Arnold asked me to give you."

"Thank you, Annie. I shall not want you to-night."

Julia broke the envelope, which was addressed

to her in pencil, and took out Edith's note, as the servant left the room.

"I have just found this old letter of yours, dear Julia, in my scrap-book," the note said. "How it got there I cannot imagine, but it must have been hidden away in it ever since that summer which you spent with us at New Rochelle. I have a fancy that it may be the very letter which we were talking of not long ago. Do you not remember my telling you that you were reading a letter when I first saw you? It is odd that I never happened to light on it before. Affectionately, EDITH."

Julia looked gravely at the letter for a moment. It was directed to her in characters which she knew quite well as those of her mother. She drew off the envelope with a touch of the awe we feel in opening something last seen by eyes which see no more. Then she perceived the photograph, which she remembered, too, although the face was younger and more beautiful than she had known her mother's. It represented a handsome woman, dressed in the extreme of the fashion of about twenty-five years earlier, — the very period of which Mr. Drayton had chanced to condemn the probable styles in illustrating his comparison, a half an hour before. He looked up now, as it happened, from the book, in which he had become absorbed again.

"What have you got there?" he asked.

"An old photograph, sir, of my mother. It is one which she sent me in a letter many years ago, and I thought that it was lost."

Julia handed him the picture, as she spoke, and, opening the letter, glanced over the faintly-written pages until her eye was caught by a sentence which referred to the photograph.

"You ask me for my likeness," it said, "but I have only a very old one to send you, child, with some stupid nonsense written on the back of it. I wish I had known you wanted one, but I have given all the last I had taken away."

"Of course!" said Julia to herself, speaking just below her breath. Then she glanced at Mr. Drayton, and noticed that he was gazing at the picture with an expression of deep sadness.

As she looked he turned it over, and read what was on the other side. There were two verses. Julia remembered puzzling over their meaning years before, and wondering, when a child, who had written them. Now, as she watched her guardian and re-read the lines, a sudden thought came to her. She noticed for the first time, with bewilderment, that the handwriting was like Mr. Drayton's own.

The verses ran as follows, seeming anything but a finished production : —

> "I have loved thee so that I could die for thee,
>   And thou hast brought me ceaseless pain ;
> Lost are the tears I shed for thee,
>   And the sighs were sighed in vain !

> "Oh, give me back the faith thou 'st taken from me !
>   Oh, give me back my youth's high aims !
> Let me live, if I must live without thee,
>   Without thy chains !"

As she came to the end of the last verse, involuntarily Julia's eyes sought Mr. Drayton's with a look of wonder, and she saw that they had followed and were resting upon hers.

"I wrote that," he said, with a bitter smile. "Of course I did not expect any one ever to see it, not supposing that the portrait would pass into other hands' than mine. I was very young at the time, and very foolish," he added, in reply to her startled look.

"And was — the picture — yours?"

"It was then. It had been given to me, but I afterwards thought it right to return it with everything else which was no longer mine."

"I do not understand," said Julia, in a frightened tone.

"Because you do not know, Julia, that I was once engaged to be married to your mother."

This idea was so surprising that Julia could hardly take it in. There was a long pause. Her brain seemed in a whirl. She had a confused idea that she should defend her mother, if possible, for some great fault, although quite conscious that she had not been accused.

"Was not she, too, very young?" she faltered at last.

"She was about my age," said Mr. Drayton, "but years older in experience, for she had lived in society from her childhood. She liked my devotion for a while, and then it tired her, and — we parted."

" And my father ? "

" This was all before your father knew her ; nor did he ever know what I have told you. He met her five years later, in Europe, and you know they were married abroad."

" I supposed — I thought my father was your friend."

" He was my dear friend, then and always," said Mr. Drayton, earnestly, — " a true-hearted, noble man ; but, as it happened, I had not told him the name of the woman whom I had hoped .to marry, and when he wrote me of his engagement I determined that he should not know, through me, what would only have given useless pain."

" How hard it was for you ! "

" Not so very hard, my child. You must not make a hero of me. I had outlived my youthful passion, and was married then myself ; but I did feel the separation from my friend, and was all the more deeply touched by the trust your father put in me, when he left you to my care." He rose as he spoke, and, stooping, kissed her on the forehead. " Good-night, my Julia," he said. " I think I will go out for a little stroll before I go to bed."

Julia sat quite still when she was alone, stunned by the shock of all that she had heard. She took up the photograph again, and looked at it long and thoughtfully, noting the strangely hard expression about the corners of the mouth, and the triumphant light in the dark, defiant eyes which were not unlike her own. Then, by some odd link of association, her memory traveled back to a scene long past, which had happened in her childhood, and became once more vivid in her imagination as if it were happening then, while its full meaning was now first revealed to her in the light of what she had just been told.

She seemed to be standing as a little girl in the deep embrasure of a window, the curtain half drawn behind her. She was listlessly looking out upon the eager bustle of a dusty New York street, when she heard footsteps in the room behind her, and a voice, her mother's voice, — she recognized it perfectly, — said in a fretful tone, " But if you will not take the child, what shall I do with her, Algernon ? "

" I did not say that I would not take Julia," answered a deep voice which she did not know, then.

" But you say that you will only take her on certain conditions. I hate conditions."

" I say that I shall require you to sign a paper giving her to me."

" If I tell you that I will give her to you, why is not that enough ? "

" I wish you to resign all future authority over her."

"Oh, if that is all, I do it now, with all my heart."

There was something so peculiarly cold and careless in the tone of this answer that the child who heard it felt the hot tears starting from her eyes, but she held her very breath with a fierce determination to make no sign of her presence. It seemed that the tone had shocked the other listener also.

" Do you not care at all for your little girl, Josephine ? " he asked, in a strange, bewildered way.

" I like you to call me that," she answered, with a softer intonation in her voice. " It reminds me of a time long past. So you care for Julia for my sake ? "

There was a pause, but when the man's voice was heard again it was charged with such controlled anger, such concentrated scorn, that it seemed as if the woman whom he addressed must have withered with the sound. " You forget that Julia's father was my dear friend. If you think that it is for your sake that I would shelter your child, you are mistaken."

What followed had been so unintelligible to the little girl who was concealed behind the curtain that Julia could not unravel it now distinctly. There had been more angry words, and then a fit of weeping. Julia recollected that something had been said about a broken engagement, a hasty marriage, and Julia's being so like her father. Then there had been a word or two of reference to the new tie which her mother was about to form. She said she wanted to forget all about the old one, of which Julia was a constant reminder.

To this the answer had been given calmly and coldly. Algernon Drayton had promised to take the child, and to send certain papers in a day or two to be signed.

All that Julia gleaned was the fact that there was some one who had known her father and cared for her for his sake, and that this might constitute a claim upon his protection, perhaps his love.

A few days later she had been sent for to the drawing-room, and formally presented to her guardian.

She remembered him quite distinctly, sitting on a sofa, and how he had risen and come forward and taken her little hand in his. She remembered the first coming home to the house in Meredith Square, and how amused she had been at Philip, whom she found a chubby little boy, in a roundabout jacket, and what good friends they had soon become. But what she remembered most, and most distinctly, through everything, was Mr. Drayton's kindness; his unfailing charity to her shortcomings, which did not seem to vex him as other persons' did; his tender sympathy when she was ill or suffering, although often shown in an odd, half-humorous way; and his real pleasure in her happiness when she had reason to rejoice.

10

CHAPTER XIII.

IT was two days after this that Miss Arnold first made the acquaintance of the unfortunate Mr. Hazzard, of whose misadventures she had heard so much. The manner of his introduction was rather abrupt, — as unexpected, in fact, to the celebrity as to herself. It happened thus : —

Mr. Hazzard had a bull-dog. He was about middle height among bull-dogs, stout and white, with a black patch over one eye, red eyelids, cropped ears, and bandy legs. His under jaw was tremendous, and his grip said to be terrible ; but he was as amiable and amenable to Charley Hazzard's behests as a bull-dog should be to those of his lawful master.

Mrs. Davering kept two men-servants, one of whose chief occupations in life had hitherto been to exercise the bull-dog. With this object the man had been in the habit of leading him forth daily, by a heavy steel chain attached to a massive leather collar, on which was inscribed in Roman letters the euphonious name of " Jig."

Now, however, that from the most active, independent, and amiable of beings, Mr. Hazzard had been transformed into a helpless, rebellious, irascible invalid, Jig's servant, Peter, was kept so busy waiting on his master that he had no time to devote to Jig, who felt the injustice sorely.

He missed his morning walk, day after day, and his temper exhibited as unfavorable a change as that of Mr. Hazzard, with even more cause: for one daily source of aggravation to Jig was the behavior of a large mongrel terrier belonging to the baker's boy, who came in the way of business every morning to the yard gate, and the moment that he beheld the nose and fore-paws of the imprisoned Jig peeping from beneath it would begin to bark and snuff and jeer at him, in the most offensive of dog language, as who should say, — " Ha, ha ! Don't you wish you could get out ? I'm not afraid of you ! " and wagging his tail the while, with a motion which seemed to express, " Look here, how free I am ! I go everywhere I please. I am not fastened with a chain."

It is not necessary to rehearse the deep growls of suppressed wrath, outraged dignity, and finally of *menace,* with which these taunts were received ; enough be it to say that repeated interviews of this excited nature having taken place, while the baker's boy was in the act of choosing the rolls from his covered cart, designed for Mr. Hazzard's breakfast, and passing them to the expectant cook through a square opening in the gate, Jig's feelings towards the baker's dog passed beyond his own control.

It happened one day, while Dr. Carey, who had gone with Philip to Washington, was away, that Mr. Hazzard declared that he must have some fresh air.

" This sort of thing," as he expressed it, could not "go on any longer," and in defiance of his friend's orders, he had himself assisted down stairs, and placed in an open barouche in which he sat with one leg stretched out, and his lame foot resting on the cushions of the seat opposite. Then, as he really entertained a deep affection for Jig, he invited that worthy dog to take the seat beside him, which Jig did, sitting upright upon his haunches, with his bowed front legs planted stiffly immovable before him.

All would have been well but that, as ill luck would have it, the time chosen by Mr. Hazzard for his first drive was a Saturday afternoon, when it is a well-known habit with bakers to send their bread about, a second time in the day, preparatory for Sunday.

It also chanced that just as the carriage reached Meredith Square, and was passing Mr. Drayton's house, the baker's boy was seeking admission at a side gate which opened upon a narrow passageway leading to the back yard, while the unconscious terrier was waiting at his master's heels, when Jig's piercing gaze detected him.

Uttering a low growl of rage, Jig sprang from

his high place of honor, miles downward in the estimation of all who knew him. In reality he was on the pavement with an easy bound, and would in another moment have fastened upon his enemy, if an unlooked-for obstacle had not come in his way.

This unforeseen occurrence was Miss Edith Arnold. She had just descended the steps of the house, in a costume appropriate for an afternoon walk, followed by Miss Prescott, when she received a sudden shock from behind. Before the unexpected force of it she tottered, and would have fallen, if Julia had not rendered her timely assistance.

At the same instant the baker's dog recognized his liberated foe, and with a howl of dismay sought shelter in the yard, the gate of which had just been opened. The baker's boy dropped his basket and made off down the street as fast as he could go, shouting, "Mad dog!" And Peter, dismounting from the box, where he had been seated beside the coachman, captured the discomfited Jig.

"Are you hurt, dear?" asked Julia, anxiously.

"I think not," answered Edith, still pale from the effect of the fright. "The dog did not try to bite me. I do not know what he wanted, but I was evidently in his way."

"That is one fashion of putting it," replied Julia. "I thought he seemed a good deal more in yours."

"My head feels rather queer."

"Come into the house and rest for a moment."

"Oh, it is nothing," said Edith. But after try-

ing to walk a step or two, she confessed that she
thought she might be better for keeping quiet.

"I think you had better give up the walk altogether," said Julia decidedly.

During this conversation, Mr. Hazzard had been
insisting that the reluctant Peter should help him
out of the carriage, and now appeared at the door
supported on a crutch, with anxious looks, which,
to do him justice, were but a faint expression of
the regret and mortification which he experienced.

"O Mr. Hazzard!" cried Julia. "How can
you be so imprudent as to bear your weight on
that ankle!"

"I can't help it," said Charley. "I had to get
out. I was feeling so badly about Jig's behavior.
I can't think what got into the dog, to fly at your
friend. Miss Arnold, is it not?"

"Yes," replied Julia, smiling, in spite of her distress, at the absurdity of the situation. "Let me
present Mr. Hazzard, Edith," she continued. "He
is anxious to apologize for the conduct of his dog."

"I hope you are not seriously hurt, Miss Arnold?" asked Charley. "I should never forgive
myself, if you were."

"Not at all," answered Edith. "I was only
startled. I shall be all right in a few moments."

They went into the house.

"Sit down here, Edith," said Julia, helping her
into an easy chair in the drawing-room; "and Mr.
Hazzard, you sit down too, please, and wait until I
get Miss Arnold a glass of wine."

The two invalids did as directed and were left sitting face to face, in a manner which rendered it essential to say something; but Charley was struggling with the disadvantage of not knowing what to say, and Edith with an untimely inclination to laugh, which, if indulged, she feared might be misinterpreted to the further confusion of the unlucky young man.

The awkwardness of the situation was suddenly relieved by the unexpected appearance of Jig. He had managed to elude Peter during his master's difficult descent from the carriage, and had slunk into the house at his heels, taking refuge under Mr. Hazzard's chair. He now ventured to thrust his nose forth, and snuff in a penitent manner, following this advance by rearing himself up and placing a deprecatory paw on his master's knee.

"Down Jig! Are n't you ashamed of yourself! Bad dog!" exclaimed said Mr. Hazzard severely. "I can't imagine what possessed you to behave so rudely!"

"Poor dog!" said Edith, touched by the evident shame of the recreant under this stern rebuke. "I assure you that he did not really do any harm, Mr. Hazzard. It is not worth while to be too hard upon him."

Jig's expression while she was speaking was worth study. He certainly understood that some one had taken his part, for he blinked hopefully at his master from the crouching attitude which he had assumed; but did he comprehend enough to realize the injustice of his position, without any means of human explanation to account for his erratic conduct, by revealing the deep sense of wrong in his canine heart, which had smouldered there and prompted it?

Partly from affection, partly from sympathy, Mr. Hazzard seemed to divine something of Jig's unhappy plight.

" He is a good dog, generally, Miss Arnold," he said relentingly.

" I am sure he is," responded Edith, "and it would be very unfair to blame him for this ebullition of energy, for nobody knows what he had it in his mind to do. It may have been some act of benevolence." Jig turned up his eyes at this moment, and looked actually saintly.

" It is partly my fault," said Charley. " I ought not to have taken him without a chain. He has been shut up for a long while, you see, Miss Prescott," he added, turning to Julia, who returned at this moment, "and he has got unruly."

" Ah! I know what you are afraid of, Mr. Hazzard," said Julia, laughing. " You do not mind Miss Arnold's thinking ill of you, but you are in great dread of her forming an evil opinion of Jig."

" I think your friend is very kind about it," answered Charley, "and it is fortunate that the dog did not knock her down."

" I am sure that he did not mean to knock me down," said Edith.

" I am sure of another thing," said Mr. Hazzard:

"that he must have given you an awful shock, and there are not many people who would take it so good-naturedly, Miss Arnold. Will you let me shake hands with you for good-by, — and you too, Miss Prescott?"

They both, smiling, granted his request, and he and Jig departed.

He was such a handsome fellow that it is possible that his looks said more than he did to soften the hearts of the two ladies ; but however this may have been, they gazed after the retreating carriage, containing Jig and his master, not unkindly, considering the annoyance he had caused them.

Julia made Edith drink the wine which she had brought her, and insisted upon her lying down on the sofa in the drawing-room.

" You must rest here for a while," she said, " before you go up-stairs. No one will disturb you, for everybody is out, and you have the house to yourself. I will go and buy your gloves and the other little things we wanted for this evening."

Edith smiled and thanked her. " I feel better already," she said, " but I will promise to do as you prescribe."

When Julia was gone, she lay still for some time, with her eyes closed. The silence of the house and the dim light in the drawing-room, which was always half in shadow from the heavy curtains at the windows, conspired to render her a little drowsy, and without expecting it she fell asleep.

The front door bell was rung once or twice without awakening her; nor was she conscious of the entrance of a person who came in through the half-closed doors of the library, with a book in his hand, while the person, who chanced to be Cecil Wilmott, was equally unaware of her vicinity. He had been told that every one was out, and having gone into the library to get a late number of the "Atlantic," which Mr. Drayton had promised to send his mother, was passing out through the drawing-room, when he was surprised to see some one on the sofa, and approaching a step or two nearer perceived that it was Miss Arnold. One arm had been used to prop herself against the back of the sofa, and her head rested upon it, with its soft light hair in some disorder. Julia had thrown an afghan over her, and placed her hat, which had been removed, with her little muff, on a chair beside her.

Cecil was so astonished that he stood still for a moment, wondering how she happened to be there. Then, instead of going away, as he was perfectly conscious that he should have done, he cautiously took up her little muff and laid his cheek against the soft fur, while his eyes dwelt upon her face. How sweet it looked in its repose! How delicate the color in the fair round cheek! What a lovely memory of a smile lingered about the corners of the pretty childlike mouth, and yet how much decision there was in the lines of the soft little chin!

"Her mouth is her best feature. It is exquisite," said Cecil to himself; but at that moment her eyelids trembled and unclosed, and her startled eyes met his. "On the whole, I 'm not sure that it is," he thought, as he lost himself in the limpid depths of her wondering gaze.

"Mr. Wilmott! How did you come here?" she asked, sitting up and looking about her with bewilderment.

"I came in through the library," said Cecil, blushing. "I was looking for a book for my mother."

"Oh! Did you find it?"

"I found it, and I found you."

"But how did I come to be asleep in the drawing-room?" asked Edith, with a puzzled look.

"I cannot imagine."

"Oh! I remember," she proceeded, in a more satisfied tone. "It was the bull-dog."

"The bull-dog!" repeated Cecil.

"Yes, — Mr. Hazzard's bull-dog. He nearly knocked me down, and I felt a little faint."

"I see," said Wilmott. "You really must forgive me for my intrusion."

"Of course." Edith smiled. "How strange you must have thought it to find me asleep!"

She rose from the sofa as she spoke, and seated herself in a chair, passing her hand lightly over her hair as she did so.

Cecil followed the gesture appreciatively.

"It is all right," he said, nodding. "Shall I tell you of what you reminded me when I found you first?"

"Of what?" she asked.

"Of that little picture on your fan which you showed me the other day. I thought you were like the sleeping lady, and I was like the fool."

"Were you here long?" she asked.

"Not very. I was just going away when you woke up."

"I am glad that I woke up," said Edith.

"Why are you glad?"

"Because the idea is very disagreeable to me of some one's being near without my knowing it. I would much rather have seen you."

"You think that is the less disagreeable of the two, then?" asked Cecil, laughing.

"I did not say that it was disagreeable at all," she said defiantly.

"When are you going to let me have the copy of verses which you promised?"

"I will get them for you now, if you like. I made it, as I said I would, the other evening."

She was glad of the opportunity to slip away to her own room and rearrange her somewhat disordered toilet.

Cecil read the "Atlantic" while she was gone, and waited very patiently. He made her take the most comfortable chair in the room on her return, having placed it so that the fading light fell full upon her face.

"Here it is," she said, opening a dainty little card-case, which she kept in a satchel at her side.

Cecil took the folded sheet of note-paper on which she had copied the verses, in a fair round hand, and she watched him while he read them, fancying that his manner was rather critical, but he smiled and thanked her.

THE SLEEPING LADY AND THE FOOL.

" O bride of sleep ! of waking gladness heir,
   Framed in thy luring wealth of golden hair,
   How nature joins with art to make thee fair
   And fatal to mankind !

" Why should each breath drawn simply for life's need
   Enhance the beauty of thy form to feed
   The longing eyes of all poor fools who lead
   Their lives too near to thine ?

" Why should unconscious movements in thy sleep,
   Thy head turned, to thy cheek the sudden leap
   Of color, with a sigh gentle, yet deep,
   Stir all a poor fool's soul ?

" Such charm has nature given to thy dreams,
   That, when in waking hours thy bright smile gleams
   On some adorer who has won, it seems,
   This passing sign of grace,

" The maiden arts which hedge about that smile
   March dignity and courtesy in file,
   Lest its receiver should grow bold the while
   Thou deftly steal'st his heart.

" Such arts cease to be dangerous, grow faint,
   Beside the living picture of a saint,
   Which makes me only long that I could paint
   Thee sleeping — I, thy fool."

Thus mused a motley fellow in a wood,
   Where he had come to sing, as he best could,
   Because his lady willed that he should,
   Or guard her if she slept.

Trembled the oak leaves in' the morning breeze,
The sunlight glancing through them played at ease
About the massive trunks, and humming bees
Filled all the air with life,

When faintly there was heard a bugle blast,
Distant at first, but drawing nearer fast.
The lady started up, " He comes at last ! "
She cried with ecstasy.

And now was echoed on the forest road
The sound of horse's feet, as on they strode,
And fleetly bore a knight, who proudly rode,
With mien gentle, yet brave.

The lady, filled with sudden consciousness,
Cast down her eyes, fearing they would confess
What, more she strove to hide she hid the less,
Her burning blushes' cause.

The knight had reined his steed in a heart beat,
One bound had brought him to the lady's feet,
Kneeling to worship there with protest sweet
And ardent vows of love.

" And art thou really come ? " she questioned low,
" Back from the fight where honor bade thee go,
To her who loved and missed and mourned thee so
She almost longed to die ? "

The poor fool listened not nor lingered more.
Much had he learned by *sight* of lover's lore,
And e'en too truly, as too sadly saw,
What such discourse foretold.

He sought a distant, lonely, forest glade,
And cast him down in a willow's shade.
He did not weep nor laugh, but gravely said,
" I am a fool indeed."

" Unfortunate young man ! " said Wilmott, as he refolded the paper and put it in his pocket. " My comparing myself to him seems to have been quite prophetic. I wonder whether the rest of the poem will come true ? "

" What *do* you mean ? "

" Oh, nothing. I was only wondering who wrote this ballad for you."

" I told you that it was written by a friend of ours, a long while ago."

" A friend of yours, or of your sister's ? "

" A friend of both ; we are very proud of his friendship."

" Indeed. May I ask why ? "

" Certainly. We admire him because he is a man, we think, of great ability, and his life has been one of the most patient scientific research."

" For which of you does he make verses ? "

" For neither. He makes them for his own amuse-ment, I fancy ; but he was always laughing at Ger-trude and calling her romantic because she believes in a great many things which he calls ' exploded fallacies,' and one day she found this which he had written, and so she has laughed at him ever since."

" Does he call you romantic ? " asked Cecil.

" Oh, dear, no ! " she answered, laughing. " He knows very well that I am not. My sister tells me that I have not an atom of romance in my compo-sition."

" I don't believe that," said Wilmott.

" Why ? "

"I think you have made quite a hero of romance in your imagination of this very individual, whoever he may be."

Edith laughed again, more heartily than before.

"That is too funny! If you could only see him, you would understand how impossible it would be to make a hero of him. Why, he wears green eyeglasses, and he is a professor of chemistry at Hoboken! He would be capable of reducing any ideal which might be presented to him to its original elements in five minutes."

"But he must be inclined to be sentimental at times, you know, to do this sort of thing," said Cecil.

"Oh, yes, he is human," she responded, with a merry smile, "but very unheroic."

"He is not like the knight on the fan then?"

"Not in the least. Will you tell me what time it is, Mr. Wilmott? I am afraid I must go up and dress for dinner."

"Why should you do that?"

"I do not want to be late."

"It wants an hour of dinner time."

"Julia will be coming home," she said uneasily, "and she will expect me to be resting, as she asked me to do."

"Is Julia such a tyrant?"

"Of course not, but she did not want me to be tired, because we are to go to the opera this evening."

"That is a polite way of telling me to go."

"I did not mean to tell you to go," said Edith, blushing.

"I am glad of that, for it is so pleasant to sit here and talk that unless you insist I would rather stay."

"But, perhaps, if you came to get a book for your mother she will be expecting it."

"Was that the only reason that you wanted to send me away?" He had risen and was leaning lightly on the back of her chair. She noticed that his manner had a certain fervor, unlike its usual carelessness of tone.

"No — yes — I do not know," she said, looking straight before her so that he could not see her face.

"Tell me one thing," said Cecil seriously, "and then I will go if you wish it."

"I did not say that I wished it. What is the thing?"

"Why do you think that I likened myself to the fool in the ballad?"

"Was it because you wanted me to tell you that you were not at all like him?" she asked, glancing up with a shy smile.

"On the contrary, it was because I felt very much in sympathy with him, having compared you to the lady."

"I suppose that was due to your having found me asleep."

"There did seem an unusual resemblance between our inward and our outward situations. Do

11

you remember the reason you said the fool had
to render him foolish — or sad, was it you called
him ? "

"I do not remember anything about it."

" Will you answer one other question ? "

" I cannot tell, until you ask it."

" It is not much. I only want to know whether
there is any knight in this case ? " He seated himself on a low footstool beside her chair, and turned
and looked up as he spoke."

" In what case ? "

"In your case ? Are you expecting some one
else ? " he asked earnestly.

She was quite taken by surprise, and there was
so much magnetism in the devoted expression of
his face as he raised it to hers that for a moment
she could not speak. Her eyes answered his, saying she knew not what, and it was with a great
effort that she withdrew them and rose from her
seat.

" I am expecting nothing," she said.

" You might give me a fair answer ! " cried Cecil, who had risen also. " I simply ask you whether
some one has been before me, some one who cared
for you ; will you not tell me ? "

She was leaning against the piano, and he was
leaning beside her with his arm upon it.

" I do not think that any one has ever cared for
me," she said, " if that is what you want to know."

"And you ? " he asked quickly. " Have you
ever cared for any one ? "

"You have no right to ask," she said indignantly.

"Then there has been some one?"

"How simply absurd!" she exclaimed, trying to laugh. "Of course there has not." She fancied as she spoke that she heard Julia's voice at the front door.

"It was a foolish question," said Cecil, "but I feel better, since you answered it."

They were both silent for a moment. Edith half regretted Julia's entrance at the end of it, in a vague, unreasonable way which she could not understand, and she felt quite sure that Cecil did. He went forward to greet Miss Prescott with his usual easy manner, but it was as though a spell had been broken.

"I am glad to see you," said Julia cordially, to Cecil. "Is that Edith? How are you dear? It is growing so dark that I did not see you at first."

"I feel better, thank you," answered Edith faintly.

"I do not think Miss Arnold is quite herself yet," said Cecil. "What a fright that bull-dog must have given her. It is too bad of me to have detained you all this time!" he added, turning again to Edith, who had risen and was evidently about to leave the room. He held out his hand as though to say good-night, but she slipped by without noticing it and escaped to her own chamber.

"How long have you been here?" asked Julia in a very quiet tone, after she had gone.

"I hardly know," said Cecil carelessly; "about an hour, I think.".

"Did you find Edith in the drawing-room?"

"She was asleep on the sofa."

"Asleep! Did you wake her?"

"Not intentionally of course. The noise of my entrance may have done so."

"Cecil," said Julia, "there is something about which I should like to speak to you. May I do so now?"

"With all my heart," replied Cecil, "but do you not think it is getting a trifle dark here? It might be well to ring for lights."

"So it is," responded Julia, crossing the room towards the bell, "and it is late, too. I am afraid I shall hardly be ready in time for dinner."

"I am very sure that I shall not," said Cecil, "and I am to dine out. I can come to see you tomorrow at any time you like."

"Perhaps that would be better," assented Julia, "or it will do any time next week. Is it not next week that we promised to lunch with Charlotte?"

"To be sure," said Cecil cheerfully. "You can talk to me then as much as you please."

CHAPTER XIV.

"But optics sharp it needs I mean,
To see what is not to be seen."
                                    JOHN TRUMBULL.

"THERE is your friend Miss Prescott, my dear,"
said Mr. Davering, in the middle of the second act
of the opera that evening, pointing to a proscenium
box which was very plainly in view from the stock-
holders' seats, among which he and Mrs. Davering
were sitting.

"Is it possible that you have only just found her
out, Buchanan?" asked his wife, with a look of
amusement. "Why, we interchanged nods before
the opera began!"

"She has her pretty friend with her," said Mr.
Davering, pursuing his investigations with the aid
of an opera glass, undisturbed by Mrs. Davering's
animadversions. "And there is that friend of
Charley's from Boston. He is talking to her. I
think, my dear, that Dr. Carey is inclined to admire
Miss Prescott. I thought he seemed quite attentive the other night at dinner."

"Did you indeed?" said Mrs. Davering uneasily, but with more respect, since this had been
the result of her own reluctant observation. "I
don't think Julia fancies him. He is too much of

a prig," she continued half to herself by way of reassurance, " but he will keep me from having her
at the house now that he has returned from Washington, and altogether I wish he would go back to
Boston."

" We must not be inhospitable, my dear," said
Mr. Davering, with good-humored malice.

His wife colored and was silent. She had hardly
noticed that she was speaking her thoughts aloud,
but had learned by experience that, obtuse as her
husband appeared, he had a perverse way of seeing
into things when least expected to do so.

" I noticed another thing the other evening," said
Mr. Davering sagely, pleased at the attention with
which his last discovery had been received.

" What was that ? "

" I noticed that Drayton was unusually devoted
to this little Miss Arnold, and I see he is talking
to her again to-night. Julia Prescott had better
look out for her friend unless she is ready to abdi-
cate in her favor."

" My dear Buchanan, who are you talking
about ? " exclaimed his wife, in profound amazement. " Do you mean Philip, or his father ? "

" I mean Algernon Drayton, of course. Who
ever thought of making love to Philip ? "

" I do not know, I am sure," said Mrs. Davering helplessly. " Miss Arnold was near me at
dinner, and I should not have suspected her of
making love to any one."

" Look at her now, then," returned Mr. Davering

triumphantly. "I do not say that she is doing it all, of course."

"The idea of Algernon Drayton's troubling himself about a shy little girl like that!" answered his wife, incredulously, but she was impressed with the originality of the idea at first, and then with the convenience with which such a discovery, if it proved to be true, would harmonize with her own plans.

She had already perceived that the task of marrying Julia to her son was beset with growing difficulties, of which Dr. Carey's admiration for the heiress was not the greatest. The chief trouble which she had to contend with was Julia's perfect contentment with her present surroundings. The girl was too happy to wish for any change. If her home were a little less to her liking she might more easily be induced to leave it, and the benevolent fairy, who busied herself so disinterestedly in her welfare, began to wonder whether she might not assist Fate a little in bringing this about. She turned her eyes as she did so towards the box at which her husband was still gazing, but saw little to support his assertion.

Mr. Drayton was, indeed, seated beside Miss Arnold, talking to her, apparently, with some earnestness. Dr. Carey, who had returned that evening from his visit to Washington, in company with Philip, seemed also to be making himself very agreeable to Julia, while Philip himself stood just behind him, and appeared to be the only person in the box who took any interest in the opera. He evidently was enjoying the singing, but just then the curtain fell, and the situation was altered. Mr. Drum Kettleby made his entrance at the back of the box, in a mood, as it seemed, to be very condescendingly gracious. He conversed for a moment or two with Miss Prescott, and then proceeded to address himself to her friend in a manner which proclaimed that she had found favor in his eyes. Mr. Drayton yielded his seat with great urbanity to the new-comer, and, after standing up and looking about him with an amiable but rather bored expression, left the box. He was a stockholder, and Mrs. Davering was presently pleased to see him making his way to where she was sitting, just as her husband had left her side.

"Good evening, Mrs. Davering. I thought I should find you here. Did not you tell me last winter that 'Carmen' was your favorite opera?"

"Did I? I had forgotten."

"You may possibly only have said that the heroine was your favorite character."

"I am quite sure that I never told you that."

"I can hardly be mistaken. You said that, or something like it, apropos of Mrs. Percy's having chosen to represent 'Carmen' at the fancy ball."

"Oh, I remember now. You were surprised at her having chosen the character of 'Carmen,' and I was not. I thought that in her the choice was quite natural."

"Why, yes," said Mr. Drayton. "I rather gathered that 'Carmen' was your ideal."

"I did not say that it was a character I should have chosen for myself."

"Ah, I see. It was your ideal for Mrs. Percy."

Mrs. Davering laughed rather nervously.

"What a satirical man you are," she said.

"To bé fair with you," continued Mr. Drayton, "I will confess that it suited Mrs. Percy's style to perfection. She looked charmingly, and she is looking very well to-night. Seeing her here reminded me of the incident."

He bowed as he spoke to a lady who occupied the proscenium box in the second tier, opposite to the one which Philip had taken for their own party. She was surrounded by quite a gay circle, in which there were more gentlemen than ladies, and was herself a very brilliant centre to the group, as she was strikingly handsome, and arrayed in some white material in which threads of gold seemed so woven that they caught the light as she moved.

"I did not know that you had such an admiration for Mrs. Percy," remarked Mrs. Davering.

"I am very apt to admire what is beautiful," said Mr. Drayton wickedly, for he knew that there was no love lost between Mrs. Davering and Mrs. Percy, although there was the semblance of a good understanding, as often happens with rival leaders of fashion.

The older lady, who had been courted for many years for her position and her husband's wealth, although she had never received so much personal

attention as the other, was jealous of the ascend-
ency which the younger one was attaining just as
her own star began to wane.

"I was just saying to Buchanan," she ventured,
"what a pretty girl Miss Arnold is."

"So she is," said Mr. Drayton heartily; "and
a very good little girl, too, I think." He glanced
up at the box as he spoke, and smiled at Julia, who
happened to catch his eye.

"I see she is in a style you admire also," said
Mrs. Davering, scoring one; "but to my thinking
there is no one as handsome as Julia."

"I am not sure that every one would consider
Julia handsome," said Mr. Drayton, looking away
towards the drop-curtain, with a shade of reserve
in his tone.

"I am quite sure that Dr. Carey does," said
Mrs. Davering.

Mr. Drayton turned again towards the box.

"Yes," he answered. "I think that Dr. Carey
admires Julia; but they are old friends, you know."

"Do not put too much faith in their friendship,"
said the lady.

"What do you mean?" asked Mr. Drayton,
with an odd note of emotion in his tone which was
otherwise carefully guarded.

"I do not know, of course," said she; "but I
am inclined to think him serious about Julia. Mrs.
Wilmott was saying the other day what a pity it is
that he is a Unitarian, when you have such a strong
objection to all forms of dissent."

" If Lawrence Carey has been making himself agreeable to Charlotte it is quite natural, as a woman and Charlotte's mother, that my sister should interest herself in his religious faith."

" You mistake me," said Mrs. Davering, with a puzzled look. " I did not say that he was interested in Charlotte Wilmott, but in Julia."

" So I understood," returned Mr. Drayton impenetrably, " and in that case he would only have me to deal with. I should be much more anxious on some other points. Whether he were a good man, for instance, one calculated to make my ward happy, and had gained her entire affection."

" Oh, but I did not say that Julia was thinking of marrying him," cried Mrs. Davering hastily, " or that she is in love with him, or anything else."

" You will forgive me for confessing that even your having said so would hardly establish so undemonstrable an assertion in my mind beyond the chance of misinterpretation."

" Oh, dear, no ! Of course not. All I meant was that I suppose Julia will fancy some one some day."

" I hope so."

" Then you will encourage her marrying?" asked the lady eagerly.

" I shall have no control over Julia's actions at the expiration of another year," replied Mr. Drayton coldly.

" It is not so much a question of control as of influence," said Mrs. Davering. " Julia is a girl

whom it is so difficult to make see her true interests."

" Pray what do. you take them to be ?" asked
Mr. Drayton dryly.

" Why, those of every girl. To make hay while
the sun shines. I wish she would learn to do that."

" Julia has known how to make hay from the
beginning, I fancy," said her guardian, " if she
wished to make it, and she has wit enough to serve
for sunshine on the dullest day."

" Yes, she has wit enough, but she is so unim-
pressionable, and what is the use of knowing how
to take advantage of circumstances if she does not
take the advantage ? Her life cannot go on forever as it is doing now."

" That is equally true of the rest of us," said Mr.
Drayton, with a sigh, and then he left Mrs. Davering, little dreaming the construction which she
would put on this innocent remark.

Miss Arnold, meanwhile, was already wearying of
Mr. Drum Kettleby's elegant attentions, and gladly
acceded to Philip's suggestion of going with him
to the front of the house, so as to have a full view
of the stage when the curtain rose. She had quite
missed Philip during his absence, and he seemed
equally glad to see her again, for since their conversation on the day of the dinner a pleasant
friendly confidence had been established between
them, and she would have been glad now to be
able to ask him a few questions about his visit to
the capitol, but although she had accepted his arm

to walk through the corridor, this might not be, for Mr. Drum Kettleby insisted on walking at her other side, much to Philip's displeasure. He chanced to have no liking for this favorite of fortune.

"The Academy is really worth seeing, you know," said Mr. Drum Kettleby. "It is a very respectable size, as opera houses go, but it is nothing this evening compared to what it is at an assembly. You will be at the Assembly, of course, Miss Arnold?"

Edith acknowledged that she should.

"That is delightful!" exclaimed Mr. Drum Kettleby, on learning that she was to appear under the wing of Mrs. Davering. "I speak for the cotillon. I trust you have not already promised the cotillon?"

"I have not, indeed, or thought of it."

"Then I may have it?"

"The Assembly is nearly a week off. Is it not a long while ahead to make an engagement?" she asked innocently

"A long while!" cried Mr. Drum Kettleby. "Why, I am astonished to find you still free to give me a dance, I do assure you."

"I had intended to ask you to dance the German with me, Miss Arnold," said Philip, in an unusually haughty tone.

"I am your guest, you know," said Edith sweetly, "and quite at your disposal."

"Oh, but I do protest, Miss Arnold," broke in

Mr. Drum Kettleby, " that that is the most un-heard-of partiality, to dance with Mr. Drayton, when I was the first to ask you."

" Perhaps you had better revoke your decision, Miss Arnold," said Philip. " It is quite unheard-of partiality to prefer any one as a partner to Mr. Drum Kettleby."

" I really do not know what I ought to do," answered Edith, opening her large blue eyes and looking from one to the other in much perplex-ity.

" Oh, but there is no doubt about it at all, you know," cried Mr. Drum Kettleby. " It is not a question of whom you prefer as a partner, of course," he conceded, with an air of modesty, " but simply of who asked you first."

" Is that really the rule ? " asked Edith, looking to Philip for counsel.

He was touched by the trust implied in her ap-peal to him, and by a certain half-confessed assur-ance which it contained that she preferred him. Indeed, so natural did the preference seem to Edith, that she was at little pains to conceal it, ex-cept so far as civility to Mr. Drum Kettleby de-manded, and Mr. Drum Kettleby was by no means thin-skinned. Philip was mollified, and made an effort to conquer his ill humor.

" I will tell you how we can arrange it," he said. " You shall dance the German with Mr. Drum Kettleby and give me the pleasure of taking you to supper."

" I will do so gladly," she answered, with a grateful smile.

"Come now, that is excellent!" cried Mr. Drum Kettleby. " That will be grand," and with this pleasure in prospect, he bade them good evening, and proceeded to pay his respects to Mrs. Percy.

The whole of this weighty conversation had not taken more than five minutes, but Edith saw him depart with a sense of relief.

" You look pale to-night," said Philip kindly. " Do you not feel well ? "

" I am a little tired," she admitted, " but what a pretty sight it is ! Ah, there goes the curtain ! I had no idea the stage was so deep."

They were standing at the opening of one of the passageways which led into the auditorium between the small boxes, exactly in the centre of the house. Looking downward over all the gay toilets in the curving rows of the dress circle, and across the crowded parquet, they were greeted by the Gipsy Scene in " Carmen." The motley groups of idlers, some playing cards, some drinking, the camp in the middle distance, and the mountains and blue valleys represented against a pale blue sky by the farthest scenery, lent so much illusion as to make the view seem to stretch away with the indefiniteness of a real landscape.

Compared with the marvels of scenic effect so often produced in the great continental theatres, there was not so much to admire perhaps as to criticise, but to the inexperienced young person from

New Rochelle, the whole thing was complete, and the music and the scene together wrought upon her fancy with almost the force of reality. "Do you know I never saw and heard a whole opera before?" she said to her companion, with a solemnity which amused him.

When they returned to the box Dr. Carey had gone and Mr. Drayton and Julia were there alone.

"We were thinking of coming to look for you," said Julia.

"Speak for yourself, my dear. I was not," said Mr. Drayton. "I was resolved upon the let-alone policy which Bo-peep originated, and which has become so popular in our day. The event proves that it would have worked well."

"Oh, the stage was so beautiful, Julia, from where we were standing!" cried Edith. "I wish you could have seen the gipsy camp as we did."

"I have been enjoying a very pretty scene myself," said Julia, "and am inclined to think that it is a mistake to roam abroad in search of distant views. Nearer ones are more to my taste, but Philip is always a rolling stone."

"Let us see some of the moss you have been gathering," said Philip.

"Look in the box opposite. Is that not an animated picture?"

"Mrs. Percy, you mean? She is hardly as good as an opera."

"She is worth fifty operas," said Mr. Drayton, "if one is near enough to hear the music."

" Perhaps she is," replied Edith, thoughtfully, "although I had not noticed her before."

" There, you see, Philip, I have the majority on my side," cried Julia triumphantly.

" You are apt to do so in espousing one so popular. There is Lawrence Carey, I see, and Cecil Wilmott. I thought, by the bye, that Cecil was due at the University supper to-night."

" He told me that he was to dine out, too," said Julia. " I suspected that it was with Mrs. Percy."

" Cecil is a young gentleman of multifarious engagements," said Mr. Drayton ; but Edith said nothing. She turned her eyes determinately towards the stage, yet she saw Cecil Wilmott all the time, seated in an easy attitude beside Mrs. Percy, and talking, as he sometimes talked to her. Meanwhile the opera advanced. The last thrilling scene was begun.

" Who is that pretty girl opposite ? " asked Mrs. Percy. " Her face is new to me."

" What girl ? " returned Cecil carelessly, " there are so many."

" I mean in the box with the Draytons. You are looking in the parquet. Do you not see the one on the left, who seems to be so much interested in the fate of Carmen ? "

Edith had become intensely excited during the struggle for life which was taking place at that moment between the faithless Carmen and her forsaken lover, and was leaning slightly forward, with her eyes fixed on the stage.

12

"Oh, yes, I see," said Wilmott. "You mean Miss Arnold. She is a friend of Miss Prescott's from New York."

"Then you know her?" asked Mrs. Percy, catching a conscious note in his voice.

"I have met her several times."

Mrs. Percy looked more critically at the eager young face.

"Does she look as pretty as that always?" she asked. "I should hardly think so."

Wilmott smiled. "Ah! that I cannot say," he replied, "I can only answer for the occasions when I have seen her."

CHAPTER XV.

"*Guil.* Good my lord, vouchsafe me a word with you.
Ham. Sir, a whole history."

SHAKESPEARE.

JULIA was engaged in making tea, a day or two later, and Miss Ruthven in making a pocket pincushion, when Edith entered, all in a glow from walking in the clear, cold air of a January afternoon.

"How did you get on, when I left you? You had no trouble in finding your way home, dear?" asked Julia.

"None whatever. Mr. Wilmott came with me."

"Oh! I see."

"Will you not give me a cup of tea, Julia?" asked Edith, with a perceptible deepening of the roses in her cheeks.

Old Rogers appeared at this moment to announce a friend of Miss Ruthven's, who was waiting to see her in the library.

"Come now, Edith," said Julia, when they were alone. "Confess that Cecil Wilmott improved the occasion by asking you to walk with him."

Edith laughed.

"We walked a few squares farther than the house, but not far. Was it a wrong thing to do?" she asked.

" Certainly not."

" I was not quite sure about the etiquette of the matter," said Edith shyly, " whether it was the custom to walk with any one who asked you."

" People are very apt to do it if they want to," replied Julia, " but if they do not, it never seems to them the right thing to do."

" There is no use in trying to talk to you about anything seriously, I suppose," said Edith, with resignation.

" Yes, you may tell me seriously what you think of Cecil Wilmott."

Edith was silent for a moment.

" If I knew, myself," she said, after a pause, " I should be quite willing to tell you, but I change my mind about him almost every time I see him." She glanced at Julia over the top of her tea-cup and added carelessly, " It seems to me that Dr. Carey admires you very much, and that you are rather hard on him."

Miss Prescott quite understood that this was a direct attempt to carry the war into the enemy's country. The device was so innocent that it amused her.

" I do not know whether Dr. Carey admires me or not," she said coolly, " but I know that I honestly like him."

" Then why do you behave so to him ? "

" I simply behave to him in a manner calculated to retain his regard. You know I am not naturally gushing."

"No, but your manner is usually playful and rather responsive, whereas you are always snubbing Dr. Carey."

"The course of wise repression which I have pursued with Dr. Carey deserves a different designation," said Julia gravely.

"But why do you pursue this course of repression, as you call it, with *him* especially?"

"Because he comes from Boston," replied Julia, dropping a lump of sugar into Edith's second cup of tea. "A Boston man," she proceeded solemnly, "has to be repressed. If you give him the slightest encouragement, he misunderstands it."

"What!" exclaimed Edith, opening her large blue eyes. "Do they advance too rapidly?"

"Mercy no!" exclaimed Miss Prescott in her impatience; "they recede."

"Oh!" said Edith, "I understand. Of course that is very disagreeable."

"Of course," returned Julia, "one does not wish for the attention of a man unless he desires to bestow it, but it is very disagreeable, as you naively remark, to perceive from his manner that he thinks you are paying attention to him."

A luncheon at which ladies only should be present being considered "the thing" in the way of an entertainment by Miss Charlotte Wilmott, she was much pleased with the idea of giving one to Miss Arnold, and it would have been difficult to imagine a more interested and excited person than Mrs. Wilmott on the morning after the conversation last recorded. Not the Earl of Leicester, when he was to be honored with the sojourn of Queen Elizabeth at Kenilworth, not Caleb Balderstone, when occupied in concealing his master's poverty from the retainers of Sir William Ashton, were more impressed with the importance of the occasion or more determined to spare no pains to make the most of their advantages; and no one who saw the elegant little repast to which the ladies sat down a few hours later would have imagined the anxiety it had caused the smiling hostess.

Cecil Wilmott had been urged by his sister to tear himself away from the professional cares which beset him at his office at the early hour of four, in order to escort the three younger ladies of the party to the State House, and thence on a round of sight-seeing, with which Cecil declared that he should be intensely bored, but still yielded to her persistence, and they had just taken coffee after luncheon, when he appeared with Philip Drayton.

On the way to Independence Hall, Cecil walked with Julia, while Edith followed with his sister, accompanied by Philip. As soon as they were fairly out of earshot of the others, Julia said, "You suggested that I should wait until to-day, Cecil, to say what I had to say to you, and I think I had better say it now."

" As you please," replied Cecil, tapping the pavement with his cane in a slightly irritated manner, " that is if you are quite sure that you had better say it at all."

"Oh! I am quite clear on that point," said Julia, quietly, "and all the more so that I fancy I can see by your manner that you know what I want to speak about."

"It would be as well to tell me, at any rate," returned Cecil.

"It is of Edith," said Miss Prescott, dropping her voice and her eyes for a moment. "Was that what you thought?"

"It does not much matter what I thought," said Wilmott. "What is it that you think?"

"I think it not at all safe for your peace of mind or hers, that you should pay her such marked attention."

"I do not think I have paid her any marked attention."

"Not marked, perhaps, in the sense of being very noticeable before the world, but decidedly *accented* to any one near enough like myself to notice the emphasis," said Julia.

"I think you are rather inclined to exaggerate," responded Wilmott, with a suppressed smile.

"You have not thought so before, Cecil, — only that I saw things as they were. Have you not often told me that I pointed out something in you before you had recognized it in yourself?"

"Yes," said Wilmott.

"And has it not usually been some folly which you were on the point of committing?"

"I believe it has."

"Now, Cecil, in this case it is not for you alone,

that I speak, but for my friend. She has a formed manner and a natural power of self-control which are deceptive, but she is very young and quite a child in experience."

" I know that."

" Yes, but you do not know, or do not stop to think, how much responsibility I feel about her."

" I don't see what I have to do with it," said Cecil.

" Her mother and sister, for her sake," continued Julia seriously, " befriended me when I was most in need of friends, and now they have trusted her to me, and I cannot see her happiness endangered without trying to save it from mishap."

" Pray, what mishap do you fear?" asked Wilmott, with heightened color.

" I hardly know," she answered, faltering a little for the first time since the beginning of the conversation.

" I do not, I'm sure."

" Yes you do," cried Julia. " We both know. It is false delicacy to pretend that we do not. There can be no doubt that it would be an unmixed misfortune for Edith if you should succeed in making her like you — better than other people."

" Why do you assume that I am trying to make her like me better than other people?"

" Because I can see that you have quite lost your head about her."

" But if I keep my heart?" asked Cecil laughing, " is not that the important matter?"

"I am not troubled about that," replied Julia. "My experience is that you are much more apt to lose your head than your heart."

"Is it Miss Arnold's head that you are troubled about then? If you will excuse the slang I will confess that it seems to me to be a remarkably level one."

"So it is," said Julia proudly; "it is as clever a little head as one often meets, and I cannot help feeling as if I were doing something disloyal in daring to question its decisions, but I should never forgive myself if I let things go on without trying to stop them."

"Do you mean that you think that she — that she might care?" asked Wilmott, with a kind of gasp.

"I do not know," said Julia quietly. "I fear lest she might care, and that would cause much misery."

"If she cared for me, I should care for her," said Cecil, in a very low tone.

"Oh! Cecil, and if you did what good could come of it? What but misery for both?"

"I don't know," answered Wilmott, "that it is worth while to consider so curiously in advance."

"That is exactly what it is worth while to do," said Julia earnestly. "I want you to consider her circumstances and yours before it is too late. Remember what you owe to your mother and sister — and — and Cecil, do not be angry with me for reminding you that this is not the first time that you have believed that you might care for some one."

" How do you know that ? "

" I know more. I know that at this very moment there is another woman who " —

" Stop Julia ! " interrupted Cecil sharply.

" I knew you would tell me that I had no right to speak of it."

" I think you are not inclined to curtail your right."

" I have done now. I am so much in earnest that I thank you for letting me speak as I have. You don't know how I love my little friend."

" Yes I do," said Cecil, and he stretched out his hand and took Julia's and then turned away, leaving her in front of the State House, which they had just reached. She saw him stand for a moment looking up at the statue of Washington, then he entered the building, and was lost to view.

" I think I did right," she said to herself, "but it was very hard to do."

At that moment, Edith and Charlotte Wilmott came up, with Philip.

" What has become of Cecil ? " asked Charlotte. " I saw him take the most touching farewell of you. One would have thought you had parted for . life."

" One would have been mistaken," replied Julia lightly, " for here comes your brother with Dr. Carey; I suppose he went to find him."

" Oh, yes, I remember Cecil did suggest that Dr. Carey should meet us here," responded Charlotte.

" It was I who asked if he might be included in

your party, Charlotte," said Philip, " as he had never been properly put through the sights."

" I don't wonder you felt a twinge of conscience when he has stayed with you so often," remarked Charlotte.

"As for that matter," said Julia, "I don't believe that Edith would have been made to do half of her duty as a stranger in Philadelphia if you had not taken her in hand, Charlotte. Philip and I make very poor hosts. We are inclined to let our guests do as they please, which is the most unprincipled thing in the world."

" I certainly think that any one returning from here, would regret not having seen Independence Hall," said Charlotte stiffly.

" Why of course I should regret not seeing it," cried Edith. " I am so much obliged to you for bringing me here."

Nevertheless, she was conscious of a certain vague feeling of disappointment when they entered the square, white-plastered room, in which she was told that the Declaration had been signed. She began to realize that in hearing of Independence Hall she must have imagined something like the hall of a baronial castle, — not that she had ever seen such a thing, but she had seen pictures of dim, lofty chambers, with carved ceilings and massive walls which were suggested by the name, and now they all vanished in the broad sunlight which streamed through the half-drawn faded curtains of the wide windows and lay on the tiled floor of the cheerful apartment in which she stood. She gazed with some dismay at the ring of stiff-looking armchairs, with covers of various materials, among which leather and horsehair predominated, and read with bewilderment the placards placed on the seats of some of them proclaiming in large letters that they had been restored to their original position by this or that family of distinction. Some of these families were so munificent as to have re-covered their chair. She was interested in the portraits of the various signers which were ranged overhead, although it occurred to her that the artists might have been more liberal with their canvas.

"You forget that it was an economical age," said Philip, with a grim smile.

"Do look at this mosaic, presented in memory of the Centennial!" exclaimed Miss Wilmott enthusiastically, pausing before a massive picture in an ebony frame, representing Washington, or rather misrepresenting him, like so many of the worthy General's portraits.

"Is it not beautiful?" cried Charlotte. "It is a gift of the Italian government."

"It is very elaborate," said Edith, to whom she seemed to look for a reply.

"Elaborate! I should think it was. Just think of the time it must have taken to make it, and what it must have cost."

Philip laughed. "I am afraid that is the principal thing one does think of in looking at it," he said.

"Very true," responded Cecil, "and as one should not look a gift horse in the mouth, we had better pass on."

Dr. Carey, who was talking to Julia, now led the way into the room opposite, which contained quite an interesting collection of curiosities and relics. There they remained for some time examining the vestiges of a highly respectable but much dilapidated past.

Philip found Edith in front of a glass case, containing an enormous silver-laced waistcoat ticketed as having been worn at the Republican Court and one would say at many a patriotic feast, exhibited side by side with the baby-clothes made for John Quincy Adams by Mrs. John Adams his illustrious mamma, the tiniest things imaginable. She could not help smiling at the contrast.

"What do you think of all this?" asked Philip.

"I like it. I feel as if I were beginning to catch the spirit of the place."

"So am I," said Philip. "I have been wondering whether the Republican simplicity and quaint sincerity of our forefathers, which it is so easy to ridicule, may not have been a necessary medium for reducing liberty from an ideal to a practical experiment."

"I think it must have been," she answered eagerly, "for I was struggling with such a fancy, too, but I should not have known how to express it as well as that."

Philip smiled. "You always know how to say

something kind," he responded, with a pleased light in his eyes.

" Do come and look at this absurd little wooden image of the Marquis de Lafayette, Philip ! " exclaimed Julia, and he turned to where she stood just as Cecil approached.

" Would you like to see the cracked bell," he asked, " which rang in independence ? "

Edith assented, and followed him from the room, across the hall, and up the staircase, to where the huge bronze bell hung, silent and solemn, beneath the steeple of the State House.

" How did it get up there ? " she asked, tipping back her head to look at it, with a wondering expression, like a child.

" It is not known," said Wilmott. " For a long while it was displayed to visitors in a sort of wooden cage, formed of the original beams and timbers on which it had once swung so freely when on duty in the steeple."

" Perhaps, being cracked, the people were afraid it might do something desperate," suggested Edith.

" It may have been something of that sort," replied Cecil, " and perhaps it was the bell itself which burst through these restraints and flew up here. All I know is that one fine day, at about the beginning of the centennial year, I saw it hanging where you see it now."

" You are an excellent *ciceroni ;* " said Edith, " you seem quite fertile in invention." She turned to him gayly as she spoke, and was surprised at the grave expression of his face. It was so out of keeping with the easy, light tone in which he had been speaking. "Are you not feeling well?" she asked impulsively.

"Very well indeed, thank you," he answered coldly.

"I beg your pardon," she returned in an equally distant manner. "I thought you looked unusually grave."

"I feel grave," he said, in a weary way, unlike his usual one, "but I am not ill. I almost wish I were."

She would not question him again, and they descended the steps in silence.

"Come and look at the square," Philip proposed, joining them with Charlotte.

They all stepped out on the sunny expanse of Independence Square, and from here Edith thought the view of the State House was much more impressive than from the other side. Dr. Lawrence Carey was delighted with it. He said there was a great deal of "tone" in the old bricks, but Edith caught very few of his remarks, as they were directed almost entirely to Julia.

She grew dispirited herself. Somehow the life had gone out of her enjoyment, and she kept with Philip and Charlotte, who talked together very pleasantly, only interrupted by an occasional remark from Cecil. After all, but a few of the sights planned for her benefit were seen, and yet, at the end of the day, she felt depressed and over-tired.

CHAPTER XVI.

"A child of our grandmother Eve, a female;
Or, for thy more sweet understanding, a woman."
SHAKESPEARE.

THEY did not see Wilmott again for several days. There were one or two small parties to which Edith refused to go on the plea of a "headache" and being "tired." Julia was surprised and puzzled, but tried, without success, to change her friend's decision. Edith had her way and stayed at home, talking to Miss Ruthven, who was initiating her into the mysteries of a new stitch, or listening to Mr. Drayton, who was fond of reading aloud, and could thus entertain them both.

There was a weary look in her blue eyes at times, and a perplexed sadness in her face, as though regretfully admitting a fact to her consciousness of the existence of which she had not dreamed; but Julia, who was very busy just then with her own affairs, did not see the look, and so could not interpret it. Everywhere that Miss Prescott went she met Dr. Carey, and she was beginning to realize that there was something in his manner a little different from what there formerly had been. People wondered that he was making quite so long a visit to Philadelphia, and the care of Mr. Hazzard, who was now able to get about by means of a crutch, did not seem quite a sufficient retaining cause.

"I imagine he is staying for the Assembly. I think Philip said he had not been to one in Philadelphia," said Julia, in answer to a question from Mrs. Davering as to what she "thought" of the matter.

Mrs. Davering, indeed, was much disturbed by Dr. Carey's lengthened stay, but her sense of propriety as a hostess, and fear that the cause of her annoyance might be suspected, prevented her from expressing herself freely on the subject even in confidence.

As for Charley, he was, as usual, fighting against his own interests with a blindness which was quite incomprehensible to his politic mother. He felt sincerely attached to Dr. Carey, and grateful to him, in his off-hand way, for the care he had taken of him, and would urge him to stay from day to day, — now for this thing, now for that, — so that his blustering cordiality quite drowned any lack of heartiness which Mrs. Davering may have shown in seconding the invitation. Besides, there was one point on which she did show equal eagerness of insistence. She would not *hear* of Dr. Carey's accepting Philip's invitation to make him a visit, and going from her house to Mr. Drayton's, any more than Charley would. It was bad enough to have him in the same city with Julia, she thought, but it would be worse to have him under the same roof.

Poor Mrs. Davering had to keep all her discontent to herself therefore, but on the occasion just referred to she ventured a question to Julia, by way of sounding that impenetrable young person, and also under the painful conviction that she was apt to know more of Dr. Carey's plans and motives than most people.

They had met in the supper-room at a little party at Mrs. Percy's. It was a very small affair, such as she was fond of giving, only ten or fifteen ladies, and the larger proportion of gentlemen, which was always noticeable at Mrs. Percy's entertainments.

"I suppose, of course, then, that he is to dance the cotillon with you," said Mrs. Davering, by way of rejoinder to Julia's supposition that Dr. Carey was staying for the Assembly.

"I do not know that it is quite a matter of course," replied Julia carelessly, " but he is, and I am glad, for I think him an agreeable partner."

"It is hard for Charley that he cannot hope to use his feet in that way again this winter," said his mother. "He is so fond of dancing!"

"Yes, and he dances so well," responded Julia, who, though far from guessing all Mrs. Davering's secrets, knew how dearly she loved to hear her first-born praised, and had besides an honest liking for the simple-hearted fellow.

"He is here to-night, you know," said the older lady, with a smile, " and he is to take me to the Assembly. You must not forget to meet me in the dressing-room, you and Miss Arnold, at ten o'clock. By the bye, why is not your little friend here this evening?"

"I do not know. I did my best to persuade her to come," said Julia, "but she would not, although Mrs. Percy very courteously inclosed a card and a special invitation; she says she is waiting for the Assembly."

"Mr. Drayton does not seem to be here this evening, either. Is he also waiting for the Assembly?"

"I fancy so," answered Julia laughing. "He has been rather lazy since his accident, and looked very comfortable when I left him, in his arm-chair, in the library. Philip was the only person whom I could induce to come with me."

"I suppose you left Miss Arnold in the library, too?"

"Yes. Edith and Miss Ruthven were both there. They are getting to be great cronies."

"Some one else is getting to be a great crony of Miss Arnold, it seems."

"Who do you mean?"

"Why, Mr. Drayton. Do you not think he is?"

"Yes," said Julia, opening her eyes a little. "He likes Edith very much, I think."

"I never should have expected it," exclaimed Mrs. Davering. "If any one had asked me I should have said it was the most unlikely thing in the world!"

"I do not see why any one should not like Edith," said Julia.

"Oh! of course, she is a very nice girl, but I should have thought him so much more likely to fancy a person of a different style. Some one older, and " —

"And what?" asked Julia haughtily.

" And — well — to be frank with you, rather cleverer, but there is no accounting for tastes. The times are certainly changed when such a society man as your guardian will let you go with Philip to a party and spend the evening quietly at home."

"It is not a subject which I care to discuss," said Julia; "but although my guardian has had some social duties to perform which have encroached upon his evenings, I can truly say that he has passed a part of every one, which he could pass, at home for many years, and I believe happily."

" Quite right, quite right, my dear. I am sure that he has done his duty by you very thoroughly, and it is natural that you should not fancy the idea of any change, but changes will come, as Mr. Drayton said himself to me the other evening."

" What did Mr. Drayton say?"

" Why we had been talking of you, and he said that of course his life could not go on forever as it was going now."

" He said that?"

" Words to that effect. He certainly spoke of himself in connection with the idea of coming

change, and I associated the remark, not unreasonably, with the possibility of his marrying again."

"Such an association may not seem unreasonable to you," retorted Julia, with flashing eyes,
"but to me it seems very disrespectful."

Mrs. Davering looked at her pityingly.

"It is foolish to get so excited about it, Julia,"
she said, "for it is certainly well to face the possibility. Of course it would be disagreeable for
you if your guardian were to marry at any time,"
she continued, in a patronizing tone which was particularly galling. "More so for you, I think, than
for Philip, because your position in the household
would be so much altered ; but if he could have
chosen a suitable person, of a proper age, I cannot
say that the step might not have had its advanta-
geous side in affording you a protection which you
have never had."

"Mrs. Davering," replied Julia, rising from her
seat, "you have said much more than I should
have allowed any one else to say, but even old
friendship does not give the liberty you are taking."

Decidedly the victory was not with Mrs. Davering, in spite of her well-turned phrases. As she
saw Miss Prescott leave the supper room on the
arm of Dr. Lawrence Carey, she experienced a
twinge of regret most uncommon with her, for she
feared that she had gone too far in the very direction in which she intended not to go. What if
the girl should not only resent her interference, as

it was evident she did, but believing all that she
pretended to discredit, should be stung by the idea
into accepting the wrong man?   It never occurred
to Mrs. Davering that Julia could be in earnest in
disavowing the bare possibility of her guardian's
thinking of marriage, for Algernon Drayton was a
man so young for his years, and so attractive to
women, that she had heard such a chance discussed
again and again, and it seemed absurd to her to
be asked to believe that it had never entered the
mind of so acute and intelligent a person as Miss
Prescott.

"It was all very fine," she said to herself, "to
get so indignant with me, but it was done for effect,
of course.   She knows as well as I do, that many
and many a cap has been set to catch him, and it
is a wonder he has not been caught before."

Julia meanwhile was floating away on Dr.
Carey's arm to the dreamy music of a waltz.

"What a very handsome girl Miss Prescott is!"
exclaimed Charley Hazzard admiringly to Cecil
Wilmott, who had just come in and was looking
rather cross.

"Yes," said Cecil, following the direction of his
eyes, "she is very handsome, if one admires that
style."

"I do not see how any one can help admiring
it," said Mr. Hazzard.

"I know you do not," replied Cecil, for it was
well known among his friends how "hopelessly
gone" — as he himself expressed it — Mr. Haz-

zard had been with regard to Miss Prescott for several years.

"I am glad to see you about again, old fellow," Cecil added kindly. "How is your ankle? — better?"

"Oh, my ankle is all right," said Mr. Hazzard, "if Carey would only take this confounded plaster dressing off. You have no idea how uncomfortable it makes a fellow."

"I rather think Carey knows what he is about," said Cecil. "You would probably be worse off without it. There is Mrs. Davering, I must go and speak to her."

Cecil liked to win his reputation for good nature easily. It cost very little to ask after a friend, but to listen to his complaints was a more serious matter, and he saw no reason why he should be bored with those of this stalwart young fellow, whose present position represented the height of worldly prosperity, whatever the future might have in store for him in the way of reverses. He had a rich mother to surround him with every luxury, a rich stepfather to indulge his every taste, a beautiful country seat to spend his summers in, the handsomest of city homes in which to entertain his friends, and a yearly allowance with which to satisfy his every whim, while with Cecil things were different. In spite of the anxious effort at home to save him from the groveling cares which beset the women of his family, he often felt the need of money, and realized without acknowledging it, the inconsistency of this sensation with the butterfly life which he chose to lead; for it took all his ingenuity to dress himself in the latest fashion, to frequent the most elegant club, to provide himself with cigars and his lady friends with bouquets, and yet avoid contracting bills which he could not pay. That he did not contract bills was somewhat to his credit. He certainly did not, but in the constant effort to live as others did on twice the money, he expended energy worthy of a better cause. He knew, in fact, that it was his duty to have turned this energy to the support of his mother and sister, for whom he was bound to work, and yet he hated work, and whenever he thought of it all the zeal with which he was always ready to throw himself into any scheme for pleasure or diversion seemed to leave him entirely. He was thinking of it a great deal to-night, which was one reason for his dullness of mood.

Cecil turned away, and Mr. Hazzard, who was left leaning by himself across the doorway, looked again for the cynosure of his eyes, but she had vanished. Only the pretty Miss Davering was to be seen, dancing with Mr. Drum Kettleby. He took refuge with his hostess, who invited him to accompany her to a small room opening from the one where they were dancing, in search of claret punch. Here they came upon Miss Prescott, resting a moment apparently from the fatigue of the waltz, while Dr. Carey stood in front of her talking very earnestly.

Mr. Hazzard provided Mrs. Percy with some claret, keeping his eye all the time on the couple at the other side of the room. She sat down on the sofa and sipped it slowly, and just then Cecil Wilmott came to speak to her.

Cecil had been flitting about everywhere, like an uneasy spirit. Mr. Hazzard took advantage of his advent to desert to Julia's side, in spite of the discouraging expression of Dr. Carey's back.

"Sit down, Mr. Wilmott," said Mrs. Percy, "you look tired." Her tones were very soft, almost caressing.

He yielded silently.

"What is the matter?" she asked.

"Oh, nothing. I am a little out of sorts," said Cecil.

"I thought you were not feeling well the other evening," rejoined Mrs. Percy. "Did not Charlotte tell me that you had been sightseeing or something of the kind, much against your will?"

"I don't know," answered Cecil, "what Charlotte said, but that sort of thing is always a bore."

"Of course it is," said Mrs. Percy, with a positive little nod of her head. "I met Charlotte at Homer's the next morning, and she told me all about it. What did you do it for?"

"To please her."

"But whom did you take to see the sights?"

"Dr. Carey for one, and Miss Prescott and her friend Miss Arnold," said Cecil.

"Ah! yes, the young lady whom I saw at the

opera last week? I was so sorry that she did not come this evening. I wonder why it was. Do you know?"

"I? Of course not. How should I?" answered Cecil uneasily.

"Look at me," commanded Mrs. Percy softly. He turned slowly towards her as though compelled by some unseen force, until he met her beautiful dark eyes. They seemed to be burning into his.

"You are a foolish fellow," she said, "to try to hide your fancies from me. This one will pass."

He watched her red lips playing over her white teeth, as she spoke, and hardly knew what she was saying.

"I think I will go away," he said.

"When?"

"After the Assembly."

She laughed. "You will 'treat' your resolution."

"Am I not engaged to dance the cotillon with you?"

"Are you? I had forgotten it."

"Have you promised to dance with any one else?"

"No, but I can, you know, if you would rather not stay."

"I would much rather stay, and I expect you to dance with me."

A ray of triumph shot from her eyes.

"How do you manage it?" she asked.

" Manage what? "

" Being in love with two persons at the same time."

" I am not in love with two persons."

" Then which is it? " She was still looking into his eyes, with a mocking smile. It showed all the pretty dimples round her chin, as she knew full well.

" Ah! which has it always been? " cried Cecil, just above his breath.

" It would be better worth while to ask which it is to be ? " she said.

" That is a question which I cannot answer," returned Cecil pointedly.

" Can *I?* " asked Mrs. Percy.

" You could have once," he answered.

" Ah! " she exclaimed, and her eyes flashed.

" Decidedly you had better go away," she added in a moment, rising with an indifferent air to return to her other guests, and Cecil happening to glance across the room noticed that Miss Prescott was looking at him. It was an abstracted gaze, but Cecil did not know it. He would not seem to avoid the meeting, although he was in no mood to talk to her just then, and so strolled over to where she sat surrounded by Dr. Carey, Mr. Hazzard, and Mr. Foxall who had lately joined the group.

" Oh, do tell me, Miss Prescott," Mr. Hazzard was saying, "what have you done with that pretty little friend of yours who was so frightened the other day by Jig? Is she still staying with you?

I have been intending to come to see you again, if you will allow me to do so."

"Do come, by all means," said Julia. "Miss Arnold is still with me, and we shall be delighted to see you."

"Why did she not come to the party this evening?" asked Mr. Hazzard.

"She has not been feeling very well. I am afraid Jig was too much for her."

"Seriously, Miss Prescott," said Mr. Foxall, "why did you not bring Miss Arnold with you? I have been looking about for her everywhere, for she promised me a dance the next time we met at a party."

"I wanted to bring her, of course," replied Julia, "but she would not come. I cannot give you any better reason for her absence than that."

"Certainly not," said Dr. Carey. "From a lady it is unanswerable."

"I wonder if he has heard that dreadful report," thought Julia. If Cecil had known how her brain was in a whirl of strange fancies, and new ideas, and she was wearied with the effort to conceal her troubled mind, he would not have feared her so much. As it was, it was the greatest relief when she turned to him with her usual friendly smile. "I am glad to see you, Cecil," she said, "for I am sure it is time to go home. Will you not see if you can find Philip, and ask him to call the carriage?"

"I will, certainly," responded Cecil, grateful for the excuse to get away.

CHAPTER XVII.

" High instincts, before which our mortal nature
Did tremble like a guilty thing surprised."
WORDSWORTH.

On the drive home Julia's mind reverted to her discussion with Mrs. Davering, and dwelt on the extraordinary report which she had retailed with a sort of startled fascination.

"I believe she invented the whole thing," she said to herself indignantly; but the more she reflected upon the matter the less likely she thought it that Mrs. Davering, who was quite devoid of imagination, could have achieved such a bold stroke of fancy.

"I was dreadfully bored this evening," remarked Philip, with a suppressed yawn. "I don't know when I have felt so dull at a party."

"It must have been something in the air. I too was longing to get home."

"That is not very complimentary to Carey."

"I do not feel especially called upon to compliment Dr. Carey."

"Why are you always so savage about him?" asked Philip, in a vexed tone. "He is certainly very good to you, and you know that he is one of my best friends."

" I am not savage, as you call it, about his friendship for you."

" But why won't you treat him fairly ? There is
that hair-brained donkey, Charley Hazzard, whom
you let hang about you, and are as gracious to, as
he pleases."

" Mr. Hazzard's hanging about me for the last
three weeks has amounted to his sending me a
New Year's card," said Julia laughing.

" That is because he has been confined to his own
house."

" Well, here we are at ours," said Julia, and as
she spoke the carriage stopped.

Philip let her in with his dead-latch key. The
lights were all out in the drawing-room. They
passed along the entry to the library, of which
Philip was just going to open the door, when
Julia placed a detaining hand on his, already on
the handle.

" What is the matter ? " asked Philip.

" Stop a moment," she said.

He took his hand away, and looked at her in surprise. She dropped her eyes and drew a long
breath.

" Now open it."

Philip did so wonderingly.

The room was quite empty. The gas was lit, but
turned down low. Only the fire was burning
brightly. Some large sheets of paper, closely written in part, but some untouched, lay with a pen
and inkstand near a low lamp on the table, attest-

ing that some one had been interrupted in writing.

Julia looked about her, with an odd, startled air.

"What is the matter?" asked Philip again. "One would think you expected to see a ghost."

"Oh! no," said Julia, "not a ghost." She sat down in a chair, and began slowly drawing off her gloves.

"I suppose every one has gone to bed, it is the most sensible thing they could have done," said Philip. "I will go and shut up the house," and he started on his nightly round to see that everything was secure before retiring himself. This tour of inspection was always very thorough and usually began with the cellar, before descending to which Plutonic region he lighted a candle which stood ready on a table in the entry.

Julia heard his footsteps die away on the cellar stairs, and the next moment one of the large doors of the drawing-room was swung slowly open and a man's figure was half visible in the firelight against the blackness of the space beyond.

She started to her feet. "Who is that?" she asked sharply.

"Who indeed," said a voice, — one she knew and loved so well that her heart was stirred at the unexpected sound.

"I am truly ashamed of myself," said Mr. Drayton, emerging from the darkness. "Do you know, my dear, that I sat up after the ladies had gone to bed, on the plea that I had some important writing

to do, with the unacknowledged intention of sweet-
ening my task by a little chat with you and hearing the first news of the party, and suddenly I became so sleepy that I felt that I must go and lie
down — why, what has happened? Are you not
well, my child?"

"You startled me so," said Julia, pressing her
hand to her heart.

He had come close beside her now, and noticed,
as the light from the shaded lamp fell full upon
her, the unusual paleness of her face.

"Sit down," he said, affectionately. "I am
sorry. I should have remembered that you probably thought yourself alone, but I have been fast
asleep and only just waked up."

"It is not your fault at all," said Julia, "but my
own stupidity. I do not know why I am so nervous to-night."

"You are a little over-tired," said her guardian
tenderly, drawing her head to his shoulder as he
stood beside her chair.

Suddenly she burst into tears, and flung her
arms round him, clinging to him like a hurt child.

"What is it? Why, what is it, my dear girl?
What has happened to give you pain?"

"Nothing, oh! nothing. Do not ask me," she
sobbed, hiding her face against his arm.

"Something must have happened, Julia," said
Mr. Drayton, in a moved tone. "I know you too
well not to be sure of that."

"Yes, there was something," she admitted, "but

it was only what some one said. It was not worth listening to. I am over-tired, as you say, and foolish."

" Was it something which Dr. Carey said?" asked her guardian, very gravely.

Julia hastily raised her head. "No," she answered, "it certainly was not."

" What was it about?"

" About you."

" Then you must tell me what it was."

" Oh! do not ask me," she cried.

"I think I ought to know."

" But it was mere nonsense — mere idle gossip!"

" It must have had some importance, to have moved you so."

" It seemed to me profane," said Julia, with flashing eyes.

" Tell me what it was."

" I don't know how I can. I was told that — that there was a report — that you " —

" That I what?"

" Were thinking of being married," said Julia, too loyal to her friend to breathe her name in such connection.

" It was profane," said Mr. Drayton solemnly.

Julia smiled a happy smile, looking up into his face.

" Oh, I could n't bear it," she whispered.

The playful light returned to his eyes. " Silly little woman," he said, and smoothed the hair ten-

14

derly away from her forehead as he spoke. Then
he stooped and kissed her. He intended the caress
to be as parental as every other that he had ever be-
stowed, but as their lips met something happened.
A sudden wave of feeling seemed to sweep them
together. His arms tightened around her for a
moment, and then dropped to his sides. He hardly
knew where he was. She had half turned away.
Then in a moment he took one of her little slender
hands in his, and raised it to his lips with a deep-
drawn sigh.

"Good-night, my child," he said, and led her to
the door, where she slipped by Philip, returning
from his inspection, like a phantom, and ran hastily up stairs.

If great works necessarily grow slowly this is
not true of great events. The unconscious prepa-
ration for them may often be gradual, but they
seem to shoot into existence at the last, and before
we conceive that they are possible confront us in
their entirety as accomplished facts.

If any one will take the trouble to recall the
period of his or her life which has been the most
decisive, and to count out the days or weeks which
went to make it, he will hardly believe that last
summer, or the week before last, was really quite
as long as that other time which meant so much
and had such far-stretching consequences.

To Julia all the night which followed was one
strange, fevered dream. She seemed to see Lawrence Carey, Mrs. Davering, Cecil Wilmott, Edith,

and her guardian, masquerading in varied groups and unfamiliar scenes. The world was topsy-turvy and all her thoughts gone mad, while all sensation was centred about one little action which was forever recurring to her memory with its first intensity of meaning. No other kiss which her guardian had ever given her had been like this one. He had not kissed her often, but when he had done so it had been as the tender protector who took the place of a father, and who always acted as if he were one. She had believed before this that she loved him as an affectionate daughter might have loved a father, who had been all in all to her lonely childhood, giving her a home and warm regard, and even a certain right over his life, by placing her at the head of his household, but she never dreamed of wishing to be more to him than this, or of ever being less, until to-night. She had been surprised and shocked at the wild pang of jealousy which shot through her at Mrs. Davering's suggestion of the possibility of Mr. Drayton's marrying again, but even that had not inspired any doubt in her of the nature of her affection for him. She was ashamed of the anger and hatred which were in her heart when the idea was conjured up of a possible wife, — a somebody who should stand between herself and him, but she little guessed their cause. She was perfectly contented. She had all she wanted. She wished for no change, and even now she desired nothing so much as that things should remain as they always had been.

If she could only live on as she had done, hold-ing the. same happy, honored place in Mr. Dray-ton's heart and home, it would be enough ; but she had an uneasy sense that this was not to be. There was something in the rapture of that kiss which left a haunting fear behind. Could they live on, in the old way, since that had been ? She wished to persuade herself that they could, and yet she al-most feared the light of day lest it should show her that the disc, in which she had seen reflected all the pageant of her life, was cracked in a thou-sand fragments, like the magic mirror of the Lady of Shalott.

Morning came at last and brought with it no sudden change. She rose and dressed early, and slipped down to the breakfast room, where the first person whom she saw was Mr. Drayton, seated at a little table near the window, writing. He looked up as she entered, and smiled at her with his kind, familiar smile.

"Good morning, my dear," he said pleasantly. "I have had to pay for my laziness, you see, by getting up early to accomplish my work."

Julia only answered his greeting with a word. Her tongue, which was usually so glib, seemed un-accountably stiff, and strive as she would to speak and look as usual, her voice sounded strange to herself.

Mr. Drayton did not seem to notice that she made none of her ordinary inquiries as to how he was feeling, or how he had slept. He went on writing steadily, while she moved about the room after her wonted fashion, drawing the curtain of a window, where she thought the light too strong, arranging some flowers in a low glass dish on the breakfast table, opening a new review, cutting the leaves of a number of " Punch " which had just come. She would often take advantage of a quiet moment like this, if she saw that he was finishing his work, to ask his opinion of some topic of the day, in which she chanced to be interested ; but she saw him fold up his papers in silence this morning, and handed him the letters she had just sorted out for him, from a pile brought in by Rogers, without a word. He thanked her in his usual tone ; but it was a relief to her when Miss Ruthven came down, and soon after Philip and Edith.

She went forward and greeted her friend with peculiar warmth.

" I am perfectly well to-day, thank you," said Edith, in answer to her affectionate inquiries.

She looked indeed the picture of health, as fresh and as delicate as a pink rose in spring.

" We missed you so much at the party last night," said Julia. " Every one was asking after you."

" Every one ! " repeated Edith laughing. "Who, for instance ? "

She flushed a little as she asked the question, although she put it carelessly.

Julia did not notice this, being otherwise absorbed.

"It is hard to remember a list of names," she said ; "there were so many. I know that Mr. Drum Kettleby did, and Mr. Hazzard and Mrs. Davering, — and — let me see — and Mr. Foxall, and Mrs. Percy, — and more besides, I think."

"They were all very kind," said Edith coldly.

"I think that thy friend Edith Arnold took the wiser part, Julia," said Miss Ruthven, "in resting quietly at home, on the evening before her first ball."

"I am sure she did," said Philip, "for Julia looks very tired this morning."

"It does not make much difference how I look," said Julia. "You know the Assembly is not my first ball."

"It is your first Assembly," said Philip, "and it is a great pity that you should not enjoy it."

"Oh ! she will enjoy it when she is there," said Edith. "Julia's looks and feelings in the evening never depend upon having had a good sound sleep the night before, as mine do. Even at school, we used to notice that the more tired she was the better she looked by lamp light. Her cheeks used to have a way of flushing and her eyes such an astonishing way of shining, late at night."

"They have still," said Mr. Drayton, who had just left his letters to come to table. Julia busied herself in making him a cup of coffee, and said nothing.

"Miss Ruthven and I had such a pleasant talk last evening," said Edith. "I was hearing all about the Revolution — the time when General Washington was quartered in Philadelphia, and then about the Republican Court, and who the worthy general used to come to visit in Philadelphia after his administration. I am to be taken to see one of the very houses which he used to stay in on the other side of the river, am I not?" she asked, turning to the old lady.

"If it should please thee, my dear."

"Of course it will please her," said Philip, "and I invite myself to be of the party. I always used to imagine when I was a boy, Miss Arnold, that Aunt Margaretta had lived herself in the days of the Revolution. She tells those stirring tales with all the spirit of an eye-witness."

"Now thou art drawing on thy fancy, Philip," said Miss Ruthven, with a gleam of gentle humor, "and crediting me with too great tenacity of life. I was only recounting to Edith Arnold some of the events which my mother has narrated to me as occurring when she was young."

"Ah! I know all about those dear old stories," said Philip, "and they are a thousand times better than the stupid entertainment to which Julia and I doomed ourselves."

"Was not your party pleasant?" asked Edith.

"Pleasant enough," said Philip. "Very much as they usually are, and we agreed afterwards that we had both wished ourselves at home, all the evening."

"One often says things which one does not mean, when one is tired," said Julia. "I really think now that I should have been sorry to miss the party."

" Sapit qui reputat," said Mr. Drayton. He too had had his wakeful hours, in the preceding night, but they had been much sadder, more bitter hours than Julia's.

They had been sweetened by none of the mystery of half-awakened consciousness to a stronger, deeper love than had been conceived of in the being he cared for most on earth. Algernon Drayton had not supposed for a moment that the knowledge of the nature of his love for Julia, of which he had been wholly ignorant until it so unexpectedly betrayed him to himself, was shared by his ward, — still less that his love was returned.

Beautiful, true, and fearless as the image of Julia always presented itself to him, it never occurred to him to think of her as anything but a sweet trust which God had committed to his safekeeping, whose welfare and happiness he was bound to seek, whose nature for its own sake it was his pleasure and his duty to develop. He felt his responsibility all the more because this charge had been a voluntary one and the girl when she had come to him had been in need of friends, and he had loved her truly and tenderly; but how or when this love had grown into the desire to keep her for his own — to join her life to his — he could not begin to conjecture; he was too utterly pained and shocked at such a thought to try. Thus to discover suddenly in himself what seemed to him

the most selfish of all impulses appeared incredi-
ble. He considered it unpardonable. He could not
forgive himself for having felt the feeling — much
less for having shown it; and thinking of Julia's
youth and innocence, he resolved that come what
might he would not drag it away in its freshness
and loveliness from its natural surroundings and
transplant it to his, to be henceforth shadowed by
the sadness of his years.

CHAPTER XVIII.

" But strive still to be a man before your mother."

COWPER.

IN view of the state of things which she had herself hastened to precipitate, Mrs. Davering had made up her mind that she must speak to Charley. She had always shrunk instinctively from letting him know that she knew of his fancy for Julia, her seeming ignorance leaving her much more free to minister to it; but it would not do to allow the prize to be carried off from under his unsuspecting eyes without opening them to what she feared was taking place. He must be made to realize his danger and pushed to some immediate action.

"I want to speak a word to you, Charley," she said, coming into the billiard-room where he and Mr. Davering and Dr. Carey were smoking their cigars after dinner.

"Yes, mother. Is there anything the matter?"

"Nothing of moment, but I should like to see you in my own room."

"Certainly." He followed her up-stairs very composedly, and sat down on a low ottoman beside the fire, in the cosy little sitting-room which opened from her bed-chamber. "Do you object to my smoking ? " he asked. " Shall I throw away my cigar ? "

" My dear son! Is it impossible to rouse you to the importance of anything ? "

" Why, what would you have ? " he inquired, innocently. " You said there was nothing of consequence the matter."

" There is nothing actually the matter now, but I am dreadfully troubled at something which may happen."

" What is it ? "

" It would be a great misfortune to you, I fear."

" A great misfortune ? "

" Yes. Would you not consider it so, if you heard that Julia Prescott was engaged ? "

Charley frowned, and was silent.

" I suppose that would depend a good deal on whom she was engaged to," he said, after a pause.

" Suppose it were to Dr. Carey ? "

" To Lawrence Carey? Absurd! Why should you think of it ? "

" Only because I am very sure that he is thinking of it. Do you fancy that it is for the sake of your company that he has lingered all this while in Philadelphia ? "

" Not entirely. He has enjoyed his visit for other reasons, of course. Philip has been one attraction."

" Julia has been a much stronger one."

" Why, he has known Julia — Miss Prescott, I mean, since she was a little girl."

"So have you."

Mr. Hazzard got up and went to the window, and threw away the end of his cigar.

"What do you want me to do?" he asked.

"Whatever you want to do. If you are willing to let things go on, do nothing."

"How can I help things 'going on,' as you call it?"

"If you cared about it, you could help it."

"Suppose I do care?"

"Then why not tell Julia so?"

Charley thrust his hands into his pockets, with a faint whistle, and took a turn backwards and forwards from one end to the other of his mother's dainty little morning-room before he answered.

"What would be the use of that," he asked at last, "if, as you think, she cares for Carey?"

"I do not think she cares for Dr. Carey."

"Then where is the danger?"

"The danger lies in him. I think Dr. Carey cares very much for her, and no one can tell what headway he may make if you leave the game all in his hands."

"I see," said Charley, nodding wisely. "Well, I won't do that."

His mother was delighted. She had hardly hoped for such a ready acceptance of her counsel, fearing that in awakening him to his peril she should dishearten him; but his heart was not faint.

Miss Edith Arnold was, meanwhile, absorbed in the preparations for her first ball; and I am forced to acknowledge that the subject of dress rose to very large proportions in her mind on this day.

She was saved any grave doubt, to be sure, as to what she should wear by the fact that her simple wardrobe only offered one suitable toilet for such an occasion, but she was a good deal disturbed lest this might not prove in all respects the thing; so she dressed early, and betook herself to her friend's door in an anxious mood.

"How pretty you look!" cried Julia. "And your dress is lovely."

"Do you really think it pretty?" asked Edith, with a shy, downward glance at the dress, which appeared to consist of waves upon waves of a transparent pink material, of which the general effect was as of a rose-colored cloud.

"Of course I do. It is charming, and suits your style so well. Come and look at yourself in my long glass. What made you think of wearing those silver ornaments?"

"They are Gertrude's. She insisted upon my bringing them with me," answered Edith, mightily pleased; "and Gertrude ordered the dress made for me in New York, so that it is all her taste. She is particularly fond of pink and silver."

"So am I — at least I like them of all things for you," said Julia. "But I must begin to get ready myself, or we shall be late."

Philip met them down-stairs, looking cheerful and handsome, and apologized for his father, who had gone to see a client at one of the hotels, he

said, and hoped to join them at the Assembly.
Then they all three rolled away in the carriage
through the damp, muddy streets, and Edith's
heart beat high with muffled expectation. She
thought of her mother and sister in their country
home, where she knew that the primitive little
household was already sinking to its long night's
rest, and then her fancy came back with a bound
to the image of herself which she had seen in
Julia's mirror. The contrast saddened her momentarily, only to add greater zest to her enjoyment when her former mood returned.

On the whole she was a happy girl as Philip
held out his hand to help her from the carriage at
the side door of the Academy, and they passed
along the carpet spread over the pavement, beneath the awning, flanked on either side by a gap-
ing, curious crowd and guarded by policemen, and
vanished from the dim world without to the bright
one within.

CHAPTER XIX.

"And e'en while fashion's brightest arts decoy,
The heart, distrusting, asks if this be joy."
GOLDSMITH.

A WALTZ was being played as they entered the ball-room, and Dr. Lawrence Carey surprised Edith by approaching and asking for the pleasure of the dance. The Bostonian had so seldom favored her with his notice that she glanced involuntarily at Julia, and saw that she had accepted Mr. Hazzard's arm, who was leading her towards a small room on the left, which opened from the larger hall at that end.

Mrs. Davering, too, looked anxiously after the retreating couple, and then critically at the pair which had just left her side, for Edith had granted Dr. Carey's request and been whirled away into the mazes of the dance.

"Miss Arnold is a very good dancer," she remarked to Philip. " I should hardly have expected it; country girls so seldom are."

" Miss Arnold is so graceful that I should have said she could hardly fail to dance well," replied Philip stoutly.

Mrs. Davering looked at him in astonishment.

"Good dancing is not always a matter of grace,"

she said composedly; "however, it seems that in this instance you would have been right."

She was further surprised, in the course of the evening, at the attention excited and received by Edith Arnold; but her interest was only partially involved in these minor events of the evening, her whole heart being set on its more important issues.

The two persons who had found a seat somewhat removed from the giddy whirl, in the small room set apart for conversation, were in Mrs. Davering's eyes the only two persons at the ball. She would have been gratified if she could have seen them, for Charley Hazzard was talking, and Julia seemed to be a not uninterested listener.

He was telling of the expected advent of some English cricket players that spring, and from cricket came to discussing lawn tennis, where they found common ground of interest, as they had often played together, and Miss Prescott was an excellent player. Mr. Hazzard gradually waxed enthusiastic.

"How pretty you used to look in that blue and white tennis dress of yours," he cried. "Do you remember?"

"No, I do not," said Julia.

"Well, I do, and I am sure you ought to."

"I never remember looking pretty, but you are right in saying that I ought to remember it if I had."

"Nonsense. Of course you do! At least, you certainly remember the dress."

" I certainly do, and I would much rather remember the beauty. It might cheer me in my old age."

" It is just like you to talk of your old age, at your first Assembly," said Charley, with a resigned air.

" It seems to show that I have postponed my first Assembly rather unfortunately long."

" Why, yes," rejoined Mr. Hazzard, with rarely facetious emphasis. " I believe you are actually *nineteen !* "

" I am almost twenty, sir, and in another year I shall be twenty-one ! "

" In another year " — these playful words suggested to Charley Hazzard all the changes which a year might bring, and he recalled his mother's warning.

" I wonder where you and I will be in another year," he said despondently.

" Why, here, I suppose, of course."

" I wish we might be together," replied Mr. Hazzard. " I mean — that is — do you think you could ever care for me ? "

" Of course. I care for you now," said Julia. " Are we not the best of friends ? "

" Do you — don't you think you might care more than that ? " asked Charley anxiously.

" What do you mean ? "

" Oh ! You *know* what I mean. You must know."

" No, I do not," she said uneasily.

" Well, I do," said Charley. " I am just distracted about you, and I always shall be! Don't you think, if you tried, you might get to caring for me?"

"Dear Mr. Hazzard," said Julia, rising, "I do care, as much as I ever could, but it is only as a friend, and I must not let you talk to me like this."

"Then you will go and marry some other fellow," said Charley desperately.

"How foolish! I am not going to marry any one. Is it possible that you did not know that I intend to be an old maid?"

"Do you, really?"

"Of course I do."

"Will you promise to tell me if you change your mind?"

Julia laughed. It never occurred to her to take him seriously. "How persistent you are!" she said. "Here comes Mr. Freeman, to whom I promised a waltz."

"Oh! Here you are, Miss Prescott, and Hazzard too. It is the first time I have seen you about, old man, since your accident," said Mr. Freeman, making his appearance at this moment. "He does not look like a sick man, does he, Miss Prescott? By the bye, may I not have this dance?"

"Hang the fellow!" thought Charley. "It is just my luck to have him come up!" But there was no help for the interruption, and he consoled himself with the reflection that if Julia would not promise to smile on him, she had at least denied the intention of accepting any one else.

Mr. Hazzard's knowledge of the fair sex was certainly not profound, or he would hardly have put so much faith in this assurance. Being deserted by Julia he went in search of Mrs. Percy, who was always rather a favorite of his; and Mrs. Davering was provoked at meeting him in the corridor, a little later, with the handsome widow on his arm, but she was much too wise a woman to show her displeasure to her son. She knew that she must not quarrel with him if she hoped to bend him to her will.

The ball was half over before Edith had gotten beyond the first novel enjoyment of lights and music and fragrant flowers. A general impression was all that she had gained until she had danced a great deal and walked in the wide corridor many times, saying actually nothing in the most excited of tones to the stupidest of partners. They were all very stupid. She was quite aware of that, but she could not help confessing that it was fortunate they were; for in the exceedingly foolish state to which her grand toilet and beautiful surroundings had reduced her, what could she have said to a clever man?

Just as she had asked herself that question, Cecil Wilmott appeared and inquired if "this" was not his waltz.

"Why, I am not engaged to you for a waltz," cried she, innocently. In truth she had not seen him before, that evening.

"You do not remember whose dance it is, I am

sure," said Cecil. " We might as well consider it as mine."

" But I do remember," replied Miss Arnold. " I promised this dance to Mr. Foxall." Her tone as she made this second remark was quite different from her first impulsive exclamation. It seemed to say that those who wished to dance with her would be obliged to ask for what they wanted. Her consent was not, it appeared, to be taken for granted.

Cecil quite understood the condition, but it nettled him.

" There would have been no use in my engaging you beforehand," he said. " One never finds one's partner at an Assembly after the room fills up."

" It would have been useless to ask me to dance, of course," she answered, demurely, " if you really thought you could not find me."

" You mean to imply that other people have been more sanguine," said Cecil, with an amused smile.

" Perhaps I do."

" But not more fortunate, for with the best intentions in the world it is very hard to find a person in this crowd."

" I suppose one must begin by looking for the person," she answered, for she had resolved that she would not easily forgive his unexplained estrangement.

" Ah! Now we are agreed," said Cecil. " That is precisely where I did begin. Come! There is no reason why you should wait for Foxall. Will you not give me the dance ? "

" I am afraid that is impossible, Mr. Wilmott, for here is Mr. Foxall."

Cecil indeed beheld that yellow-haired gentleman advancing through the crowd, for Mr. Foxall, who was highly imitative, had perceived with respect the growing estimation with which society was welcoming Miss Arnold, and had proceeded to fling himself at her feet, in a metaphorical manner practically illustrated by his engaging her five dances ahead, and waiting about in a nervous way during the fourth dance for the happy moment when he could claim her hand. It was not likely therefore that he would be much behind time, and Cecil bit his lip as he noticed the contented expression with which he approached his partner.

" Of course, if you prefer Foxall, I have nothing to say," he remarked, in a very low tone.

Edith had not time to answer ; Mr. Foxall was already at her side, saying nothing very earnestly on the subject of their dance ; but she raised her eyes suddenly and shot at Wilmott the only reproachful glance which they had ever given him.

Cecil was melted in a moment. " Can I take you to supper ? " he whispered, following as the triumphant Foxall was leading her towards the ballroom from the corridor where the meeting had taken place.

" I am engaged for supper to Mr. Philip Drayton," she answered softly, turning back her head a little.

" Then I shall come for a dance just afterwards,"
said Cecil. " Do not forget."

She smiled in answer without looking at him,
and the next moment was lost to sight among a
hundred other waltzers, and again resigned herself
to the gay spirit of the moment and the new charm
of charming. It was not unnatural that she should
enjoy her triumph, and no small compliment for a
little homebred maiden to find herself admired and
courted in such a brilliant scene ; but she was conscious that these things alone would not have made
her happy. She knew that since those last words
of Cecil's she felt unreasonably lighter-hearted, in
spite of her determination not to be reconciled.

When Philip came for her to go to supper he
found her seated on a sofa in the entry with quite
a little group about her, of which Mr. Foxall was
one, and the rest was composed of three of the extremely young gentlemen whose acquaintance she
had made on New Year's Day. They were still
a good deal occupied with their kid gloves, and
were further trammeled on this occasion by scru-
pulously kept dancing-cards, to which they were
continually referring in order to determine their
movements, as a mariner to his chart and com-
pass.

Philip stood still for a moment without speaking.
Edith was evidently full of fun, and was amusing
the young gentlemen very much, although how she
managed it Philip could not tell, being conscious
of the difficulty of the task and too far off to catch

what she was saying. He was quite near enough, however, to see how pretty she was looking; nor was he the only person who was alive to this. Among others, Cecil Wilmott, who happened to be passing, had paused also, though unseen by Philip. There was a fascination to him in watching the girl, which he thought it safe to yield to, since she did not know that he was near; and he noted the exquisite whiteness of her neck and rounded arms, the softness and purity of outline of her face, the changing light on her fair hair, which was drawn back and fastened by a silver arrow in a wavy knot behind, and the quiet sincerity of her blue eyes as the merry smile died out of them, which seemed to preclude the possibility of guile. Cecil breathed hard as he looked at her, and something rose up in his throat, which he gulped down with an impatient sigh, as he turned away.

"Are you ready for supper?" Philip asked, advancing a step or two so as to speak to Edith across Mr. Foxall, which he could do very easily, owing to his greater height.

"Oh, yes, I am quite ready," she answered, gladly, and the other men made way, as she rose to take his arm with the happy confidence with which he always seemed to inspire her.

"It is better to go now," he said, approvingly, "for we are a little late to get good seats." He led her towards the stairs; descending which a sudden turn brought them to a broader flight at one end of the supper room, on which a crowd of ladies in dresses of every shade and color were sitting, while their busy cavaliers flew about to supply their wants; and looking across from the top of the steps where they stood, Edith saw another stairway equally wide, at the opposite end of the room, on which was a like assemblage.

The accidental combination of colors, mellowed by distance into harmony, formed an exquisite rainbow effect of bright and tender tints, still further enhanced to her admiring eyes by a background of tall green plants.

Below were small tables arranged on either side the room for the lady patronesses and other matrons of distinction, while a cloud of black coats about the long table in the centre shifted uneasily to and fro, a dark undulating ring, in the midst of which the daintily spread feast with flowers and fruit and glittering glass, lighted with tall wax candles, looked all the more brilliant.

"Here is Cecil. He will wait here with you a moment," said Philip, "while I find you a seat."

Edith hardly heard him; she was absorbed in the scene before her, and could not withhold a faint exclamation of delight.

"So you like your first ball," said Cecil.

"Oh, very much." She had not turned her head to look at him, but she recognized his voice. "I do not see how I could help it," she added, with a happy little sigh.

"Do you mean that you would if you could?" asked Wilmott.

" I mean that my will has nothing to do with it."

" A woman always likes a thing better for that, I believe," said Cecil.

" I am not sure," replied Edith, doubtfully, " but I think a man never likes a thing unless he has determined to like it."

" You are mistaken there," said Wilmott. " A man often likes what he has determined that he should not like."

" Would and should have different meanings. I did not say that a man always did his duty."

" But you credit him with very great strength of will."

" I think when a man does a thing he generally knows that he is going to do it."

" For all that, it may be a sort of fatality," said Cecil.

" How a fatality ? " she asked, turning suddenly towards the speaker, but he shook his head at her mischievously for all answer to her question, and at that moment Philip returned.

" I have found Julia," he said to Edith. " Would you like to sit beside her ? "

" I should, thank you. Where is she ? "

" Just below."

He gave her his arm, and as they were moving down the stairs to join Julia, who was seated near the bottom among a group of girls, but with a place beside her which she had evidently been keeping for Edith, they saw a very handsome woman dressed in gold-colored brocade, who had

been looking in vain for an empty table at the side
of the supper-room, come to the foot of the stairs
and point with her fan to the seat which they were
seeking, and the gentleman with her seeming to
approve, she glided into it with such a gracious
smile to Julia that it would evidently have been
quite impossible to dispute her right.

"How provoking!" exclaimed Philip.

"Will you not sit here, Miss Arnold?" asked
Miss Louisa Mortimer, who happened to be near.

"Thank you. You are very kind," said Edith,
as Miss Mortimer made room for her. She was indeed glad to sit anywhere rather than near the
dark-haired beauty, in whom she had not failed to
recognize Mrs. Percy. Philip went off to get her
supper, and presently she saw Cecil Wilmott approach the stairs from below and stand for a moment, with an indifferent air, beside the banister,
half leaning against it. Mrs. Percy, who had been
talking languidly to Julia, chanced to glance up
and met his eyes. Edith noticed that he started as
though he had not been conscious of her vicinity,
but the next moment he bent down and said something to her at which she laughed and shook her
fan, then he sprang lightly up the stairs and was
once more beside Edith, before she realized that he
was coming.

"Have you not begun your supper yet?" he
asked.

"Not yet. I have just found a seat."

"We shall be too late for our dance. It is too

bad. I wanted to have it before the room re-filled."

"We might postpone it until the next Assembly," said Edith.

Cecil glanced at her quickly. She was decapitating a pansy.

"What has made you angry?" he asked.

"Nothing. I am not angry," she answered, without raising her eyes.

"Here is some salad, Miss Arnold," said Philip, who had approached with a plate and a glass.

"Oh, thank you!" She looked past Cecil at Philip, with a soft grateful smile.

"She has learned some of the ways of the world," thought Cecil.

"Let me hold your champagne for you," he said, taking it as he spoke from Philip's hand, without making the slightest motion to surrender his seat.

"Thank you, I need not trouble you," said Edith quietly, offering to take the glass which Cecil held just out of her reach. Philip looked at them both, colored slightly and turned away.

"You need not trouble me, at any rate," said Cecil. "Holding your glass is no trouble, but there is something in your manner which leads me to fancy that you would rather like to trouble me."

Edith looked up quickly, and her eyes met his. They did not sink or falter, but flashed out an indignant light which lent a new aspect to her face.

"You are mistaken," she said, and seemed half

inclined to quarrel with him for an instant. Then, as though struck with the want of dignity of such a proceeding, she smiled at her own childishness. Just then Philip returned.

" I am going to ask you, Philip," said Cecil, uneasily, "to let me carry Miss Arnold off for a waltz which she has promised me."

" If Miss Arnold wishes to be carried off, I have nothing to say."

" Of course she does. It is our only chance to have our dance quietly, before the crowd gets back."

" Can I not get you something more, Miss Arnold? " asked Philip.

" Nothing more, thank you."

" Then you will go with Mr. Wilmott? "

" I certainly promised him the dance."

Philip bowed in silence.

The music was playing in a dreamy sort of way when Edith and Cecil reached the dancing hall. Only a few couples were moving about slowly over the polished floor, although numbers of elderly ladies, who had been taken early to supper, had returned and were seated together chatting in groups, with an occasional unfortunate damsel stranded beside them.

" How unhappy they look! " cried Dr. Carey. " They seem exposed like Andromeda to the mercy of the monster Gossip and bound hand and foot by Conventionality, while Theseus has returned to the supper room (after his custom in this latitude) to further refresh himself before undertaking the deliverance."

"Pray what does Theseus do in Boston?" asked Miss Prescott, for she and her partner formed one of the slowly revolving pairs.

"Oh! Andromeda is not so tightly bound there."

"Perhaps she knows how to defend herself?"

"She may know a little better how to avoid requiring defense."

"That is fortunate," said Julia.

"Why?"

"Because I am afraid there is no Theseus to come to the rescue."

"Theseus is a very commonplace person, of course, with us," said Dr. Carey. "He has neither the cap of darkness with which your hero is furnished (that I take to be ignorance) nor the wings of Mercury to raise him above eating his supper at the same time that Andromeda eats hers, and if he has slain no beautiful Gorgon with whose head to petrify her enemies, he fails to desert her afterwards."

Wilmott, meanwhile, and Miss Arnold were floating in time to the music. They had both danced many times that evening, but to each this dance seemed different.

"How light you are upon your feet," said Cecil softly.

"I am very fond of dancing. Are not you?"

"Yes. With some people. It sounds stupid, but I feel as if you and I could dance forever without growing tired."

She smiled, without raising her eyes.

" Who gave you those flowers which you prize so much ? " asked Wilmott.

" What flowers ? "

" That hat full of pansies," he said provokingly, for he had noticed that she kept it on her arm, although she had left her other bouquets on a chair, for convenience.

" I do not prize them so much," she answered.

" Well, waiving that; who gave them to you ? "

" I do not know."

" Oh, come now, that is absurd. Of course you know."

" No, I do not."

" Do you mean to say that Philip sent them anonymously ? "

There was just a perceptible pause, and then she said, " What leads you to think that Philip — I mean Mr. Drayton — sent them ? "

" I know who you mean, for I saw my cousin choosing them at Pennock's," replied Wilmott, coolly. " Of course I had a shrewd suspicion of whom they were for, but it never occurred to me that he meant to make a mystery of it."

" They are very beautiful," returned Edith. " How kind he was to think of me ! "

" I thought you said a little while ago that you did not prize them ? "

" Now that I know who sent them to me, I do prize them," said Miss Arnold. She seemed thoughtful for a moment. Perhaps she was remembering how unwillingly Philip had resigned the hope of dancing with her for that of taking her to supper, and that she had hardly interchanged two words with him that evening.

"What are you thinking of?" asked Cecil.

"Oh, of nothing!"

"Will you look at me?" he said earnestly.

"What for?" she responded, still continuing to avert her gaze. They were almost alone now in the centre of the room, and waltzing very slowly.

"I want to see whether Philip is really such a lucky fellow as you would have me believe," replied Cecil.

"You are mistaken in supposing that I would have you believe anything," she said.

Cecil looked longingly into her sweet downcast face.

"I would give a great deal if you would let me see your eyes," he said.

She hesitated, and then raised them half reluctantly to his, but dropped them in an instant.

"Thank you," he whispered, and just then the music came to an end.

They paused near the chair on which Edith had carefully deposited her two bouquets. It chanced to be Cecil's chair for the cotillon, but Miss Arnold's flowers had been pushed on one side, and a huge bunch of crimson Jacqueminots occupied their place.

"I beg your pardon," said Mrs. Percy, who was seated beside the roses. "I had no idea those

were yours, and naturally put mine there for safety :
— Miss Arnold, is it not ? "

Edith started involuntarily, and then turned to
the lady, who had risen, while Cecil performed an
introduction.

"I hope Miss Arnold will forgive my unconscious rudeness," she said. "One gets in the
habit of being a tyrant, and confiscating one's partner's seat."

"Very naturally," returned Edith. "It is I who
should apologize for the intrusion."

"There is certainly no reason why you should
apologize," said Cecil in a vexed tone. "I told
you to put your flowers on my chair."

"Yes, I have no doubt you are to blame in the
matter," replied Mrs. Percy, displaying all her
dimples, with a sunny smile. "After all, it is Mr.
Wilmott who is responsible for my red roses, too,"
she continued, turning again to Edith, and then with
a careless glance at the young man which seemed
at the same time to claim him and to depreciate
her possession, she glided away with Mr. Freeman,
who had stood impatiently by during the conversation, waiting for the last waltz before the cotillon.
The music had begun again. Wilmott looked very
cross.

"Will you dance once more ? " he asked.

"Thank you, I think not," said Edith, coldly.

At this moment Mr. Drum Kettleby approached.

"Everything is ready, Miss Arnold," he said,
deferentially, "whenever you would like to begin

the cotillon. Our seats are the first two, at the
upper end of the hall; may I conduct you to them?
— But no, I beg pardon! I see that they are bringing in too many chairs at that side! It will make
a crowd. I will return in an instant." He darted
off, leaving Edith still on Cecil Wilmott's arm.

"We had better walk towards my seat. You
can leave me there," she said gravely.

"Are you to dance with Drum Kettleby?" asked
Cecil, in a tone of extreme surprise. "Why, that is
a great honor," he added, as though quite forgetting his ill-humor.

"Is it?" asked Edith, with a faint touch of
scorn.

Wilmott did not seem to notice her tone. "Drum
Kettleby leads the cotillon," he said. "That is
really very nice."

"Oh, it is delightful!" returned Edith, giving
vent to an odd bitterness which she could not re-
press.

"I assure you," pursued Cecil seriously, "that
there are hundreds of girls who would give their
eyes to have Drum Kettleby ask them for the cotillon at the Assembly."

"What do they obtain in return?" asked Miss
Arnold satirically.

"Well, they get a beautiful bouquet to begin
with," said Cecil, smiling, as he regarded her bur-
den of flowers. "Do you know," he continued,
"I thought of course you were to dance with Philip
Drayton."

"I wish I were!" said Edith heartily. "He asked me to dance with him."

"And you were previously engaged? Well, it is no small honor to lead the cotillon in the foyer of the Academy," pursued Cecil, in a manner which Edith inwardly condemned as sententious, but she knew that her own irritation was unwarrantable.

"How I do wish you could put on my ball dress," she said hotly, "and lead it with Mr. Drum Kettleby! I am sure you would appreciate the honor so much more than I do."

Cecil grew very pale. "When you have been a little longer in society," he said, "you will understand more about these things."

Edith was cooled at once. They had reached the end of the room, where a bank of flowers concealed the orchestra. She slowly withdrew her arm from that of her companion, and turned so as to face him with an air of quiet disdain.

"I may be mistaken, Mr. Wilmott," she said, "but I do not think that a prolonged acquaintance with society will lead me to understand you any better than I do at present."

She never knew what Wilmott would have answered, for at this instant, Mr. Drum Kettleby suddenly returning and clapping his hands, the music for the cotillon began, and Cecil was obliged to repair to his partner, nor did he again approach or speak to her in the course of the evening, which was perhaps not unnatural.

CHAPTER XX.

" Some natural sorrow, loss, or pain,
That has been, and may be again."
WORDSWORTH.

THE morning after the Assembly was dull and cheerless. Julia complained of a bad headache and did not come down to breakfast.

At about noon Edith sallied forth in thick boots and a brown ulster for a solitary walk. It was the first that she had attempted since she came to Philadelphia, and there was a spice of adventure in the undertaking which recommended it to her in her present mood. It was quite within the range of possibility that she might lose her way, but she intended by her discretion and self-possession to render such an event extremely improbable.

She wished to be quite to herself, unmolested by any of the Drum Kettlebys of her acquaintance; and so, avoiding the neighborhood of the Square, turned her steps along Eighteenth Street, crossed Chestnut and Market, and would have continued her direct course, being a good deal absorbed in her own thoughts, if the breadth and stateliness of Arch Street had not arrested her attention and determined her to choose it rather than the one she was pursuing. She remembered hearing Julia say that the inhabitants of the older part of Arch Street were chiefly Quakers, a people whose ways seemed peculiarly mysterious and interesting to Edith ; and then Mr. Drayton had once teased Miss Ruthven by telling her that when he was a boy it used to be the fashion to walk in Arch Street of a Sunday afternoon to see the pretty Quakeresses sitting at their windows, Miss Ruthven maintaining that this was a base scandal. Edith found herself gazing wistfully at the large, old-fashioned houses, half hoping to see a rosy-cheeked inmate with delicate frilled cap and muslin kerchief peeping from between the curtains of the wide windows, and quite unconscious of the rarity of the Quaker garb among the younger members of the society in her own day.

As she passed on, thus divided between her thoughts and fancies and her naturally keen interest in the objects about her, which no amount of preoccupation could entirely destroy, she was quite startled to see a well-known face gazing out abstractedly from one of those very windows.

It was no merry, girlish one, such as she had been picturing to herself, but that of a very grave young man, whose gravity when his face was in repose made him look much older than his years.

Philip Drayton, for it was he, chancing to withdraw his eyes from the opposite side of the street where they were fixed with a certain stern patience, saw the compact little figure of Edith Arnold, close to him, as it almost seemed, with the sweet face

upturned to his; and at the same moment a voice
from behind summoned him, and he was obliged to
turn away from the pretty vision, which when he
looked again, was gone.

Edith passed on, at a loss to imagine how he happened to be there; but it was not of Philip she had
been thinking at the moment that she recognized
him, but of another person. She had indeed been
driven out to walk by the half-acknowledged need
of a quiet hour in which to reconcile her conflicting feelings with regard to this person, and the unexpected sight of Philip jarred upon her reverie.
It brought his kindness suddenly to mind, and her
own shortcoming in deserting him on the previous
evening, of which she was distinctly conscious.

She tried to assure herself that it was nothing, —
Philip probably had not thought of it again. He
certainly had made no effort to detain her, but she
began to wonder why he had sent her those beautiful flowers if he did not care for her society? Was
it his custom to take so much trouble for people in
whom he felt no interest? and why had he sent
the flowers anonymously? It would have been a
great deal pleasanter, she thought, to know whom
they came from. She might have thanked him
graciously and been saved all regret upon the subject, whereas now she retained the uncomfortable
conviction that she had ill requited his generosity.

Just as she had thought of this, she heard hasty
steps behind her, and, turning, saw Philip hurrying
to overtake her.

"Where are you going, so far from home, Miss Arnold?" he asked.

"I do not know," she answered. "I only came out to walk."

"But why did you choose such a damp, muddy day?"

"Oh, I am well protected, and you know in the country we go out in all sorts of weather."

"Do you? It is not a common trait with country people," said Philip. "But then, you do not exactly come under that head."

"Why not?" asked Edith. "I am a country girl, of course."

"Not exactly. I have always noticed that there is a distinction to be made between country people and people who live in the country. You belong to the latter class."

"You like the country, do you not?" asked Edith.

"Very much. I should live there if I had my way; — but shall we not turn here? This gets to be more of a business street as it goes on. I have an hour to myself unexpectedly. What do you say to our spending it at the Academy of Fine Arts? There are a few good pictures there just now."

"I should like that," she said. "I am quite curious to know what you were doing in that house in Arch Street, where I saw you, a little while ago?" she continued, when they had turned the corner of Broad Street and were walking towards the Academy.

" For the moment I was not doing anything."

" So it seemed, but I fancied it was hardly like you to be doing nothing."

" I should have been as much surprised as you were," said Philip, " if I had been told yesterday that I should be there. The truth is that my father was summoned by an old friend and client to make an alteration in her will, and as he was just leaving town he sent me instead. I was kept waiting for about ten minutes only to hear that she had decided to leave her will as it was. I was really delighted to hear it, for I had caught sight of you as you passed the window, and knew that by hurrying a little I should have a fair chance of overtaking you."

" And you never gave a thought to the unfortunate heir, who may have lost thousands by the old lady's change of mind ? "

" On the contrary, I am inclined to think that it was just the other way," said Philip. " She probably only sent for my father in a fit of temper, thinking that she would do awful things in the way of disinheriting her descendants ; and perhaps the very fact of being obliged to open her intention to a stranger, instead of to an old and tried friend who might have understood her special cause of aggravation, had something to do with her change of purpose, in which case you see that her heirs apparent or presumptive have as much reason to be pleased as I had, — I will not acknowledge that they have more."

"That is a very fine compliment," said Edith.
"I think I must make you a courtesy;" and she
turned to him on the first step of the Academy,
which they had just reached, and dropped a mock
reverence with an air of comic humility.

Glancing up from this, her eyes encountered
those of another person bent upon her with a half
satirical expression which did not quite conceal a
look of pain.

She lowered them instantly, acknowledging the
presence of Cecil Wilmott — for it was he — with
a somewhat constrained bow.

A moment later, his light overcoat was receding
in the distance and Edith was climbing the drab
stone steps which lead up to the galleries, with
Philip by her side, but he noticed that she did not
laugh again; her mood was changed.

Julia meanwhile, having summoned her maid, to
ask for a cup of tea, not long after Edith went out,
was handed, with the tea, a little note from Mr.
Drayton, whom she had only seen for a moment at
the ball the night before, as he had come very late
and left early, without waiting as usual to escort
them home. She hastily opened his note, which ran
as follows: —

"DEAREST JULIA, — I seize the only moment I
have to write to you, as I am called to Washington
on business. I cannot tell how long I may be detained — possibly a day — possibly a week; but
will return as soon as I can, you may be sure" —

Here Julia rang again for her maid. " Has Mr. Drayton *gone ?* " she asked.

" Yes, Miss Julia, he left early this morning."

" That will do," said Julia.

The woman hesitated for a moment before leaving the room, although she understood that Miss Prescott wished to be alone. She could see from her young mistress' expression that she was deeply troubled, and could not bear to go without a word of consolation.

" Miss Ruthven seen to the packing of his things herself, Miss," she said at last, timidly.

" That was very kind on the part of Miss Ruthven," said Julia. " Now you can go, Emily." And Emily went. Her mistress sank back on her pillow and lay very still for a while, until her eyes fell again on her guardian's note, and she remembered that she had not finished reading it. She took it up with a sense of apprehension strangely at variance with her usual contentment in reading anything from him. Somehow, she felt as if he had suddenly gone a long way off from her. This unexpected journey, undertaken without a word of warning, seemed to have carried him much farther away than Washington, but the style of the note, when she resumed it, was not very formidable : —

" Now for a word in confidence, dear Julia. I would rather have spoken it, but take my only opportunity to say that I should not be surprised if Philip's friend, Dr. Carey, should seek ere long to see you. I fancy that he wishes to speak to you of

something which he has very much at heart; and so
I should like you to know that I think him an excellent young man, with strong common sense, fair
ability, highly cultivated, who has made a good
choice of a profession. In short, that if you should
be able to listen to him as he desires, he is not apt
to give you reason to regret your choice.

" At all events, do not decide hastily, my child.
Take time to consider, and believe me as always,

" Affectionately and faithfully,

ALGERNON DRAYTON."

As she finished reading the note, Julia sprang
out of bed, and began her toilet with a sort of
desperate energy. It seemed to her that she could
not stay shut up in one room any longer.

It was a little odd that a few moments later
there came a knock at her door, and a card was
handed in, on which was inscribed the name of Dr.
Lawrence Carey.

" Did you say that I was not well, and not able
to see any one ? " asked Julia.

" Yis, I jist did, Missy," said Rogers, speaking
from the other side of the door. "I said you
had n't ben down to breakfast, and I did n't know
eff you 'd be coming down to lunch; but he say eff
you be a-thinkin' of comin' down he 'll jist step in
and wait."

" Say that I have a bad headache and shall not
be down for half an hour at least," said Julia, not
chancing to be in a mood to soften this announce-

ment, but she knew that if her visitor persisted in staying spite of such discouragement she must see him. He was so intimate at the house that were she to deny herself altogether, on the plea that her head was aching too badly, there would be nothing for it but to remain up-stairs, and she felt just then as if she needed air. The whole house was not large enough for her! She dressed hastily, therefore, and came down stairs with rather a bad grace.

She and Dr. Carey, whom she found standing near the centre-table in the drawing-room, in rather an uneasy attitude, had had a polite dispute during the German cotillon which they danced together on the previous evening, and Miss Prescott knew quite well that his coming this morning was an overture of peace. She had an anxious feeling, indeed, that it might signify something more, for even before her guardian's warning she had begun to be conscious of an increasing difficulty in keeping on purely society topics with him, and the hostile measures which she had adopted had been partly a ruse to ward off the evil hour which she feared now was approaching. She would not show the white feather, however, and, much as she had hoped to find the field unoccupied, marched in and faced the enemy with a bold front.

The preliminaries passed off very well.

Their dispute chanced to have been on the subject of Ralph Waldo Emerson, of whom Dr. Carey was a very warm admirer, and whom Julia had proceeded to attack upon some passing mention of his name, out of a pure spirit of contrariety, little dreaming that a great critical author was, ere long, to adopt the same method of dealing with the same subject.

Dr. Carey now appeared like a recording angel, with two volumes under his arm, one of essays, one of poems, and Miss Prescott was soon reduced to silence by the eloquent testimony which he heaped up before her from the poet's own mouth and out of the very brain of the philosopher.

She was quite content to sit quietly at her end of the sofa and listen to all that there was to be said and quoted in opposition to her rashly-expressed opinion. She even encouraged her visitor to read much more than he had intended, because, in the first place, she had taste enough to enjoy what he read, and, in the second, it was so good to have his attention thus happily occupied and the current of his thoughts turned into so safe a channel.

But Dr. Carey had not come for this. It was sweet to make a convert to one of his favorite authors, but much as he admired him he had decided that there was some one else whom he admired more, and on this occasion Emerson had merely been a subterfuge covering a yet deeper subject of reflection to his young apostle.

"There is a life of him, by Conway, just out," he said at last. "I shall have to send it to you."

Then they talked of other things.

Dr. Carey felt, it seemed, that the limit to his stay in Philadelphia had come at last.

"I have been away much longer than I intended," he said, "and there are a hundred things which need attention at home."

"Are you glad to go?" asked Julia carelessly, realizing an instant after she had spoken that she had better not have asked the question.

"I am not glad," he answered.

"Society here is very pleasant, certainly," said Miss Prescott, choosing to give a broad interpretation to his words; "but we who live in it tire a little sometimes of seeing always the same faces."

"I was thinking only of the friends of whose society I do not tire," said Dr. Carey.

"Indeed, no. I often wonder what you and Philip find to say to one another when you shut yourselves up for one of your long talks," said Julia. "I do not think Philip is an easy person to talk to, fond as I am of him."

"I do, but then he is equally tolerant of me, which every one might not be," returned Dr. Carey, with unusual meekness. "You said just now," he continued, in a studiously matter-of-fact tone, "that you sometimes wearied of society here. Do you think you would be willing to live anywhere else?"

"I do not know that I should," she answered, more seriously than she had yet spoken. "To be tired of a thing is not always to be sure of liking a change."

"Certainly not, but it is apt to render one willing to try change."

"Not if one knows the world, I think," replied Julia, with a sigh so genuine that a student of human nature could hardly have suppressed a smile at the inconsistency of her apparently bright prospects with her sad philosophy.

Dr. Carey had never a very keen sense of humor, and was too much in earnest just then for it to have been stirred, even had he possessed such a faculty. Julia was, he thought, the most complete woman whom he had ever met. There was a dependence and an independence about her which appealed to him equally, touching two sides of his own character — his love of domination and a natural dislike to being made too far responsible for anything. Then he thought her handsome, in rather a rare style of beauty, and was unconsciously impressed by her social ease and tact. In truth, he did not know himself how much of her surroundings were admired by him as a part of herself, but felt a vague uneasiness at the thought of transplanting her, for her own sake, which increased the difficulty of asking her to become his wife.

Seeing that he was allowing a pause which might become dangerous, Julia spoke again.

"Talking of change," she said, "I think I should like to go abroad."

"I was not thinking of that," said Dr. Carey, "when I asked you if you would like to try a change, but it was a stupid remark ; pray forget it. I came to-day prepared to be selfish, to talk to you of my own hopes and wishes rather than of yours."

"Oh! I have such a bad headache!" cried Julia. "I am sure I shall not be sympathetic. Do not you think you had better wait for some other time ?"

"Unfortunately I cannot. I am obliged to return to Boston to-morrow. I am very sorry that you have a headache, but I must say my say."

Julia protested no more. There was something in her visitor's tone which convinced her, even more than his words, that protest would be useless. He must say his say, and she must listen to it. A passive part was never an easy one to her, and to be obliged to listen to the unburdening of another heart when her own was struggling with a new sense of misery was doubly hard ; but she had an unusual power of mastering emotion.

She rose from her seat on the sofa and walked over to the piano, which was open. She sat down before it and struck a few soft chords, and then turned towards Dr. Carey a quiet, attentive face.

"I am listening," she said, calmly and very gravely. "What is it that you have to say ?"

Carey rose also. It was not half so easy to speak his mind, now that he was requested to do so, as he had thought it would be a few moments before while she seemed so unwilling to let him speak. His heart sank at the unchanging stillness of her face. He thought it augured ill for him, but he was too much of a man to let a faint heart overcome him.

" What I want to say is simply this," he said, suddenly resolving to dispense with all preliminaries which might have led up to his request. He drew near and rested his crossed elbows on the piano, while he bent towards her in a determined attitude. " I want to ask you to be my wife. Will you ? "

" Do you think it is a question of will ? " she asked.

" *Can* you, then ? "

" I cannot." The words were not said ungently, but deliberately. A refusal was never more unmistakable since the memory of man, but Carey did not seem to heed it. It has been hinted that he had some experience of Julia's temperament which might incline him to believe it the reverse of docile. Perhaps he fancied that the decision of his manner had roused a spirit of opposition.

" You do not mean that," he urged gently. " Think for a moment. I care very much for you. It is hardly necessary to tell you that."

" Why ? " she asked.

" Because I think you know it. You must have seen how I was getting to feel," he replied, with a tremor in his voice which he vainly tried to calm.

Julia shook her head.

" Did you not know what was coming ? " asked Dr. Carey.

"Indeed I did not, in time to avert it."

"Then will you not think now, whether you might not love me and be my wife?"

"Ah no!" she said. "I never could."

There was a pause.

"You have not given me open encouragement, of course," pursued Carey presently, while the hot blood surged into his face; "but"—he hesitated. "You must have known that your very contrariety attracted me. Did you not?"

Julia dropped her eyes.

"It ought not to have," she said, with a faint smile.

"Ah! But it did. Everything about you does. What you do, and what you leave undone."

"I am at least not responsible for that," she said demurely.

"Julia! You are trifling with me."

"Dr. Carey, I am not, and I have not given you the right to take the liberty you are taking in calling me by my name!" She rose angrily as she spoke, and turning from him stood for a moment looking out of the window.

"Julia! Julia!" he repeated, vehemently, in a tone of genuine feeling, which touched her, in spite of her determination to be cold.

She faced him with an agitation which she vainly strove to conceal.

"What can I do?" she asked, with trembling lips. "This is very painful for both of us. Surely it had better come to an end."

17

"Did you mean what you said to me? Will you not think of it and give me an answer at some future time?"

Julia looked perplexed. It happened that her guardian's last words in the note she had received from him that morning flashed across her mind. "Do not decide hastily," he had said, but as she thought of his advice, she only grew more determined that she would not follow it. In all things else she would take his counsel, she thought, but in this he was not fitted to judge of what was best for her; then, too, she had a duty, a hard one, to the young man who stood before her waiting for one word of comfort, which he would translate into a world of hope.

"If I consented to that," she said sorrowfully, "you might really tell me, with reason, that I had trifled with you."

"No, I should not."

She clasped her hands together and her face grew pale.

"I must not deceive you or myself," she said. "It is utterly impossible for me to answer as you wish, now, or ever."

CHAPTER XXI.

"This is truth the poet sings,
That a sorrow's crown of sorrow is remembering happier things."
TENNYSON.

MRS. PERCY was alone. She was seated near
the window in her own drawing-room, trying to
catch the fading light on a bit of artistic embroidery to which she was applying the finishing touches,
turning her head from side to side as she did so,
with a critical air which became her well.

A small tea-table near the fire was spread for
afternoon tea, with an easy-chair near it, which
opened its arms most soothingly to a weary passer-
by, and a slender-legged papier-mache one ready
for a more energetic guest, but the tea hour was
passing and no one had come.

Mrs. Percy herself had been so busy with her
work that she had not thought of ordering in the
kettle, and just as she was about to do so, two visitors were admitted. One of the late comers was
tall, angular, and rather awkward in his movements; the other, somewhat below him in height,
lithe, active, as graceful as a man can be in these
modern days of absence of all effectiveness from
male costume.

It chanced that this visitor entered the room a

little in advance of his companion, and the lady, who was just turning from the window with her work in her hand, smiled on him, a sweet, triumphant smile, which he knew how to interpret; but there was an expression in his face which she did not understand until the taller man came in ; then she darted a sudden, piercing glance at Cecil Wilmott, in whose hand she had already placed her own, and said in a dry tone : —

"So you have been very thoughtful, and brought Dr. Lawrence Carey with you ? "

"Yes, I have literally brought Carey," said Cecil, answering as in good faith. " Here is a man, Mrs. Percy, who would have left town without coming to wish you good-by. He wanted to express his regrets through me, but I told him he must bear them in person."

" What, is Dr. Carey a deserter? Will he not dine with me after all ? " asked Mrs. Percy, turning to the Bostonian and holding out to him the little jeweled hand which she had rather hastily withdrawn from Wilmott.

" I regret to say that I must return to Boston," said Dr. Carey stiffly, "and so cannot have that pleasure."

" So soon ! " exclaimed Mrs. Percy, with a downward inflection of her expressive voice ; " but I am glad at least of this pleasant opportunity of seeing you. You must sit down, and if Mr. Wilmott will kindly ring for tea, I will make you a cup which shall be good enough to tempt you to return to us."

She did not look at Wilmott as she mentioned his name, but made a gesture towards the bell, which he instantly obeyed.

" You have been bored with our stupid city, Dr. Carey, I am sure," she said.

" No, not exactly," he answered, studiously non-committal. He was thinking what a fool he had been to allow himself to be forced into paying this visit when in anything but a mood for conversation. He had only done so in consequence of an elegant little note which he found awaiting him that afternoon, and which must be answered in some way.

" This woman will not rest satisfied until she has formed some theory to herself of why I am going away," he thought, uneasily. " There are days in a man's life when he might be spared a cup of tea ! " Indeed, he had managed to take a hasty leave of his hostess, Mrs. Davering, by pleading an unexpected necessity of starting for home that night.

" But you are getting very tired of life here," persisted Mrs. Percy. " Confess, now, that you are longing to be once more in Boston."

" On the contrary, I should have liked to stay longer, but found that I could not."

Unconsciously he put this assertion in the past tense, poor fellow, endeavoring to give it force.

" All the clever people at home are growing importunate. I know how it is," said his tormentor, nodding gayly. " Here is your cup of tea."

" My dear Mrs. Percy, we have very few clever

people in my native town," he said, carrying the war into the enemy's country. "None to compare with some whom I have met in yours."

"You are determined to leave a pleasant impression behind."

"I am speaking rather of that which I shall take with me."

"How she does manage to make every one pay her compliments," thought Cecil.

"The cleverness, you mean?" said the widow to Carey. "Of course you will. And does Mr. Wilmott go with you to Boston?" she asked, sweeping round upon her other visitor, with a teacup in her hand. "If you took him you would at least take a lively impression."

"I do not expect to go to Boston," said Cecil Wilmott, to whom Mrs. Percy seemed to look for an answer to this question. "Why did you think so?"

"Oh, for no reason," she said carelessly, "and so I fancied it might be true. It is always the unexpected which happens."

"I have been thinking of going away for a week or two," said Cecil, "but only for a visit to my uncle, in New York."

"Ah, now I remember," she said, "that you told me you were thinking of going away somewhere, and as you came with Dr. Carey I thought it possible you might be going with him."

"I am sorry to have to hurry off, Mrs. Percy," said Dr. Carey, who saw in this diversion a chance of escape, "but I have an engagement with Mr. Hazzard, — to dinner, in fact. We dine at the club, and I go afterwards to the train, so that I cannot keep him waiting."

"Indeed? Then I shall not see you again," said Mrs. Percy. "It is too bad that you must go," she added, with a faint show of reluctance, but even good acting had not been able to conceal from his rather obtuse vision that something was going wrong between herself and Cecil Wilmott. He did not care a sixpence what it was so long as it gave him an opportunity of quitting the field in good order, for his wounds were beginning to cry out, and he could not bear the pain and smile much longer.

"Were you afraid to come before?" asked Mrs. Percy, in a mocking tone, as soon as the door had closed on Dr. Carey.

"There are very few things of which I am afraid," said Wilmott.

"Then I am not one of them?"

"Hardly." He took the hearth-brush, as he spoke, and began dusting some stray cinders into the fire.

"Are you afraid of this little Miss Arnold?"

"Why do you ask?"

"It is evident. Are you not running away?"

"I am not afraid of her in the sense which you mean."

"How, then, are you afraid of her?"

"I do not intend to say."

"Oh, the transparency of man! And you think I cannot guess?"

"I think you cannot."

"Will you acknowledge it if I guess rightly?"

"I will acknowledge nothing."

"Stupid! Have you not already in that very speech acknowledged everything? I know your secret. Shall I tell you what it is?"

"As you please." He was leaning against the mantelpiece, frowning a little, as he looked into the fire.

"You give me permission?" asked the widow in a bantering tone. Cecil did not see the look of indecision which came over her face as she vainly tried to read his own, but he suspected that her questions were not merely prompted by the love of teasing. She was deeply interested in the answers, and for some reason or other she wanted to gain time.

"It is one of two things," she was saying to herself. "I will try the least likely. His manner of denying will teach me more than a confession."

"You give me permission?" she repeated aloud. Cecil waved his hand impatiently.

"Then, Mr. Vanity, you are afraid to stay here for fear this young lady may grow too fond of you."

Cecil blushed hotly. "Absurd!" he said, trying to laugh.

"Of course it is absurd. The truth is always much more absurd than an invention."

"Some people have a genius for invention," replied Cecil, "which enables them to reproduce the absurdity if not the truth."

"Are you not inclined to credit me with some knowledge of you?" asked the lady.

"A little. Why?"

"Well, then, I will tell you another thing about yourself. You brought that Bostonian here with you this evening simply because you were afraid to trust yourself with me alone, and you would have gone with him when he went but that you were still more afraid of leaving me in anger."

"That is partly true," said Cecil; "the last part."

"The first part is the truest."

"However positive you may please to be," rejoined Cecil, "your supposition of my reason for deciding to go to New York is entirely groundless."

"I believe it is," said Mrs. Percy musingly, "for two reasons. First, you are too selfish to take so much trouble for the sake of any one; and secondly, because if you had only been going for that reason you would not have feared to see me."

"If I had feared to see you, Reta, why should I have come?"

"Why, indeed?" she asked, with a sudden smile which brought out all her dimples. "The inclination must have been a little stronger than the dread. I believe you are fond of me, you foolish boy, but this new fancy has taken a very strong hold on you. You are much farther gone than when I last saw you."

Cecil did not speak for a moment. He strode

impatiently up and down the room. Presently Mrs.
Percy came to his side, and laid her hand caress-
ingly on his shoulder.

" Cheer up," she said. " There is really no danger of your taking that young woman seriously."

" Reta," he returned, taking her hand in his,
" you have always been a very sweet friend to me."

" Only a friend ? " she asked archly.

" I wanted you to be more to me once, but —
you refused me. That was a long while ago," said
Cecil.

" And since then you have only been a friend ? "

" I have tried to be. Part of the time you were
bound to another."

" That too is past."

" Ah, yes ! " cried Cecil, dropping her hand and
renewing his walk to and fro. " It is all past, and
no doubt some day this will pass also ! "

A look of anger and pain had come into the eyes
of Mrs. Percy.

" Then you really have decided that it is this girl
whom you care for ? " she asked, in a bitter tone, out
of which she vainly tried to put all feeling. She
knew it was an unwise question, and would have
recalled it the moment after she had spoken.

Cecil looked at her regretfully.

" Why will you make me say such things ? " he
said. " I have not decided ; it has been decided for
me — by the fates, I suppose. I had better say
good-by, Reta." She had sunk down on a low seat
before the fire, with her face turned from him.

She neither moved nor answered for a moment, and for a moment Cecil stood before her, waiting. Then he walked over to a corner table where he had left his hat, and coming back held out his hand.

"Good-by," he said again.

"Good-by," she answered softly, without turning her head towards him or seeming to see the outstretched hand. "I suppose I shall hardly see you again."

"Oh dear, yes; you will see me to-night, if you go to Mrs. Waverley's," replied Cecil, cheerfully. "I have no doubt I shall take you in to dinner."

"Then you are not to leave town immediately?" she exclaimed, in an altered tone.

"I hardly know," he said. "Soon, if not immediately."

She turned and looked up into his face. "Is it to be a last resort?" she asked, and this time, she laid her hand in his.

"Perhaps," he answered, and so he left her.

CHAPTER XXII.

" Where passion leads, or prudence points the way."
ROBERT LOWTH.

CECIL left Mrs. Percy in a curious frame of mind, and he concluded while he was dressing for Mrs. Waverley's dinner that he had better start for New York the next day. Chance would have it that he was seated beside Mrs. Percy at dinner, even as he had suggested that he might be ; but the lady's mood was quite changed since he had left her in the dusk and the firelight.

She was more brilliant than usual — quite the centre of admiration ; but she took no more notice of Cecil, than if he had been the most indifferent of her acquaintances. As for Wilmott, he was unusually silent. He had one more farewell visit to pay, to which he looked forward with mingled feelings of pleasure and apprehension, and he was trying to decide that it would be wiser not to pay it. Having determined to run away, why test his resolution by another interview with the siren from whom he had resolved to fly ? asked Prudence. To which Cecil answered that it would be treating the members of his uncle's household very cavalierly if he went without " saying good-by " to them, and this flimsy excuse was all that his disinclination to such a course required to condemn it.

His nature was averse to prudence, and much more ready to rush hastily into action than to bear patiently the results of its own temerity. He went to dinner in a state of indecision as to whether he should or should not depart the next morning without seeing Edith Arnold again, but when dessert was served his mind was made up. He excused himself from rejoining the ladies, and was soon on the way to Meredith Square.

As he neared the house he was determining to avoid anything like a tête-à-tête with Miss Arnold, which he felt would hardly be a wise experiment, but to treat her in a kindly, friendly manner which should harmonize, as far as might be, the slight inconsistencies of conduct of which he acknowledged himself guilty on former occasions.

Rogers, who had received instructions that the ladies would see no one that evening, took his time about answering the bell.

" No, sar. Miss Prescott, she got a very bad headache and can't come down no more to-night; and Miss Arnold, she 's with her; and Miss Ruthven, she 's gone out with young Master Philip to a Star Lecture. There ain't nobody at home, nor ready to see nobody ! " concluded that worthy negro.

" Has Miss Arnold a bad headache ? " asked Wilmott.

" Well — I ain't heered about that, sar," said Rogers, looking puzzled.

" Take up my card to Miss Arnold," said Wilmott, in a clear, decided tone which surprised himself, "and say that I should like to see her if she can leave Miss Prescott for a little while, as I am going out of town to-morrow."

It was not until the reluctant Mercury had departed with his message, and he was looking dreamily into the library fire, that Wilmott recollected his prudent resolve to avoid a tête-à-tête. He pulled himself together with a start, and then remembered that it was too late now to draw back, but he could at least keep the other half of his resolution. He could be as kindly and as friendly as he pleased. Five minutes elapsed after he had come to this conclusion, and he began to wonder whether after all he was to have an opportunity of trying it. Then the door opened quietly and Edith came in.

She came slowly, putting up her hand as she did so to shade her eyes from the light. Her face had that pale tint which often comes of having been some time in a darkened room, and Cecil fancied that there was a slightly tremulous movement about the corners of her mouth. Her hand, too, trembled just a little, he thought, as he took it in his, but she withdrew it almost instantly, so that he had not time to be sure.

Could it be possible, he thought, that this shrinking little girl was the scornful young lady who had turned upon him so disdainfully as she uttered her parting words at the Assembly? Or, again, was this quietly moving figure the same which he had seen so full of life and animation, on the steps of the Academy that morning? What had caused the change? It was an unwise subject of speculation; and a silence had fallen between them, after the first polite interchange of greeting, which was equally unfortunate. Edith was the first to break it.

"I am sorry to hear that you are going away," she said.

"It is a bore to have to go just now," replied Cecil.

"Because there is so much that is pleasant going on at home, I suppose." Her manner was quiet and cold.

"Have you forgiven me for being so disagreeable at the Assembly last evening?" asked Cecil, abruptly.

"It is I who should ask to be forgiven," she said, with a smile and a faint blush.

"Perhaps you should. I think you were a little hard on me in your thoughts," rejoined Cecil, "but I erred in speech. In fact, I made an ass of myself, and quite deserved anything you might choose to think."

She did not answer for a moment, and then she changed the subject. "Where are you going?" she asked.

She had seated herself in a low chair with a high carved back, on the other side of the fire-place, just opposite to him, and her face was half turned from him, bringing the delicate outline of her features into distinct relief against the dark marble mantel-piece.

Cecil noticed that she wore the same dark green traveling dress in which he had first seen her. Somehow he fancied that there was a significance in this little fact.

"I am going to New York to stay with my uncle," he said, in answer to her question.

"And why do you go now, since you say that you would find it pleasanter to stay at home?"

"Oh, I don't know." He took a little carved wooden paper-knife from the table and began playing with it.

"I think you had been with your uncle in New York when I first met you," said Edith.

"Yes," answered Cecil. "Did you see me when I first saw you?"

She smiled.

"I fancy you did, and yet through the whole of that dreary detention you never gave me a chance to say a word to you."

A slight frown crossed her brow. She raised her head a little. "No," she replied quietly.

Cecil laughed merrily at her little air of offended dignity. "You evidently do not think it your duty to amuse chance acquaintances in railway trains," he said. "Your manner now reminds me forcibly of the reserve in which you wrapped yourself on that first evening. Even after I told you who I was, I had to struggle with all my might to elicit the interesting bits of information which you strove so tenaciously to withhold."

"I do not think I succeeded very well," said Edith, demurely.

"No, not very," replied Cecil. "That sort of thing does not go down with me."

"If I should not see you again," she said gravely, "I shall not forget how kind you were in befriending me on the first evening of my arrival."

"Why should you think that you will not see me again?" he asked with a sudden change of tone. "Do you expect to be gone before my return from New York?"

"That depends upon how long you stay there," returned Edith, laughing.

"It also depends upon how long you stay here."

"I cannot tell you that," she answered.

There was a pause, in which she rose. "I wish you a very pleasant journey," she said, and held out her hand to Cecil, who had also risen. Her easy, cordial manner exasperated him to the last degree.

"You seem in a great hurry to get rid of me," he remarked.

"Not at all," she answered blandly. "I fancied that you were ready to go."

She reseated herself as she spoke, opened a little leather wallet which hung at her side, and took out some fine crochet work in colored silk, through which she began plying the needle diligently.

Cecil leaned against the mantel shelf in gloomy silence. As he watched her busy fingers, her head slightly bent, and the composed expression of her face, it suddenly occurred to him that the situation which he had anticipated was reversed in this interview.

18

It was Edith who was being kindly and sedulously friendly, and he who was wondering at the change in her and inwardly chafing at its inconsistency with certain shy, sweet glances which he remembered only too distinctly.

Had she never really cared for him at all then? Had she felt no response to the attraction which had been so strong with him? Common sense should have told him to rejoice in the certainty that his idle fancy had hurt no one, but common sense was silent. He was alive to no feeling but an irresistible desire to make her care, almost to make her suffer for the pain which he was feeling, as the last moments flew past in which he could be with her.

"What are you making?" he asked.

"A little silk purse," she answered in a practical tone, without looking up.

"It is very pretty. May I see it?"

As he spoke, he held out his hand, which touched hers as he took it.

"For whom are you making this?"

She smiled, and looked up archly.

"Suppose that I should tell you, for Mr. Drum Kettleby?"

"I should not believe you."

"Then, as I do not like being doubted, you must guess for whom."

"Will you not give it to me?" he asked, surprised at his own boldness.

She laughed. "The purse is for my sister," she said.

" Then will you not make one for me ? Is it too much to ask ? "

She did not answer for a moment, but lifted a fire screen from the table and held it before her face.

" I want to take something to my sister made with my own hands, to show that I have thought of her while I have been away," she said, at last.

" And you do not want to give me anything to show that you have thought of me ? "

" I have thought of my sister."

" But not of me ! " he returned, with a bitterness which startled her.

" I have not thought of making you a purse," she replied, quietly.

He handed it back to her and turned away.

" I wish I had never thought of you," he said.

She glanced up at him shyly, with one of her old appealing looks.

" Would you really care for a purse if I made it ? " she asked.

" You know I would ! " he cried vehemently. " There is nothing I want so much."

She was surprised at the eager, triumphant light in his eyes.

" Do you promise to make it for me ? " he continued. She smiled and nodded.

" Give me your hand on it, then ! "

She drew back a little. She was frightened, she hardly knew why, he seemed by his manner to make so much of so little.

" I will certainly keep my promise," she said, without seeming to notice the hand which he held out to her.

But Cecil was in no mood to be gainsaid. A moment before he had been profoundly discouraged. Now he once more commanded the situation.

" If you will not give me your hand," he said, " I must know the reason. Have I done anything to offend you?" He bent over as he spoke and looked earnestly into her face. She grew very pale.

" I am not offended," she answered faintly, and a shy, frightened look came into her eyes.

Cecil drew a long sigh of relief, and possessed himself of one of her hands without further question. She tried to withdraw it, and failing, started to her feet, but Cecil still held the hand fast between both his own.

" Edith! " he whispered. " Edith! I love you."

" Hush! " she said, while the color began to return to her cheeks. " You must not say that."

" I must and I will. I love you! I love you!" he cried, vehemently. " Do you love me? "

She was silent, for she was making a gallant struggle for self-possession.

" You did not come here to say this," she replied, at last.

" Perhaps not," he answered, " but what of that? What difference does it make whether I meant to tell you? Do you not believe me when I say I love you? "

"It makes all the difference," said Edith, answering the first part of his question only. Again she tried to draw away her hand, and this time succeeded.

"If you did not mean to tell me," she proceeded quietly, "it is best you should not do so."

"But I have told you," he said. "What is done cannot be undone."

"Yes, it can," she answered quickly; "or, rather, it is not done, since you did not mean to do it."

"It is," he replied, firmly. "I have spoken and you have heard me, and I must hear my answer. Do you love me?"

She had been drawing away unconsciously, step by step, and he following her, until she had reached the corner of the room nearest the fire-place. She placed her hands on the back of a tall old-fashioned chair near the window, and drew it in front of her for support, under a sudden sense of weakness which had come upon her rather than to protect herself against him, but he misunderstood the action.

He paused instantly, and folded his arms across his breast.

"I await your decision," he said. There was a long silence. Cecil had dropped his eyes and did not see the effort which she made several times to answer him. At last the words came very slowly.

"You may think it strange," she murmured, "when I tell you that I might have cared for you, but it is all that I can say."

"You mean, then, that you do not?" he asked, raising his eyes and fixing them on hers.

"That is all I can say," she repeated.

"But you must say more," said Cecil. "Do you mean that you do not care for me?"

"No," she answered, faintly.

"Not at all?"

"Not in that way."

"Then how do you know you might have cared?"

She was silent.

"Believe me," he pleaded, "you must care a little, or you could not be sure of that."

"I only know," said Edith, in a low voice which trembled very slightly, "that I do not love and trust you as I should do the man I married."

"Why not?" he asked, almost with defiance.

"It may be," she replied, more firmly, "because you have not sought my love."

"What can you mean!" cried Cecil. "Surely I have. Am I not seeking it now?"

"For the moment you are."

"For my whole life, Edith! Why will you be so cruel?"

"Do you think me quite blind," she asked, "and quite stupid? Do you think I have not seen how you tried not to care for me?"

"What difference does that make, even if it be true?" he answered slowly. "Suppose that I tried not to care and yet did care in spite of it, does not that prove that my love was all the stronger?"

"How can that be?" she answered. "You acknowledged a little while ago that you did not come into this room even intending to tell me that you loved me!"

"I am beginning to think that you never have cared!" he exclaimed bitterly. "You do not know what it is to love or you would think that of as little consequence as I do."

"I certainly think it of consequence," she said.

"Then you doubt my love?"

"Ah, no!" she cried, impulsively, pained by the pain his face and voice expressed. "It is not that"—

He drew a step nearer and held out his arms, but still she shrank away from him.

"It is not that I doubt it," she said desperately, "but that your love does not seem supported by any strength of purpose."

"And so you do not trust it?"

"No."

Cecil turned without a word and left the room.

CHAPTER XXIII.

" Who is this that darkeneth counsel by words without knowledge? " — OLD TESTAMENT.

" WELL, you know, dear, we must give something."

" Must we ? "

" Oh ! How stupid men are ! " cried Mrs. Davering, looking hard at a wax candle which was stuck into a curiously wrought sconce attached to her writing table. On the table lay some note-paper and a pen with a fanciful penholder, beside an ornamental inkstand. They all looked as if they had just come out of a shop, for Mrs. Davering did not write very often.

Mr. Davering stood on the hearth-rug in his wife's boudoir. He was indeed warming his coat tails, but with none of that truculent air of sovereignty which one associates with the action. He looked meek, on the contrary, and rather dispirited, although there was nothing despicable in his meekness. It evidently only arose from the depression with which a gentle nature regards the decision of another which he does not share nor disagree from strongly enough to oppose.

" Why must we give something ? " he ventured to ask.

" There are such simple reasons," said his wife, disdainfully, " that I should think even you would see them." She drew an impatient sigh, and then, as though resigning herself to the inevitable, began to explain. " What I propose to give in this instance," she concluded, " is something a little different from the rest of the world. I think of having private theatricals, and as it seems hardly worth while to turn the drawing-rooms upside down, I think of taking the little theatre, which will hold my guests quite comfortably, and then letting them come home to supper."

" But, Helen, I have quite a feeling about private theatricals — and who will act in them ? " asked Mr. Davering in dismay.

" Do not trouble yourself about that, Buchanan," said his wife, nodding her head contentedly. She had indeed talked herself into quite a good humor, and Mr. Davering realized the inutility of any further protest. He therefore left her ; brooding, as he went, on how much he had always disliked private theatricals, and how well Mrs. Davering knew it.

Fate meanwhile was being kinder than he hoped; for when his wife opened the answer to an elegant little note which she proceeded after this conversation to dispatch to Julia, she found to her dismay that Miss Prescott declined taking part in any theatricals.

Being aware that her whole object in proposing this troublesome form of amusement had really

been for the sake of bringing Julia and her son
Charley together, one may imagine that for the
moment Mrs. Davering was completely crushed.
Indeed Mrs. Wilmott, who chanced to drop in for
a neighborly chat in the course of the afternoon,
found her friend in an unusual state of depression.

"I can't think what has come over Julia," she
said, after confessing her grievance.

"I do not think that Julia has been looking
at all well lately," replied Mrs. Wilmott kindly.
"She always misses Algernon when he leaves her,
and you know he is in Washington now, with the
possibility of a longer absence."

"That is another person whom I counted on to
help me with my play!" exclaimed Mrs. Davering.

Mrs. Wilmott shook her head with an air of
commiseration which was very aggravating to Mrs.
Davering in her present vexed mood. "I am
afraid, Helen, you will hardly get Algernon to interest himself in the matter just now. He is a
good deal taken up with some important lawsuit
which has required his presence in Washington,
and it is just possible may take him abroad. I had
a letter from him yesterday morning asking me
whether I should be willing to go to Heronsford
and take Charlotte, in case he had to be away
through the summer. You know Aunt Ruthven
always goes back to her own house in Germantown
in the spring, and he is anxious to secure suitable
guardianship and cheerful surroundings for Julia.

I wrote at once to say that I would do so with much pleasure."

Mrs. Wilmott quite forgot at the moment that she had been specially requested not to communicate this piece of information to any one until Mr. Drayton's return. There was something so pleasant in having the opportunity to disclose in an easy off-hand way the fact that she had been asked as a *favor* to go to Heronsford. It would prevent there being any danger of Mrs. Davering's supposing that her presence and Charlotte's there was merely an act of Christian kindness from Algernon, to save them expense through the warm weather when town would be unbearable.

Mrs. Wilmott was so often the recipient of Christian kindness that she was sensitive upon the subject, and at this moment a most brilliant plan occurred to her. " I have it ! " she exclaimed with kindling interest; " why should we not get up a little parlor opera, instead of a play ? We could find one with just two or three characters, and perhaps Julia would play the accompaniment."

" Who would sing in it ? " asked Mrs. Davering.

" Well — there is Charley. He has really a very fair baritone, and Cecil sings a little."

" But who would sustain the rôle of the heroine ? "

" I do not know of any one who would both sing and act well, except Mrs. Percy," said Mrs. Wilmott, thoughtfully.

" Dear me ! " exclaimed Mrs. Davering. " How tired one gets of Mrs. Percy. She is always everywhere. I am quite sick of her affected French songs! I can't think why they take so."

" She has a great deal of dramatic talent," said Mrs. Wilmott, " although I confess I never like to see too much of that sort of thing in private life. It makes one feel as if one could not tell what was real about a person, and how much assumed for the occasion."

" Well, to do her justice, she did not assume to care when her husband died," retorted Mrs. Daverring.

" What would you have? She had married for money, and with his removal disappeared the only obstacle to her enjoyment of it; but she is a very fascinating woman to men," said Cecil's mother, with a little sigh.

" After all it is only her voice, which is a matter of the least consequence to me at present," said Mrs. Davering majestically.

She walked over to the bell, and after ringing for the carriage, stood still a moment, pleasing herself with the idea that a " parlor opera " would sound very different from private theatricals to Mr. Davering. " I will see Julia to-morrow, and ask her about the accompaniment," she said aloud. " I do wish Cecil were to be here to arrange things for me. I could make him stage manager, if he did not feel equal to singing."

" It is very possible that Cecil may return in two weeks," said his mother, with a proud sense of her son's importance. " He did not expect to stay

longer than that. I will write to him and tell him
of your plan, if you like, and urge his coming as
soon as he can."

" Do. That is a kind woman ; and now come
with me for a turn in the Park and I will drop you
at home, on my way to call on Mrs. Percy ; I shall
find her in a little after five o'clock."

When she went to call on Julia the next day
Mrs. Davering was told that Miss Ruthven and
Miss Arnold were out and Miss Prescott was engaged, but on sending in her card, with a particular request that she might be allowed to see Miss
Prescott, was ushered into the library, where she
found Julia sitting alone.

She did not look well. Mrs. Davering was impressed with this fact, and would have remarked
upon it at once, but for something cold and rather
constrained in Julia's manner to herself, which
rendered her a little less at her ease than usual.

The truth was that, as sometimes happened to
this lady, in the absorption of her own affairs she
had temporarily forgotten her keen interest in
those of others, and until thus reminded of it, both
the cause of the somewhat formal terms on which
she and Miss Prescott had remained ever since
Mrs. Percy's party, and the formality itself had
quite escaped her memory.

Now, however, as she sat opposite to Julia in
Mr. Drayton's library, the conversation of that
evening came back to her quite distinctly, and she
recalled how indignant Julia had been ; but she

kept her thoughts to herself for the moment, and rushed into the details of her new project.

Julia listened, but with little display of interest; and when Mrs. Davering at length preferred her request that she would play the accompaniment for the parlor opera, said quietly that she was sorry that she could not grant it.

" Are you afraid you would be nervous at playing before so many people ? " asked Mrs. Davering anxiously.

" It is not so much that," said Julia calmly; " but I do not wish to undertake anything of the kind at present."

" You are really not looking well," said Mrs. Davering, changing her tone to one of patronage; " but I am sure you will regret your decision, for it is best to keep up in these cases, no matter how badly one may be feeling."

" Thank you, I am quite well," said Julia. " I am only suffering the reaction from a headache."

" That is all you will acknowledge, of course," said Mrs. Davering, who, feeling herself thwarted in her pet scheme, was determined at least to have the satisfaction of firing one parting shot; " but I was really sorry to hear of Mr. Drayton's proposed departure. If you felt so badly at the idea of your guardian's marrying, my dear, how must you feel at the prospect of his being away all summer ? "

" Mr. Drayton has only gone to Washington a day or two on business," said Julia proudly.

" Oh, yes, I know," said Mrs. Davering. " I did

not mean *now*, of course. I meant when he crosses
the ocean for two or three months. It will really
be hard on you, dear, to be left at home. I remember when you were ill abroad and missed seeing so many of the sights, you were always talking
of the things you would see the next time Mr.
Drayton took you to Europe." The shot had hit
the mark. Julia grew quite white for a moment
and her lips quivered; then she made a great effort
at self-conquest, and rose as though to usher her
visitor politely from the room.

Mrs. Davering, although she was standing and
had proposed to go, was not in any hurry about it,
but Julia felt that she could not endure inactively
what she was suffering. She must do or say something. What she said was : —

"Helen, you were very kind to me at that time
which you have just spoken of, when I was ill, and
I have considered you until lately as a friend; but
it was a friendship born of circumstance, not of
real sympathy or understanding, and — it has come
to an end."

"Dear me! How melodramatic! Why, your
headache has made you quite imposing. And how
tall you look in that maroon-colored peignoir! It
is really becoming. Au revoir, my dear!"

Julia did not take in the sense of these last words
of Mrs. Davering's. She only realized that at last
she was gone, and turning slowly from the door to
which she had accompanied her, sank into the nearest chair with a sense of stupid misery.

It was *true*, then, — not a dreadful possibility, but a fact, — Mr. Drayton was going to Europe, and she was to be left, and all the world had heard it, except herself. She did not know how long she had been facing this idea, when suddenly she heard the street door open. A light, firm step was coming through the entry.

It paused before the library door, and then the door opened; and without turning her head, she knew that Mr. Drayton was in the room. She rose mechanically, and stood stiff and still, not looking at him or speaking.

"Why, Julia? Is that you, dear?" he said affectionately, coming towards her and taking her two cold little hands in his.

"Yes, Mr. Drayton." Still she did not raise her eyes, or smile.

"What is it, my child? Are you not well? I am afraid you have been going to too many parties, you naughty girl!"

"Yes," said Julia, raising her eyes at last with a strangely hard look in them. "I have been going to too many parties." There was a faintly satirical smile about the corners of her mouth.

Mr. Drayton dropped her hands and turned away. He stepped to the fire, drew off his gloves and began warming his hands. "How are Miss Ruthven and your friend Miss Arnold?" he asked, presently.

"They are very well," said Julia coldly. "Philip and Edith have gone to ride on horseback. Would you like a warm cup of coffee after your journey?" she asked, in a kind but slightly weary tone.

"No, thank you, dear. The journey is not a very long one. There are several matters, however, about which I am anxious. Perhaps I had better go down to the office."

"Oh no, do not! Philip will soon come back, and then you can talk them over with him," she said earnestly, coming to his side, and forgetting for the moment, in her solicitude, her feeling of wounded pride.

"Why, that was spoken like your old self, Julia!" said Mr. Drayton, turning to her with his sweetest smile. "Let us sit down, dear, and have a little talk." He drew her to a seat beside him on a low lounge by the fire. "Come, tell me all that has happened since I went away," he said.

"Not much has happened *here*," said Julia, with some accent on the last word.

"Did a certain young gentleman come to call, as I predicted, and wish to discuss a certain delicate subject?" asked Mr. Drayton, with an attempt to be playful, which for once was rather a failure, on account of the anxious expression of his face.

"Whom do you mean?" inquired Julia, fixing her direct gaze upon him.

"I mean Dr. Carey," said Mr. Drayton, looking into the fire.

"Yes, Dr. Carey came to call," said Julia, coldly. "He came to say good-by."

"That was not all, Julia?"

19

"It is all that I care to remember."

Mr. Drayton turned and gave her one long searching look, which Julia bore unflinchingly with something of defiance in her eyes.

"Are you quite sure of that?" he asked. "Do you not think that you will change your mind?"

"I am quite sure that I shall not."

He put his arm gently about her. "Julia," he said, "there is something which I must tell you; and the sooner it is said, the better, I suppose."

He paused for a moment, and then began again more hurriedly.

"I have just decided, my dear, to accept that case of which I spoke to you a few weeks ago, the one which involves my going abroad, and I have to sail very soon, — next Monday, in fact."

She listened in stony silence. It was nothing new to her, only a little more sudden — a little sooner than she had thought possible. At last, she said : —

"I heard that you were going abroad for the summer, through Mrs. Davering, this afternoon. It is true, then? I did not know whether to believe it."

Her throat felt very dry. It was with difficulty that she succeeded in pronouncing her words, but she spoke clearly enough and rather coldly.

"It is quite true," said Mr. Drayton, "but I do not know how Mrs. Davering heard it." His face wore a serious, troubled look, which at any other time would have aroused Julia's sympathy, but it seemed as if some evil fairy had transformed her usual tenderness into the haughtiest indifference, so far as her manner was translatable. Perhaps some such thought occurred to Mr. Drayton; for seeking anxiously a cause for Julia's altered demeanor, he suddenly hit upon Mrs. Davering as the evil genius who had wrought the change. It was a great relief to have some one to blame other than his ward or himself.

"Has Mrs. Davering been talking to you again about me?" he asked quickly.

"Oh, no," said Julia. "She said nothing but what I have told you."

"Nevertheless, you felt wounded at hearing it from her first, rather than from me. Is that not true, Julia?"

"I should have supposed that I might have been told as soon as any one," said Julia calmly, "but it makes very little difference, since you go so soon. I" —

Her voice broke off suddenly, and she turned away her head. Mr. Drayton hastily withdrew his arm. He rose from his seat and began pacing up and down the room with firm set lips, a glow on his cheek, and a brilliant light in his dark eyes.

The excitement of his manner had a quieting effect upon Julia, and restored the self-control which she feared she had been about to lose. There was comfort in the assurance that this parting, which was so hard for her, was after all not such an easy matter for him; and then, quickly as he had withdrawn from beside her, there had been, at the instant of his doing so, something like a lightning flash of sympathy which had passed from him to her. She knew by a sudden instinct that he was feeling more than he wished her to imagine, and the discovery gave her courage to say what she could not have said without this gleam of hope.

"Must you go away?" she asked.

He did not answer, so she spoke again.

"Is it necessary to take this case?"

"No, it is not necessary."

"Then why do you do it?" she inquired, in a softer tone.

"For many reasons. It is not only gratifying to my ambition to have been asked to take it, but if I conduct it well it will increase my reputation both here and abroad; and then the change of air and scene will no doubt do me good." The last part of this speech was uttered in so sad a tone, and the first part with so little of the buoyant expectation which the words would have conveyed, that Julia exclaimed, —

"I do not believe you really want to go!"

Mr. Drayton walked away towards one of the book-cases at the side of the room. He took down a book, opened and looked at it. His back was towards Julia, but she saw him raise his hand to his eyes. It might have been to shade them from the light, but she fancied that he brushed away a tear.

"I do not think it will do your health as much

good to go as to stay here," she said, earnestly. "If you are not feeling strong you will need to be cared for. It will be lonely among strangers."

He did not answer for a moment, and then he turned once more towards her, with the kind smile which she knew so well.

"My dear girl must not believe me so selfish," he said, "as to be thinking only of what is good for me. I am thinking also that it will be best for her to have a little less care, — to be thrown more entirely with younger people; for when I am here I am unconsciously selfish, and monopolize her time a little too much, without meaning to do so."

He had drawn near to her and taken her passive hand in his. Her whole heart rose to her lips in one wild protest against the fate which seemed closing about her.

"Oh! if it is of *me* you are thinking, do not, do not leave me!" she cried.

"I must," said Mr. Drayton, in a strange, stern voice. "I must leave you for your sake and mine. It is best for both of us."

Julia said nothing then. What could he mean? Was it that after all he was tired of the responsibility which he had undertaken in the care of her? Did he fancy that she was becoming too exacting, too dependent on him? Did he suspect the reason why she had answered Dr. Carey as she had done? Oh horror of horrors! Why had she shown her sorrow to him? A feeling of despair had suddenly succeeded to her passionate grief, and she was dumb with a sense of suffering which could not be expressed.

She did not know how long it was before he left the room. She remembered afterwards that he had come close up to where she stood by the table in the centre of the room, and just touched her forehead with his lips, and that she had not moved or raised her eyes, and then he had gone — yes, he had gone !

When she realized that, she stretched out her arms with a low cry of pain. Her hands touched the back of a heavy leathern arm-chair, the one in which her guardian always sat, and she clung to it as to a living thing and clasped it in her arms, sinking down until her head rested upon its cushioned seat, and weeping there as if her heart would break.

CHAPTER XXIV.

" The blood more stirs
To rouse a lion than to start a hare ! "

SHAKESPEARE.

EDITH meanwhile had gone to ride with Philip, as Julia said. The promise had been of long standing, and its fulfillment postponed from time to time, until Julia took it in hand and insisted that it should be fixed for to-day.

She had set her heart upon Edith's wearing her riding habit and riding her horse ; which, as she was very fond of the horse, was a proof of the enthusiastic nature of her friendship, for she had never allowed any one else to ride him. Indeed, until the time of his accident Mr. Drayton and Julia had ridden together constantly ; but during the press of the gay season Miss Prescott had not found time to ride with Philip, who had been condemned to go alone.

Edith, who was feeling a little dispirited just now, was not very enthusiastic about the ride, and a little incident happened as they were about to set forth which plunged her into a sad abstraction, very unlike her usual alert interest in the things about her, and must have made her rather a dull companion.

It chanced that as they came out of the house a boy was standing on the door-step, holding a note. Philip, recognizing in him his own office boy, put out his hand mechanically and took it.

"Is any one waiting?" he asked, quickly.

"No, sir. Mr. Wilmott give me the note before he went away."

"Why did you not give it to me yesterday, then, or this morning?"

"It ain't for you, sir. He told me to bring it up here when I'd get a chance, and I ain't had a chance before," said the boy.

Philip glanced at the address. "I beg your pardon, Miss Arnold," he said, in a changed tone. "It seems that this note is for you."

Edith blushed hotly as she took it from him, as much from surprise as embarrassment. Her first impulse was to put the note in her pocket, and wait for a more suitable moment to read it; then it occurred to her that such a course would add to the appearance of something prearranged between herself and Cecil, and she decided to open it at once, but on breaking the seal perceived that it only contained the verses which she had copied for him, and which he had returned. There were a few words written on his card to say that after what had passed between them he did not feel that he should keep them, and that was all. The whole matter was unimportant, evidently the result, in Cecil, of a passing feeling of pique; but the little action wounded her, and the tears sprang to her eyes unbidden, as she thrust the paper hastily out of sight and joined Philip on the pavement, where he had been apparently absorbed in the inspection of the horses and conversation with the groom while he awaited her coming.

He helped her on horseback without speaking, and they rode for some distance in silence. Had Philip been a ready man he would have begun to talk at once upon indifferent topics; but if he succeeded in not seeming to notice his companion's mood, he was far too much distressed by it to be capable of acting the part he would have chosen.

At last Edith roused herself, and began questioning him about some beautiful gardens which they were passing, on either side of a broad street, with many grand-looking houses standing in the midst of them.

" Why have I never been in this part of the city before? " she asked wonderingly. " How fine it is. Who lives here? "

" Some of the most worthy people in town," replied Philip; " but, living where we do, we do not happen to know them, and are not often led in this direction either for business or pleasure."

" If I lived in Philadelphia I should live here," said Edith decidedly.

Philip smiled. " I do not wonder that this part of the town impresses you favorably," he answered. " It is much more beautiful than our own, but we are very conservative, and cling to our old haunts."

At this moment a lady rode by, in a dark-green

habit, whom Edith recognized as Mrs. Percy. She bowed graciously, as did also the cavalier who was accompanying her, and who proved to be Mr. Hazzard.

"Are you going to the hare and hounds, Drayton?" he called out in passing.

"No, I was not," said Philip. "In fact, I had forgotten that the hunt was to-day." And then, turning to Edith, as if a sudden thought had struck him, asked, —

"How would you like to see the hare and hounds, by the bye, Miss Arnold? We might go to the meet, and to Heronsford afterwards. It is on the way."

"I think that would be delightful," replied Edith. "You know I want to see Heronsford very much."

"Never fear. I will certainly take you there," he answered, " but it is rather a rare chance to see the hare and hounds at this season of the year. This hunt has been gotten up rather as an experiment, because we have had such mild weather for the last few weeks, and they do not usually begin until a month or two later."

They had left the pavements by this time, and, turning their horses at the next cross-road, passed along a country lane, and then on into another, until they found themselves at the gate of a long avenue, which led up to an old-fashioned gray stone house. In a field near the house were a number of open and close carriages, filled with people, and of ladies and gentlemen on horseback, some of the latter dressed in red coats, which proclaimed that they were to join the hunt.

Philip dismounted, and went to speak to the lady of the house, who might be seen in a pretty little basket phaeton, wearing a jaunty hat, and nodding with kindly hospitality to all new-comers. She drove up presently to welcome Miss Arnold, and recommended a certain spot to her and Philip as likely to give them the best possible view of " the start."

They had just taken their places on the side of a hill, according to her directions, when the "hare" passed them, moving quite deliberately, and with none of the fear in his eye of coming pursuit which might be associated with his character.

He appeared about forty, was dressed in a velveteen riding-suit, mounted on a strong-looking chestnut, and carried a bag, strung over one shoulder, from which he drew a handful of small bits of white paper, which he scattered on the ground to make the trail. A lady rode beside him, glancing at whom Edith perceived the inevitable Mrs. Percy.

"The hare will be allowed twenty minutes' grace," said Philip, "that he may be well in advance of his pursuers before they set upon his track."

During the pause which ensued Mr. Hazzard rode up.

"Good afternoon, Miss Arnold. How is Miss Prescott to-day? I was sorry to hear yesterday that she was not feeling well."

" She is better, thank you, but not quite herself,
yet. Do you not miss Dr. Carey very much, Mr.
Hazzard ? "

" Miss him ! I should think I did. I hardly
know where I am without him. I don't see why
on earth he should have insisted on going away ! "

" I miss Carey, too," said Philip. " What a
good fellow he is ! I wish I could have seen more
of him while he was here. He has always stayed
at our house when he has been in town before, you
know, and I quite envied you for having him with
you."

" Ah, yes, I stole a march on you," replied Mr.
Hazzard. " You see I had been on to Boston last
winter, and Carey was so confoundedly kind to me
that I wanted to get a chance of giving him some
fun ; but with my usual luck I must needs go and
sprain my ankle, which was sorry fun enough for
both of us."

" Your ankle seems as well as ever now," said
Edith, glancing at his riding-boot, the fine proportions of which did not seem in any way disturbed
by the leg within.

" I still have a little trouble in walking," he answered ; " but I am as good as any man in the sad-
dle. Will you not remember me kindly to Ju —
to Miss Prescott ? I came yesterday on purpose to
ask her if she would not ride out here to-day with
me. By Jove ! I believe they are going to start,"
he added. Looking where he pointed, Edith saw
that the huntsmen had all formed in a line across

a broad valley in front of them, a few rods behind
a green hurdle which had been arranged for the
first leap.

While she looked, Mr. Hazzard had joined their
ranks just as the word was given, and they were
off. They all took the hurdle successfully, and
then came flying by in a wild rush for the end of
the field, where the topmost rail had been consider-
ately withdrawn from the fence in several places.

Philip and Miss Arnold had only intended to be
spectators of the scene, which was pretty enough
in the bright winter sunshine ; but as the hunters
swept by them, the horse which Edith was riding,
being a young one, suddenly became excited. He
plunged and kicked and struggled for his freedom,
and then, taking the bit between his teeth, without
further ado joined in the race, so that before she
realized what was happening she had dashed down
the hill and was riding with the others.

They were fast approaching the fence, and she
had never practiced leaping ; she felt giddy with
excitement, but the next moment Philip's voice
sounded in her ear, and she was comforted to find
him still close at hand. He had held back a little
at first, fearing to incite her horse still further, but
now he came swiftly to her side.

"Give him his head," he said calmly, as they
neared the fence. "That will do. Now your whip,
and raise him a little. Bravo ! " he cried, as she
found herself, to her own infinite surprise, on the
other side of the barrier, with Philip still beside

her and his strong hand on the bridle, beneath which her horse seemed quite submissive.

"Oh! I am so glad," she exclaimed breathlessly. "And thank you ever so much for taking such good care of me."

"Why, you are a famous horsewoman," replied Philip. "I had no idea you meant to do such desperate things."

"Indeed, I did not mean them, either," she said contritely. "I am ashamed to say that I could not manage my horse."

"I know all about it," answered Philip reassuringly. "No one could have restrained him, I think, with the temptation so near. I should have been more thoughtful in choosing our point of observation. How do you feel about it now? Do you want to follow, or shall we turn back?"

"Oh, let us go on," cried Edith; and then seeing that Philip looked troubled, she added, "I will do whichever you think best."

"I think it would be a little safer not," he said.

"But must we turn back? It is so ignominious."

Philip laughed. "Suppose we take a medium course," he suggested, as they came to a road which led off to the right of the one which the others were following. "Let us strike down this path; which I think will lead us out so that we can see the hare again," he continued, turning their horses' heads as he spoke, and they were soon riding through a thick wood. Huge bare trunks of trees stood out on either side of them, the naked boughs of which with their thousands of little branches formed a fine network overhead, so interlacing that the pale February sky was only faintly visible between.

The sound of the hunt soon died away in the distance. There was no noise but the rustle of the dried leaves as they crumpled beneath the horses' feet.

" How ghostly this is," said Edith. " It is a great contrast to the gay scene which we have just left. If I were alone, I think I should be quite frightened."

" Why, what are you afraid of ? "

" I am not afraid — with you." She looked up at him frankly and trustfully, as she spoke. Perhaps the sense of security which his presence always inspired was increased at the moment by the pluck and presence of mind which he had shown in the last half hour. " I wish that I had had a brother, and that he might have been like you ! " she exclaimed, impulsively.

Philip started. He cast an earnest glance at her unconscious, smiling face, and then turned away with a deep sigh. " I think we must hurry a little, if we are to reach the other side of the wood in time to see the end of the hunt," he said.

They quickened their horses' pace, and soon heard the far-off winding of the horn which denoted the whereabouts of the hare. It was used in this instance by the lady who accompanied him.

" Why did you not want me to follow the hunt?" asked Edith.

" Because the leaps become more and more dangerous as the chase goes on."

As he spoke, they emerged from the wood on an open field which sloped away gradually towards a little stream winding along between two swampy banks. · Just as they did so the hare leapt the stream, closely followed by Mrs. Percy, and then the whole pack of hunters came flying across, helter skelter, some sinking into the mud and water up to their horses' knees.   After this, a mad race began for the top of the field, which, as the horses were beginning to feel the effect of the run, was hard for them, but the riders urged them on with redoubled speed, each excited with the hope of coming in the first.

At last the hunt was over.   The hare and Mrs. Percy had just escaped being overtaken, and Mr. Hazzard had been the nearest to the capture.

" How   about   Heronsford?"   asked   Philip. " Would it be wiser to postpone it for another day?"

" We will if you say so."

He smiled at her evident disappointment.

" I meant only in case you were tired," he said.

" But I am not tired."

" Then we will push on, by all means.   After all, we have not far to go."

Their way led them through a shady country lane bordered with fine old willows, and after passing several cosy looking farms, and here and there a country-seat, brought them at last to the gates of Heronsford.

The avenue curved in a long sweep and crossed a rustic bridge, bringing them in sight of the house some moments before they reached the door. Edith had been pleased with the little sketch which she had seen of it, but was not at all prepared for the stateliness and grandeur of the original. It was built in an English Gothic style, with carved stone ornaments, very finely executed, in the pointed arches above the doors and windows.

The gabled end of a pointed roof was presented to the approach, adorned with numerous little stone spires and pinnacles, and the chief entrance was protected by a carved porch in three Gothic arches from which a few steps descended to the ground.

The main body of the house formed an angle with this projecting wing, and built into the structure was a long line of slender sculptured pillars, through the intervals between which the windows of the drawing-room could be distinguished, opening on a sort of stone piazza like a cloistered walk; while on the left another wing jutted forward, inclosing an irregular strip of lawn, and terminating in a low turret.

The whole building was of a rough, faintly tinted gray stone resembling granite in texture, but evidently softer and easier to carve; and the longer Edith looked the more attractive it appeared, among the dark foliage of a wide-spreading group

20

of Norway pines, and covered at one end with a veil of ivy.

" Do you like it ? " asked Philip turning towards her eagerly.

" Oh, very much ! " she answered. " Everything about it is so in harmony and so beautiful. How could you think of all this yourself ? "

" I did not think of it all," said Philip modestly. " I wish I had."

" Did you not plan it yourself ? " she asked.

" I planned it, but I mean to say that the forms themselves are not original. They have been repeated hundreds and hundreds of times."

" The combination is original," said Edith, " and although I have only seen the forms in pictures, I doubt if I should like them so well if you had invented them yourself."

" I did not intend to say that I could invent forms as good."

" If it were possible that you might," she answered, " they would not have the same associations. There is a charm in the ideas which these awaken, which add to one's enjoyment. I can fancy some royal prisoner, for instance, looking from the solitary window of that turret chamber, or an astronomer, or a misanthrope ; or I can imagine a brown-robed monk pacing that cloistered walk."

" That tower contains my collection of curiosities," said Philip, " and I fear there is never any face but my most commonplace one to be seen from it."

"I wonder which you look the most like, a king or a philosopher?" she questioned gayly.

"You have a lively imagination indeed if you could fancy I looked like either," said Philip.

Edith colored a little. "Oh! no, I have no imagination at all," she responded demurely.

They had reached the door now and Philip had thrown the reins to a groom and stood beside her horse ready to help her to dismount.

"Why do you say that?" he asked.

"I have always been told so."

"I do not believe it," said Philip. He was holding her at arms' length, with a wistful look in his eyes of which he was hardly conscious.

"It is all the result of your imagination," asserted Edith, "which has set my stupid brain to working."

This was too dangerously sweet, and suddenly realizing that he had thrown precaution to the winds, Philip set her on her feet just in time to receive the welcome of a graceful red setter, which came bounding up to greet them.

"Down, Larry! Down, I say!" exclaimed his master.

"Oh!" cried Edith, "can this be Larry? Why, he does not look as if his leg had ever been broken!"

CHAPTER XXV.

" The worst is not
So long as we can say, *this is the worst.*"
SHAKESPEARE.

IT being once decided that Mr. Drayton was to go abroad in a few days, time seemed to fly by on wings of which the motion might almost be felt and heard. Sunday morning came, and he went to church with Julia and Edith as usual, the only unusual circumstance being that Philip, who was not much of a church-goer, accompanied them.

It has been mentioned that Mr. Drayton was an Episcopalian, and very simple and earnest in his belief. He might be seen at the corner of his old-fashioned family pew in one of the oldest churches in Philadelphia as often as Sunday morning came, but there was none of the pomp and circumstance of the typical *pater familias* in his manner of attending the service, and never the faintest reproof conveyed in word or look to any one who chose to remain away.

Philip availed himself of this privilege very freely, but when Julia was a little girl she had begged to be allowed to go to church with her guardian, and they had always been together since.

Edith Arnold never forgot the impression made

upon her by her first Sunday in Philadelphia, the
deserted aspect of the town, the air of starched re-
spectability of the other church-goers whom they
met on their way to the morning service, proceeding solemnly two by two as though assisting at a
funeral, or the stillness of the streets.

It seemed to her an awful silence that fell on the
great city at the end of every busy, giddy week,
and she could not shake off the impression that
some serious misfortune was about to happen, when
she heard the chiming of the bells.

As she was waiting for Julia at the foot of the
stairs in the front entry, on this particular Sunday,
Mr. Drayton looked out from his library and asked
Edith if she would not step in for a moment, as he
wished to speak to her. She assented quietly, and
taking the chair he offered near the large end window, looked up inquiringly.

"Perhaps you have heard, my dear, that I am
going abroad unexpectedly?"

"Yes, Mr. Drayton, I was so sorry to hear it."

"I am very sorry, too. I feel it most for Julia's
sake, as you may imagine," said Mr. Drayton,
speaking hurriedly. He paused, and then said, "I
want to ask if you will not do me the great favor
of remaining with my ward as long as possible after I am gone?"

"I will, indeed, as long as I *can.*"

"And can you not stay long?"

She looked embarrassed. "My mother and sister have been growing impatient for my return,"

she said, hesitatingly; " but I will write to my mother and tell her of your having to go away, and I think she will let me stay."

Mr. Drayton looked much relieved. " I shall consider it as a personal kindness if you will do so," he said. " Julia is very fond of you, and you may do more than any one else can to divert and cheer her. She will make an effort to go into society for your sake which she would not make for her own, perhaps, — and I think society is good for her."

Edith was touched by the tenderness of his tone. " I will do all that I can," she said, " but I wish that you were not obliged to leave her. Julia cares for so few people that her feelings are very intense for those whom she loves."

" I know it," said Mr. Drayton. He turned to the window and was silent for a moment. " I would rather, Miss Arnold, that Julia did not know of my having spoken to you on this subject," he said, presently.

" I will say nothing about it," said Edith, rising, and as she spoke he opened the door, for they both fancied that they heard a step on the stair. It proved, however, to be Philip, who came in with his usual grave demeanor.

As the whole party walked together, the fact that Mr. Drayton and Julia hardly spoke to each other on the way to church was not noticeable; but it was communion Sunday, and when they came out alone half an hour after the others and walked side by side, still without speaking, the silence became oppressive.

It was the last of many Sundays that they had walked home together like this, but not like this. Whether talking or silent, with "oh, what different feelings!" thought poor Julia, as she struggled to keep back the flood of sweet old memories which threatened to break down her self-control.

"Next Sunday you will be on the ocean," she said at last, in desperation. She shrank from imagining the future, but it was easier to face it calmly than to think of the past.

"Yes, I suppose we may have reached Queenstown by Sunday," said Mr. Drayton, with that stupid assumption of cheerfulness which deceives no one on such occasions.

"Queenstown — so soon!" exclaimed Julia.

"You are right," he returned, hastily. "We could hardly reach there so soon, certainly not at this season."

"Are not voyages at this time of the year — more dangerous?"

"They are longer, but as to the danger, it is quite a matter of chance at any season. There are a few times, of course, which are considered exceptionally safe for crossing or exceptionally hazardous, but this does not happen to be either," said Mr. Drayton.

He did not renew the subject, and Julia, who had not the courage to speak again, was for once thankful when they reached the house, so much did she dread some word or look which might dispel her outward composure.

It was fortunate for her that the rest of the day was so occupied with the necessary preparations for Mr. Drayton's departure that there was no time to think. She had always taken a pride in performing certain little womanly offices for him, and she would not relinquish them now of all times, when they seemed to be the last faint links connecting her with a past which was fast slipping away from her.

She dropped here and there a silent tear as she folded one of his coats, or between the piles of his clean handkerchiefs, when none were by to see her weakness, but at dinner she wore a brave front, and all through the afternoon until the moment of parting was close at hand.

Mr. Drayton, who was to sail from New York early the next morning, had told her that he must leave home on Sunday evening, intending to go on board that night; and towards dusk Julia crept into the library, where he was giving a few last directions to Philip, with such a dull sense of misery at her heart that she was glad of the twilight which sheltered her from sympathizing eyes.

Miss Ruthven and Edith were in the drawing-room waiting to say " good-by," and presently Mr. Drayton went with Philip to speak to them, but Julia did not follow. She sat down quietly at one corner of the familiar old fire-place, and felt that she could not bear to hear the commonplace last

words, which must be said in the cheerful family
farewell.

It seemed to her an interminable time before she
heard Philip start up, declaring that they would be
late, in energetic tones. He went out to see after
the carriage, and then his father came back into
the room, and Julia knew that he was standing beside her. She had risen, and he was holding out
his hand. She raised her eyes slowly until they
met his. One long look passed between them, and
then he opened his arms and folded her to his
heart, bending over her as he did so a face filled
with the tenderest, most protecting love.

"Julia, my dear, dear child," he said. "God
bless you!"

He put her gently from him after that, and left
her without daring to take another look. In the
entry he met Philip coming to hasten him; they
both went out together, and soon the retreating
wheels of the carriage told Julia that he was really
gone.

It is Miss Thackeray, I think, who, with that
pretty gift of insight, half satirical, half tender,
which she has inherited from the genius of her father, gives thanks to Heaven, somewhere, that we
are not always young!

To those who know how keen a sorrow may be,
for comparatively little cause, when felt with un-
accustomed nerves by one who never dreamt its
power, and is thus unprepared to fight with it, this
is properly a cause of thankfulness; but there may

be two classifications of the causes of great sorrow.

First, that of its being new and bringing a kind of terror to the imagination, as well as a rending of the heart ; and, second, that of its actual intensity, for like every other passion it is capable of almost infinite shades of force.

There can be little doubt that the bitterest is not that which comes as a stranger, but as an old acquaintance ; as an enemy often met and striven with, but never vanquished. The poor hunted spirit which such grief pursues knows every far-off sound of its awakening, every step of its approach ; and when he feels that he can fly from it no longer, but must turn and see its face, his very breath is stopped with anguish, and his mental pain may be compared to the worst physical torture ever devised by tyrant.

It is not asserted that Algernon Drayton suffered from grief like this, but there was a strange mingling in his love for Julia of past and present associations which added to its strength, and his self-reproach, at having permitted himself to covet that which he considered a trust, added to it the sharp prick of regret. Of Julia's own feelings, he told himself that they were those of an affectionate daughter who had not known any parental care but his, the sense of whose estrangement from her mother had added to her love for him.

"She could not love me better if she were my own child," he said, and tried to make himself happy with that thought. How much sympathy there was between them! What perfect understanding of each other's moods! How glad Julia would be to see him on his return! How happy their life would be when they were once more together — but stop! Where were his thoughts traveling?

He remembered that he had deliberately planned to come away from home in order to give her an opportunity to form some attachment which would separate her from him. After Julia was married could they live together as they had done? He had thought once that this could be. The time had been when he looked forward to taking her children on his knee as he might do those of Philip, but that time was past.

He knew now that he never could live in the house with Julia and feel that she was married to another man, — that some other had the *first* right with her, and he was only second in her love. When he realized this he was a very unhappy man, and he paced with long strides up and down the damp deck of the steamer, which was only waiting for daylight to put out to sea.

Meanwhile, in her darkening chamber, through the long hours of the winter evening, Julia knelt motionless with her face hidden from sight. She did not know how time was passing. She did not know that she was there; she only knew that he had left her and that she was alone.

It was Edith who first came to her to try to offer

comfort, although she little knew how much it was needed. She wound her soft arms about her friend, however, and laid her cheek to hers, and by and by Julia consented to lie down, while Edith sat beside her in silent sympathy.

CHAPTER XXVI.

IT was the middle of February when Mr. Drayton sailed, and the news of his safe arrival had not reached home before the day appointed for Mrs. Davering's " Parlor Opera " approached.

He had written once by the pilot and once by a ship crossed at sea. Both were short, affectionate notes in which he spoke regretfully of his enforced absence, mentioned that the ship was comfortable and the passengers agreeable, and ended with kind messages.

The style of these communications was, unconsciously perhaps, much more reserved than his tone had ordinarily been in writing to Julia, and what she noticed most was the entire absence of his usual vein of playful humor. These weeks were very hard to her, for she did not fairly understand why she suffered. She was always conscious of a dull, weary pain of spirit, a physical restlessness, and showed a tendency to take offense easily at little unintentional acts or omissions in others, which was very foreign to her usual disposition.

They were sitting together in the library one

evening when two notes were handed to Julia, one
for herself and one for Edith, who had left the
room to get something a few moments before.

" It is an invitation to a theatre party from Mr.
Hazzard," said Julia. " I do not care to go."

" I think thou shouldst make an effort for thy
friend's sake," remarked Miss Ruthven.

" So I would, if I thought it would give her
pleasure," replied Julia. " I will go and find out
how she feels about it." She left the library,
and presently she and Edith came back together.
Edith, it seemed, was delighted with the prospect
of the theatre party, so it was decided to accept
Mr. Hazzard's invitation.

" By the bye, Edith," said Miss Prescott, as she
sat down to her writing table, " what have you done
with the notes ? "

" I left mine up-stairs."

" Yes, but what did you do with mine ? "

" I thought you took it."

" No."

" Then I must have put it in my pocket."

" No doubt," returned Julia, " for talking of notes,
here is one which I found in the pocket of my riding habit. You must have left it there after your
ride last week." As she spoke she drew from her
workbasket the crumpled envelope containing the
verses returned by Cecil.

Philip recognized his cousin's handwriting, knowing it well, and noticed that Edith received it with
a bright blush.

Immediately the whole scene connected with the note came back to him. He remembered how embarrassed she had seemed before, when he handed it to her, how surprised he had himself felt at Wilmott's having written, and her evident perturbation afterwards. Then he recalled the fact, which he had learned accidentally, that Edith had seen Cecil alone on the night before he went away, and all these trifles tended to confirm a suspicion, which had crossed his mind once or twice before, that some understanding, possibly a secret engagement, existed between Edith and Cecil. The only fact which seemed to him inconsistent with such a possibility was that of her having gone to ride with him, on the very day after Cecil's departure. He had it not in his heart to accuse her of frivolity or lightness, and yet, to his strictly loyal nature, this little action and another, that of her having mislaid Cecil's letter, seemed to point to a thoughtlessness of conduct of which he was loth to believe her capable towards the man whom she meant to marry. It was all the harder to be just to her, that he felt in his heart how fatal the course of circumstances had been to him. " I do not believe I really cared, before that ride," he said to himself ruefully.

When he realized that he had allowed his inclination to wander in a forbidden direction, he resolved that for the future he would hold it better in check.

Thus it happened that a week passed without his doing more than to interchange a hasty greeting with the two girls, or a few affectionate words with

Julia after breakfast, and as during this time he went nowhere in society, there were none of the chance meetings which might have taken place away from home.

At the end of the week, however, he appeared to have modified his enthusiasm for work, for although they saw no more of him in the house they occasionally met him in society.

Edith was surprised to find that he now seldom came to speak to her, but he would stroll into a corner of the room from which he could see that part in which she happened to be, or, if chance led him to approach her, would pass by with a courteous bow. She did not know how to interpret this change of deportment at first, and feared that she had unintentionally given him cause of offense ; but after the first one or two occasions, when she looked at him with a troubled, mystified expression, or smiled upon him in his distant corner, or glanced up with surprise when he passed her, she ceased to show that she was disturbed by his conduct. He thought her manner serenely indifferent.

Meanwhile the season was at its height. Edith and Julia were pressed with engagements on all sides. Breakfasts and luncheons, afternoon teas, dinners, dances, followed one another in bewildering succession. There was so much to be done and so little time to do it in that the two girls had little opportunity for interchange of thought, and each had imperceptibly become more shut up in herself and less confidential than in the early part of Edith's visit.

This inexperienced young person had undergone an indefinable change in a few short weeks which struck Cecil Wilmott very forcibly the first time that he saw her after his' return from New York, which chanced to be at a small cotillon party given by Miss Mortimer. In the first place, Edith had become the fashion. It was very easy for a pretty stranger to do that, especially if in addition to an attractive face and figure she had sweet manners and a supply of small talk.

Dinner parties, opera parties, luncheon parties, were made for her. She and Julia were asked everywhere, and Edith, at least, seemed unwearying in her enjoyment of this new life of gayety, so different from anything which she had ever known before.

Mr. Drum Kettleby and Mr. Foxall vied with each other in delicate attentions and monopolizing suggestions of walks, and talks, and dances, which they strove to bespeak so long before the occasion as each to outstrip his rival, and Edith turned an amused face on either without seeming to care very much to which she was talking, or what he was saying; so very deep had this young lady from New Rochelle become in the course of six weeks of fashionable society.

Julia meanwhile had not regained her usual looks and spirits. She went out almost as indefatigably, but with a lack of enjoyment which Edith could not fail to detect in her languid air and the wearied expression with which she often returned.

21

Her displeasure with Mrs. Davering had somewhat blown over, but had left a coldness of manner and of feeling, with Julia, which nothing as yet had dissipated. She had, indeed, consented, with reluctance, to be present at the representation in the drawing-room theatre which Mrs. Davering was to have for the benefit of her friends, but her consent had been wrung out of her by the earnest supplications of Charley Hazzard, who was all this time, poor fellow, falling more and more deeply in love, while Julia still looked upon him as the friend of her childhood, — a good-hearted boy. She consented quite unsuspectingly to his entreaties to be allowed to ride with her sometimes, and she and Edith had gone together to a theatre party given by him in their honor. He was, of course, liable at any time to be tripped up in conversation by this fair young athlete, and to find the heels of his wit kicking against the sky, but if Julia laughed at him she did it to his face, while beneath the laughing there was a hearty liking which she was at no pains to conceal. Charley was triumphant, for he was convinced that his mother's timely warning to him to declare his affection for Julia just when he had done so had been the undoubted cause of Miss Prescott's rejection of Dr. Carey; and although a good deal frightened by her threat of remaining an old maid, he hardly believed she would adhere to her resolution always, and sooner or later he confidently hoped to win her hand, having no suspicion of the existence of any other rival than the one whose suit he, by his clever tactics, had defeated.

Mrs. Davering was pleased to find that he was very much interested in the plan of the parlor opera, and on the evening before his mother's entertainment, Edith and Julia, who were sitting with Miss Ruthven in the library, were surprised by Charley's entrance with Cecil Wilmott.

Edith hardly dared to look at the latter. His coming at all seemed very strange to her, but Julia evinced more pleasure at seeing Cecil than she had shown at anything for some time, so that Charley Hazzard seemed a little hurt, and Julia, yielding to his persuasion, rose and consented to go with him into the drawing-room to play "something."

"We hardly expected thee so soon, Cecil," said Miss Ruthven, who, in her meekly dignified way, evidently took the whole credit of his visit to herself.

"Oh, I got back a week ago," replied Cecil. "It was a little sooner than I expected, myself, but I came in obedience to a summons from my lady mother."

"I saw you at Miss Mortimer's party the other evening, Miss Arnold," he added, turning to Edith, "but I think you did not see me."

Edith blushed, but said nothing, so Miss Ruthven took up the conversation again.

"Thou hast not told us why thy mother sent for thee," she said.

"Heaven knows why!" returned Cecil, and then

noticing that the old lady looked quite shocked, he added hastily, "She meant it all right, of course. She had engaged my services to Mrs. Davering, it seems, as stage manager and general sufferer for all the faults of a somewhat faulty performance at the little theatre."

"That is where Julia and thee are going together to-morrow evening, my dear, is it not?" asked Miss Ruthven, turning to Edith, who saw that she must enter into the conversation.

"Yes, Miss Ruthven, that is where we promised to go. Who sings in the operetta, Mr. Wilmott?" she asked, lifting her eyes to his face for the first time.

"I hardly know," said Cecil, "the performers have been changed so often. Charley and Mrs. Percy take the principal parts. Mrs. Davering wanted me to sing baritone, but I respectfully declined. If you only knew how tired I am of the sound of it you would not mention the word operetta!" he exclaimed impatiently.

Edith laughed.

"Why, the sound is the very thing of which thou shouldst not tire," said Miss Ruthven reprovingly.

"I am afraid you are too critical," said Edith.

"I should like to hear your opinion on that point when you had sat through a rehearsal," said Cecil grimly.

Just then Miss Ruthven rose and gathered up her work, and left the room.

Edith became very much absorbed in some lamp-lighters which she was making. Cecil took Miss Ruthven's seat, a little nearer to her than he had been before.

"I am glad to have this opportunity of speaking to you, Miss Arnold," he said, "for there is something which I want to say."

She glanced up at him with a shade of apprehension which he did not fail to detect.

"You need not be afraid that I am going to renew the conversation which we had when I last saw you," he said satirically, "but what I have to say to you certainly bears upon that. It assumes that what took place that evening may not have deprived you of all friendly feeling for me. Has it or has it not?"

"Surely not," she said.

"Then," pursued Cecil, "perhaps you may like to know that I thought very seriously about all that had passed between us, afterwards, and it seemed to me that you were quite right in accusing me of infirmity of purpose."

"I did not say that."

"You may not have used those words, but you expressed that idea; and I resolved that if you would accept me for a friend, instead of a lover, I would try to prove to you that I had a little more backbone than you supposed."

Edith was much moved by this confession.

"You are very good to care what I think of you," she said.

"Then you will let me be your friend?"

"I will indeed." She put her hand in his calmly and gently, and so he went away.

The whole of this short interview with Cecil came back to Edith quite distinctly that night when she was going to bed, and she became vividly aware that Cecil was no longer the magician that, with all his faults, he had been to her before he went away. He appeared an agreeable young man, nothing more. Was it because she had been going more into society merely, meeting more people and growing accustomed to being admired? She was very sure that it was not, and quite indignant with herself for such a thought. Then was it for some particular reason, conscience asked, on account of some special person who had absorbed her interest?

"Oh dear, no!" she said half aloud, and with an effort to escape further self-examination she rose and moved to the toilet-table, where she began combing and braiding her long, fair hair, but her own countenance, which she saw reflected in the mirror opposite wore a very shame-faced expression.

In truth, she suddenly realized that there was a person who had begun lately to monopolize much of her thoughts, and that for the last ten days, she had noticed his looks, his manner, where he sat or stood, with a distinctness which provoked her with herself. She extinguished the gas and jumped into bed, with a determination to turn her mind in some more profitable direction for the future; but just as she was falling asleep she was aroused by the sound of footsteps and started up to see a bright light shining from the crevice beneath her door.

She sprang out of bed, lit the gas, and opening the door, was surprised to see Julia in her dark red dressing-gown, with her feet thrust into a pair of loose slippers, and a lighted candle in her hand.

" Why, what is the matter ? " she cried, for there was a strange, wild look in Julia's face which frightened her, and her hand, when Edith grasped it, was quite cold.

Julia came in slowly, without speaking, and set down the candle, looking about her as she did so with wide, staring eyes.

" Speak to me, Julia," said Edith. " What is it ? "

" I had to come to you," she answered, in a low, horror-stricken voice.

" Of course, it was quite right to come to me, if you were troubled about anything."

" I could not bear it ! I could not stay alone with it ! " exclaimed Julia, still speaking low, but with a tone in which there seemed pent up such an intensity of suffering that Edith, moved to pity, put her two arms about her, and drew her to the bed, where they sat down side by side.

" You certainly should not be alone," Edith said. " Will you not tell me what it is which has disturbed you so ? "

Julia did not answer for a moment, but turned her head round again and looked about the room in all directions; then she hid her face on Edith's shoulder.

"Oh! Edith, I can always see it, even when I close my eyes!" she cried.

"For Heaven's sake, Julia, tell me what it is you see! Have you been dreaming? Or has something really happened?"

"It was all so sudden," said Julia. "I was sitting by the fire in my dressing-gown, thinking, as I often do. I had been sitting a long while, I hardly know how long, when I heard a voice behind me speak my name, — and Edith, it was Mr. Drayton's voice! Oh, you need not look incredulous, — I heard it quite distinctly; so I jumped to my feet, and the whole side of the room was dark, but in the midst I saw him standing in a gleam of light. I knew it was my guardian, and he was holding out his arms to me as he did on that last day, but I could not go to him, something held me back, and in an instant he was gone, and then there was a roaring in my ears like the wild rushing of water, and I kept seeing his face before me everywhere, as if floating upon the air, whichever way I turned, but oh! so changed! Edith, Edith! something has *happened!*"

She shrank still closer to her friend and clung to her with a sort of desperate fear, which was so real, that it infected Edith herself, in spite of her efforts to be calm.

"Hush, dear Julia, it was only a dream!" she said. "There is nothing in it, dear."

She tried to soothe her as she would a frightened child, but Julia shook her head.

"I am sure it was his voice," she said. "It is not like any other!"

"I think that you probably dropped asleep without knowing it," replied Edith, "and you were suddenly awakened by some sound in the street. Some one may even have spoken your name, — but not to you, dear, to some one else, — and you know your guardian's voice so well that it was quite natural you fancied that you heard him call. It is easy to be deceived into thinking that we hear a sound with which we are very familiar," proceeded this young philosopher.

"But is it not very strange, at any rate," said Julia, "that nearly two weeks have passed and he has not been heard from?"

"I thought you had heard from him twice."

"Oh, yes, on the way; but I mean that we have not heard of his safe arrival."

"There would not be time for you to hear of that; certainly not by letter."

"No, not by letter, but by telegram. The arrival of a steamer is always telegraphed by cable, and I have been looking vainly for any notice of the Bohemia."

"Ah, now I see the whole cause of your bad dream!" exclaimed Edith. "You have been worrying yourself about that without ever saying a word to any one, and the idea of some misfortune has taken hold of your imagination. Depend upon it you will hear to-morrow that all is well."

" Do you really hope that ? " asked Julia, raising her head and looking into her friend's face very
earnestly.

" Certainly I do," she answered cheerily. "Now
get into bed with me, dear, and we will go to sleep
and forget all about it."

" You are very good to me," said Julia wearily.

" Ah, dear Julia, you do not know how I love
you."

" And so do I love you," returned Julia, as a
softer light came into her anxious eyes. " But I
am afraid I cannot go to sleep."

Nevertheless, Edith persuaded her to try, and in
a shorter time than she had hoped, Julia did sleep
quite soundly, as though worn out with emotion,
her hand still clasped in her friend's and their
heads resting on the same pillow ; but Edith lay
awake for a long while.

In spite of the good sense and decision with
which she had succeeded in quieting Julia's agitation, the story which she told made a strong impression on Edith's mind, and it was several hours
before she succeeded in throwing it off.

At last she too slept, and did not wake until
quite late the next morning, when to her surprise
she found Julia up and dressed, but with the same
sad, patient face as usual, for the day had brought
no news.

CHAPTER XXVII.

" Like ships that sailed for sunny isles,
But never came to shore."
HARVEY.

ON returning from his office the next afternoon Philip glanced into the drawing-room before going up to dress for dinner, and saw Edith sitting with her back to him, looking out of the window. She was all alone, and, yielding to an impulse, he allowed himself the unusual pleasure of going in and addressing her.

She started slightly at the sound of his voice, and answered his greeting with a look of surprise which led him to realize more than he had before how odd his conduct must have appeared to her of late. He grew suddenly shy under the consciousness, and began to wonder what he could say which would make it seem natural that he should have spoken to her now.

" Would you like to see the evening paper?" he asked at last, unable to think of anything less stupid.

" Thank you," said Edith, tranquilly, " I have seen it."

" Indeed?"

" Yes, Julia sent for it," replied Edith gravely.

"She is hoping for a telegram to announce the arrival of the Bohemia."

" Ah, I see. We should hardly hope for that yet, I think," said Philip.

" Do you really not think so?" she inquired eagerly, glad of this opportunity of allaying her doubts.

" Certainly not. Why do you ask?"

"I think Julia is a little anxious at not hearing."

" Oh, there is no reason for anxiety," said Philip, sitting down beside her on the sofa as he spoke. " The Bohemia belongs to a line which is proverbially slow and sure; besides, voyages are always longer at this season of the year."

"I am very glad to hear you say so, in order to be able to speak more reassuringly myself. I confess that Julia's fears had made me a little nervous."

" You must remember that Julia has an anxious temperament," returned Philip, smiling. " I was afraid she would begin to look for news long before it could get to us, but it has seemed to me of late that she was in better spirits. Whom did I hear her playing to last evening?"

" Mr. Hazzard and Mr. Wilmott were both here," said Edith, " and Mr. Hazzard urged her to play, but I thought she only did it not to seem disobliging."

" Possibly," answered Philip. " Have you seen much of Cecil Wilmott since he came back?" he added, with an attempt at carelessness.

" He came to see us for the first time last even-ing."

Philip knew he was on dangerous ground, but the temptation was tremendous. He wanted to know the worst.

" I want to ask you a question," he said.

" What is it ? "

" Will you tell me whether you had not met Cecil before since his return ? "

" Why do you ask me that ? "

He was silent for a moment, then he said, —

" I had several reasons for asking, but pray do not answer if you do not wish to do so."

" I had not met him before," replied Edith, slowly.

" Or heard of his change of fortune ? "

" I do not know what you mean."

" I meant that I did not know whether Cecil had told you that he had suddenly come into quite a large sum of money through the generosity of his uncle in New York."

" He did not tell me," she answered gravely ; " but I am sincerely glad to hear it."

" Cecil has done a very fine thing, I think," said Philip, " for as soon as he got home he had a deed executed by which he settled two thirds of this money permanently on his mother and sister."

" Did he really ? " cried Edith, with a look of keen pleasure. " Do you know that you have made me very happy by telling me that ? "

" I am glad to have been the means of giving you pleasure," returned Philip, with just a touch of bitterness, and then took himself to task for his folly. He had wished to tell her himself of this good action of his rival, taking a sort of sad comfort in the fact that, with all his faults, Cecil was a better fellow than many persons had given him credit for, but the sight of her joy at hearing it was hard to witness, so inconsistent is weak human nature even in the strongest and best of us.

After spending the early hours of that evening in working as usual, Philip returned to the house at nine o'clock, and had just dressed to go to the Drawing-room Theatre, where he had promised to join Edith and Julia, when his attention was arrested by a shout, heard through his window, of a newspaper boy, who was passing on the opposite side of the street.

"'Evening Telegraph!' Extra edition! Terrible disaster at sea! Midnight collision in a fog! The steamer Bohemia sunk off the coast of Ireland!"

Philip rushed to the window and flung it open. The voice was growing more distant, but the next words came to him only too distinctly, "Sixty persons supposed to be lost! Others rescued by the Cornwall." Philip's heart gave a great thump against his ribs and then seemed to stand still. For one instant he felt as if he could not move. The next, he was tearing headlong down the stairs, — was in the street and in hot pursuit of the newsboy. Then he had overtaken him, and was returning with a copy of the fatal paper. He came back into the house quietly, for he had left the street-door open, and unfolded it beneath the gas-light in the entry with a trembling hand.

There was the same heading, word for word, which the boy had repeated. There was no mistake in the name of the steamer, as he had hoped.

The account of the accident was dated from London, on the morning of that same day. Philip read it with a sinking heart.

" The Anglo-American steamer Bohemia [Captain Waterman] which sailed from New York on the —— of February, for Liverpool, and arrived at Queenstown at daybreak on the 11th instant, came in collision last night at midnight, during a heavy fog, about eight miles east of Dungarvan, in St. George's Channel, with a vessel reported to be the Scotch Mull of Cantyre, from Glasgow for Cork, in ballast. The Bohemia at the same time was on her way from Queenstown to Liverpool. One hundred and fifty-four of her passengers and crew were saved by the iron screw steamer Cornwall, and landed at Liverpool.

" The following is a list of the saved passengers as far as known."

Then came the list of persons who had been picked up by the steamer Cornwall, and carried · safely into port. Philip looked in vain among them for his father's name. Further details would be furnished whenever received, the paper said. That was all the comfort that it gave him. ·

As he still stood staring blankly at it, feeling too

much stunned to think, the door of the library opened and Miss Ruthven came out.

" I thought it was thy step, Philip, which passed in such haste."

" Yes, Aunt Ruthven."

" What is the matter, Philip ? " she asked. " Thou dost not look well."

" Oh ! Aunt Ruthven, something dreadful has happened."

" Come hither, Philip. What hast thou there ? A newspaper ? "

Philip came close to her and took her withered hand. He felt very much like laying his head on her shoulder and giving way to his grief, as he might have done in years gone by, when he would come to his old aunt with his childish troubles, but he strove to remember that he was a man and must guard against too sudden a shock to her.

" What is that ? " she said again.

" It is this evening's paper, Aunt Margaretta, and there is something in it which has made me very anxious."

" What is it about, my dear ? "

" About my father," he said.

" Something concerning his business, Philip ? Has something gone wrong with any of the trusts which he left in thy keeping ? "

" No, thank God, it is not his honor, but it is bad enough."

" No danger to his life ? " she asked faintly.

" There has been an accident to the ship in which

he sailed. He may be saved, of course, but his name is not mentioned."

"What, then? Algernon is not lost? Speak, Philip!"

"I hope not, Aunt Ruthven, but I do not know."

"Ah! my poor boy," cried the old woman, stretching towards him her trembling arms. Philip led her to a chair in the drawing-room and knelt beside her with his head in her lap.

"How can I bear the uncertainty?" he asked. "How can I tell Julia?"

"Strength will be given thee, my son. God will not forsake thee," she said, tenderly enfolding him. "Oh! Algernon, Algernon," she murmured, "that I should outlive thee!"

Philip soon started up and began pacing the room.

"I wish I could avoid speaking to Julia," he said, "until we know more. There may be better news in the morning."

"Yet would it be kinder that she should hear it from thee than from a stranger," returned Miss Ruthven. "If it is in the paper, may not this report reach Julia at any moment?"

"That is true!" cried Philip. "I must go to her at once. Good night, dear aunt."

"Good night, Philip."

As he strode through the street in the midst of his misery and doubt, the wish again occurred to him that he could save Julia the anxiety which he was suffering.

22

" If I could only get her safely home ! " he said to himself. " If I could only get her home."

He made his way up-stairs, when he reached the Theatre, and through the gay throng of people who stood about the entrance of the auditorium.

There was a scene being enacted at that moment. Mrs. Percy, who performed the part of a peasant girl, was singing, and coquetting with her own sweet reflection in a spring of mimic water. Mr. Hazzard, her valiant adorer, was dressed as a French soldier, and watching her from a stage concealment. Edith and Julia were sitting beside Mrs. Davering and fortunately not very far forward in the audience. Julia, who had the inside seat, looked pale and weary. Her eyes had a sad, far away expression which showed that she was not in sympathy with the scene about her.

Edith, on the other hand, was full of life and enjoyment. Her face beamed with animation, and even at this moment Philip was provoked at the sight of Mr. Drum Kettleby occupying the seat just behind Miss Arnold, and leaning forward from time to time in the pauses of the song to speak to her with amiable patronage. Philip was presently beside them.

" I beg your pardon, Drum Kettleby," he said, hastily, " but I shall be greatly obliged if you will let me have your seat for a moment."

" Certainly, certainly, my dear fellow," said Mr. Drum Kettleby. " Take it by all means." Nevertheless he looked at Philip in some surprise when he quietly took it and turned his back upon him without further ceremony.

"Turn your head this way, Miss Arnold," said Philip to Edith. "I have something to tell you which I do not want overheard."

Edith turned her head instantly. He had spoken in a low voice, but unconsciously used a tone of command which she instinctively obeyed.

"What is it?" she asked quietly.

"I have heard some bad news," said Philip, "and I do not want Julia to know it. Do you understand?"

"Yes," replied Edith. A sudden change swept over her face. "Do you wish to tell me what the news is?"

"It is about my father," said Philip, hurriedly. "Of an accident to the ship in which he sailed, but he himself may be safe."

Edith's eyes flashed up into his with a quick glance of sympathy and understanding, which gave a kind of comfort.

"You see the thing is in the evening paper," he went on, "and I wish above all things to guard against its reaching Julia accidentally. How can I get her home?"

"I can do it," said Edith.

"How?"

"I will say that I am tired, and do not want to go back to Mrs. Davering's to supper."

"That will do," said Philip, "tell her that I have gone to call the carriage, please."

" Had you not better speak to her yourself?"

" I can't," he answered. " I am afraid to have her see my face."

Edith looked up again, and noticed what a pale, stern face it was.

" I am so sorry for you," she said impulsively.

" Thank you. I know you are. We must only hope that things are less dark than they seem. Do not let any one have an opportunity of speaking to her if you can help it. You will find 'me below."

He went, and Edith turned to her friend, whose attention happened, very fortunately, to have been engaged by Mrs. Davering during Philip's short interview with her.

" Do you care very much about going to Mrs. Davering's to supper, Julia?"

" No. Why do you ask?"

" I feel rather tired. Would you mind if I asked you to come home with me now?"

" Certainly not," replied Julia. " We will go as soon as the opera is ended."

" So far so good," thought Edith, " but who might not come and talk to Julia after the opera was ended?"

" Do you think it is necessary to wait till the end?" she asked nervously.

" Are you in such a hurry? Perhaps you do not feel well?"

Edith jumped at the excuse; anything rather than what she feared. " To tell you the truth," she said, " I think the air is rather oppressive."

"I see," responded Julia. "You feel faint."
She looked about her anxiously. "I wish Philip
were here. You know he promised to come for us."

"He did come a moment ago, when you were
talking to Mrs. Davering," said Edith, with a desperate effort to appear unconscious. "He said he
would wait for us outside."

"Did he, indeed? Then I will explain to Mrs.
Davering, and we can go at once."

There was very little stir made, for they glided
quietly out in the midst of a loud burst of applause
at a duet from the tenor and the prima donna.
Philip was waiting at the foot of the stairs. He
offered his arm instinctively to Julia. It seemed
to him, poor fellow, that she needed all the support
which he could give her, but Julia drew back.

"Take Edith," she said. "She does not feel
well. Help her to the carriage, Philip."

"Do you not feel well, Miss Arnold?" he asked,
in a tone of genuine concern. "Why, I thought" —
He was going to say that he had thought she was
looking remarkably well, when a slight warning
pressure on the arm which she had taken somewhat
enlightened him as to the cause of her sudden in-
disposition.

He was haunted with the fear even on the drive
home that they might meet some belated newsboy
who would shout the dreadful secret into Julia's
ears as it had come to his, but they reached the
house on Meredith Square without further incident.

CHAPTER XXVIII.

"But oh, the heavy change now thou art gone!
Now thou art gone and never must return ! "

MILTON.

THE morning papers brought no comfort to Philip. He rose early, after a sleepless night, and walked down to the news office, giving orders that his absence should not be mentioned, and that all papers were to be taken unopened to his bed-chamber, especially that they were not to be shown to Julia under any circumstances.

When he reached home again he had realized that almost all the little hope to which he had clung was gone. He could not conceal his great bereavement from himself or keep it from others any longer. The first thing that he heard in coming into the house was that Julia had asked for the paper, and being told that Philip was "reading it," had requested Rogers to get her another. The poor old family servant, only half suspecting that some great misfortune hung over the house, was beside himself to know what to do, when, fortunately, his young master came.

Philip went into the dining-room where Julia was sitting by the fire alone. He knew she was thinking of his father, for this was an hour in the day peculiarly associated with him. Mr. Drayton had always been full of life and mischief in the morning, being so much more boyish in this respect than Philip, that the few moments before breakfast seemed quite to belong to him.

Julia looked up as Philip came near her, with a slight start, as though aroused from some sad thought.

"Is there any news of the Bohemia, Philip?" she asked.

Philip felt himself grow pale. "The ship has been heard from," he answered.

"How? Where? Has it arrived safely?"

"No, Julia, it has not arrived."

"Has something happened, Philip?"

"Yes, there has been an accident — at — at sea."

"I knew it!" she exclaimed. "O Philip, your father — is he safe? Tell me!"

"I hope so."

"What have you heard? Where is the paper? For pity's sake do not keep it from me! What hope is there?"

This was the hardest question for him to answer which she had yet asked. Philip opened the first of two folded papers which he held.

"This one came first," he said, gently. "It is the account of a collision. The Bohemia was run into by another vessel and a hole made in her side. Here is a list of a number of the passengers and crew who were saved."

Julia's eye was upon him as he uttered the last

words. He knew only too well what it was asking. There was a pause.

" And his name is not there ? " she said at last.

" Not there, but this is only the list as far as known."

" O God ! " she cried, and buried her face in her hands. Then suddenly she withdrew them and pointed to the other paper. " Not there either ? " she asked. " Read ! Is it not there ? "

" No, Julia, not as having escaped," he said, mournfully, " but still he may be saved."

" Let me see, please, please," she murmured ; and Philip reluctantly gave her the paper which had come · that morning, and turned a little from her, for he was sick at heart.

This is what she read : —

" Further particulars of the Bohemia disaster show that she was near Helvick Head, about three miles from shore. She was struck on the starboard side amidships, and sank in less than twenty minutes. Distress signals were given and responded to by the Cornwall, proceeding up the Channel, which made all haste to the rescue. There were nine boats on the Bohemia, four of which were crushed in the collision. Five were got off, but one, being overcrowded with passengers, was sunk. All the boats pulled away from the doomed ship, leaving the captain, who refused to desert his post. The last boat was commanded by the first officer, who did all he could to induce the captain to leave the ship.

"The following who appear on the steamer's passenger list have not been accounted for."

" I thought you said his name was not there," said Julia hoarsely.

" You know what I meant, Julia."

" Then you saw it on this list ? "

Philip bowed his head. Julia read on with a terrible eagerness. The personal accounts of several passengers were given in full. She stopped at one headed by the names of two ladies whom she knew in New York, and pointed half way down the column to another name. Philip had seen it too.

The older of the two ladies wrote as follows : —

" About forty-five minutes after eleven o'clock at night, without the slightest warning of the proximity of any vessel, a bark appeared on our right, and crashed into us just above the funnel, making a big hole. My daughter and I were in our stateroom. We were awakened by the crash and rushed on deck, where the boats were being put off. Every one was crowding into them, and we saw one sunk before our eyes from being overloaded.

" We women were powerless against the rush of strong men, for many of the crew were trying to save themselves. We were beginning to give up hope, when our friend, Mr. Drayton, saw us and made way for us, assisting us into the last boat. We begged him to follow, but there were nearly forty in the boat already, and seeing a number of sailors trying to get on board, thus endangering the lives of all, Mr. Drayton cut the ropes himself and set the boat adrift, saying good-by to us. We were too much laden even to attempt the rescue of any persons floating. We rowed to the Cornwall, which stood by during the night.

"At daylight the topmast of the Bohemia and her fore and main-yards were visible above water, but there was nobody in the rigging."

Julia started up with a low cry.

"Of course he was not there!" she said wildly, "he was *here!* Don't you see? He came here."

"What do you mean, Julia?" asked Philip, bewildered.

She clasped her hands above her head.

"That was it," she murmured, speaking more to herself than to him. "He died like a hero! Like a hero!" she repeated, with a wail, "and he came to me!" Her large, dark eyes were fixed in a sort of stare. Presently a mist seemed to come over them. She tottered and stretched out her hands to Philip, who just caught her as she would have fallen senseless on the floor.

It was the beginning of a long illness, a protracted fever, in which Julia lay tossing for weeks between life and death. She had the less chance of recovery, the doctor said, that her health had been giving way, and she had evidently overtaxed her strength for weeks before the shock came.

No one could be more patient and loving than Edith in this time of trouble, except perhaps Miss

Ruthven. The two together devoted themselves night and day to the care of Julia, but neither of them was strong enough to bear the long-continued strain, and at last they were forced to allow the assistance of a trained nurse.

It was a sad sight to see Philip Drayton in these days. He went about with the look of a man upon whom some great blow had fallen, and who was stunned by it, so that none of the little outward circumstances of life were real to him, but like things acted in a play. He had never known, himself, with what a worshipful dependence he looked up to his father, until he felt that he was gone.

He was always making inquiries and searching the papers for some possible clue, which should give him the right to indulge a faint hope that Mr. Drayton might, after all, have escaped. The captain of the lost steamer, who had been picked up by a Welsh vessel, floating on a bit of wood, and carried to Caernarvon, was reported at one time to have said that he believed there was " another steamer " near the wreck, which had saved many lives ; but when this report was sifted it proved to have been the Cornwall to which the captain referred, on which the name of every passenger saved was well known to poor Philip.

Another day he turned away with a shudder from the following short despatch, dated from Dublin :

" One female and two male corpses were landed yesterday at Tramore. One body is apparently that of an officer of the ill-fated Bohemia, and one of a passenger, — it is thought an American. His watch, which was found on him, had stopped at 12.15, no doubt the hour the ship went down, that fateful night."

Edith Arnold, who happened to be in the room, had taken the paper from Philip's hand. She drew his attention to the concluding sentence.

"That was just the hour," she said, "when Julia believes that she saw him."

"Poor Julia!" sighed Philip. "I know she thinks that she saw him."

"Do you know, I can hardly help believing it myself?"

"That my father actually appeared to Julia?"

"You know she came to me on that very night," said Edith, "only a few moments afterwards, and told me all about it. I was impressed even then by the story and by her manner."

"I never heard that before," said Philip gravely. "What time was it when she came to you?"

"It was exactly twenty minutes past twelve. I know, for I looked at the little French clock on the mantel-piece, when I lit my light."

They were both silent for a little while.

"I shall write and get the description of this watch," said Philip, presently. "If it seems worth while, I will go to Ireland. Where are you going?" he asked, as Edith rose.

"To Julia. She may want me," she said, and glided from the room.

He did not see her again for several days. She

was so constantly engaged with Julia that they rarely met, except by accident, or when he went to the door of the sick room, as he did morning and evening to ask the tidings.

Then he would interchange a few whispered sentences with Edith or Miss Ruthven. Would be told of " a little better night," " not quite so much fever," or " a little less restlessness," as the best news which he could hope to hear, and go down again to his solitary breakfast or dinner with a dull sense of misery which was not the best incentive to appetite. There was no denying that he suffered very much from loneliness added to his grief. Cecil Wilmott and Charley Hazzard came constantly to inquire for Julia. The latter sent her the most beautiful flowers, and carried about with him a very mournful face, poor fellow, while Cecil showed the sincerity of his interest in many little ways. He also came out very unexpectedly as a help to Philip in his professional cares just at this time; but in spite of the fact that his cousin had really gone to work in earnest since his return, there was not more sympathy between them than there had been.

There may have existed a secret cause for the want of intimacy now which prevented them from being more in each other's company; but certain it is that Philip saw very little of Cecil except when thrown with him by the necessities of business.

As Philip sat in the study one afternoon, the door opened, after a muffled ring at the bell, to admit Rogers with a card. He had a pleased expression as he handed it to his young master, and Philip glancing at it read the name of Dr. Lawrence Carey.

"Show him in, — or wait, — where is he? I will go to him!"

Philip opened the folding doors long closed between the library and drawing-room, the usual obscurity of which was increased by the bowed shutters of the front windows, — a token that the house was in mourning. Dr. Carey was sitting near one of them. He rose and came hurriedly towards Philip, holding out both hands.

"My dear fellow!" was all he said, words which may be rendered in a hundred different tones, but then their hands were clasped together in a manner which could not be mistaken.

"I was thinking of you the other day," said Philip. "You were the only person whom I wished to see."

"And Miss Prescott?" asked Carey, with an earnest look of inquiry.

"She is about the same. Perhaps a little less well to-day."

"Then she is not out of danger?"

"The doctor will not say so."

Dr. Carey turned his back to Philip and walked to the window.

"It was good of you to come," said Philip.

"I could not keep away," he answered.

"I am glad of that," said Philip simply.

CHAPTER XXIX.

" How wonderful is death, —
Death and his brother sleep ! "

SHELLEY.

DR. CAREY stayed two nights and a day. His visit was a great comfort to Philip, but it is doubtful whether he gained much consolation from it himself beyond this, for Julia steadily grew worse, and yet Carey was forced to return on the second morning after he had come. Philip went with him to the train and promised to write often, and so they parted with heavy hearts.

Mrs. Wilmott and Charlotte, coming to ask after Julia the next afternoon, were shocked by the servant's answer, — "The doctor says Miss Julia is very low."

"I must speak to Mr. Philip!" said Charlotte, pushing by old Rogers who would have closed the door again, and bursting in upon Philip, who was sitting alone in the library, for Charlotte had a very kind heart, but was not always considerate of the feelings of others. "How is Julia, really?" she asked impetuously. "Is she worse?"

"Yes, Charlotte."

"Do you think she — cannot live?"

"God knows," answered Philip.

"Oh, mother! There is hardly any hope!" cried Charlotte, turning to Mrs. Wilmott, who had followed and stood behind her in the doorway.

Just then there was another ring, and Mrs. Davering's voice was heard inquiring.

"This is too much," cried Philip. "I cannot see that woman!"

"I will go and speak to her," said Mrs. Wilmott. She went to do so, and Philip slipped out and ran up stairs at the same moment, leaving Charlotte alone. He knew she intended to be kind, but he could not bear her well-meant sympathy just then. He had a desperate feeling that he was being shut out forever from Julia, that perhaps at this instant her spirit was passing away, and here were all these strangers crowding in to take possession of his life, which had been spent near her and near his father.

He crept softly along the passage and through the room adjoining hers, in which Miss Ruthven slept, to the door of Julia's chamber.

He was determined to see her. They had kept him from her all these days because the excitement would not be good, they said: and what had come of it? Had she a chance more of living, for his banishment?

There was a screen in front of the door, standing silently behind which, he could hear her labored breathing, and now and then a faint flutter, as of some one fanning her. The light was dim in the room, although it was bright enough outside, for it was only four o'clock of a spring afternoon.

Peering fearfully from behind the screen he saw that Edith was by the bed, which was just in front of him, and Miss Ruthven and the nurse were whispering together in the doorway of a room which opened on the other side. Edith was bending very close to her friend, with a look of love and anguish which he could not mistake, even from where he stood.

At this moment his hand was touched from behind by some one. He turned, and to his surprise saw the doctor holding out something towards him. It seemed to be a yellow envelope. He stepped back and took it mechanically. He did not feel the least interest in it. Then he opened the envelope in a stupid sort of way and gave a great start, putting his hand over his mouth to keep himself from crying out. It was a telegram.

"Is it true?" he asked of the doctor, with a look of frightened gladness, the like of which the good man had never seen before.

"I will soon tell you," he answered, stepping unceremoniously behind Philip and reading the message over his shoulder.

It was dated "Gibraltar, March —," and ran thus: "Rescued by ship Mary Brown, for this port. Have written. ALGERNON DRAYTON."

"It is signed with my father's name," said Philip.

"Yes. It was evidently sent by him."

"And he is living? Would to God it had come sooner! To think that Julia will never know!"

" Do you suppose that she would rejoice in it as you do ? " asked the doctor.

Philip stared at the medical man in amazement. " Why, I thought you understood, doctor, that this — this terrible report was the whole cause of her illness ! "

" The shock — of course — I understand that, and that she had previously been in a frail state of health; but was she very much attached to your father ? "

" She has been perfectly devoted to him all her life," said Philip, with tears in his voice.

" Ah! Well, if that is the case," said the doctor, cheerfully, " I think there is some hope yet ; otherwise I should hardly feel justified in saying that there was."

" What do you mean ? "

" I mean that in the state into which Miss Prescott has unfortunately sunk in spite of all our efforts to prevent it, nothing will save her but some great reaction, if it can be safely brought about. It is a dangerous remedy in her weakened condition, but hers is a case of extremity. If she is not roused she will almost surely pass away in the sort of stupor which has been creeping over her for the last twenty-four hours."

Philip looked piteously into the doctor's face. " What can be done ? " he asked, " and how ? "

" I think if she could only be made to realize your father's safety all might yet be well."

" But do you think that possible ? "

" It is just possible only, but it is worth trying. As she has not seen you before, it might not be a bad idea for you to try."

Philip nodded. " I understand," he said eagerly. He was all alertness and attention now. " How had I better do it ? "

" Suppose you go in and take her the telegram ? I will see that the other door is closed, so that there may not be too many people, and will be ready here in case I am wanted."

He went out through the entry, and Philip waited until the door on the opposite side of the chamber was softly closed. Then he glided into the room.

Julia was lying in the centre of a huge, four-post bedstead with heavy chintz curtains. Her little figure looked so slight and frail — more like a child's than that of a full-grown woman — that he could hardly believe that it was hers. One of her poor thin hands was clasped in Edith's. That was a good sign, Philip thought. It showed that she had not entirely lost consciousness. But what troubled him most was her breathing, — it came with so much effort, although she was propped up with pillows.

As he approached the bed, Edith looked up at him with tear-stained eyes. He met them with a steady gaze. There was a sort of reserved strength in his manner, which had changed utterly in the last few minutes, and seemed to hold a kind of subdued hope.

He gently withdrew Julia's hand from Edith's, and took it in his own. Then he leaned towards her and whispered her name.

" Julia."

The dark eyelashes trembled, although her eyes did not unclose. He felt sure she had heard him.

" I have something to tell you, Julia."

Her eyes opened now with an inquiring look, but they wandered away from Philip in an instant, as though nothing were able to fix her attention.

" It is something about my father," said Philip.

She turned her face slightly towards him, with an expression of apprehension.

" There is good news," said Philip.

Her little hand, which had lain so lifelessly in his, suddenly grasped it spasmodically. Her eyes shone like two stars, and gazed up at him with a desperate eagerness of entreaty.

" He is saved, Julia."

Her lips moved now, although he could not distinguish what they said. He bent over her and caught the words : —

" How do you know it ? "

It was so like Julia to ask that, even in this supreme moment. He recognized the old doubting spirit which had haunted her from childhood.

" He has telegraphed to me from Gibraltar," he answered, holding up the telegram as he spoke, and speaking very distinctly.

The dying girl uttered a low cry, — the first sound above a whisper since the day before, and withdrawing the hand which Philip held, clasped it in the other with a look of passionate thanksgiving.

She remained in this attitude for several moments; then her eyes gradually lost their lustre, the lids drooped over them, her head sank a little sideways on the pillow, the labored breathing ceased. Was it sleep, or was it death?

The doctor, who had entered the moment that he heard her voice, bent his ear over her anxiously. He cautiously inserted his fingers round the wrist of one of her hands, which still lay clasped together on her breast. He shook his head and asked for some ammonia.

The nurse went for it, and, with old-fashioned prejudice, brought at the same time a mirror. They were all there now, — Miss Ruthven standing behind Philip with her hand upon his shoulder, a mixture of hope and anxiety upon her wrinkled face; for she had just heard of her nephew's safety, and yet seemed in the dread presence of the enemy whom he had escaped.

While the doctor was pouring out the stimulant the nurse approached the mirror to Julia's lips. Every one bent forward involuntarily, and a dim cloud of mist appeared on the surface of the glass. The doctor managed to insert a teaspoonful of the ammonia between her lips, and a faintly warmer tint replaced the deathly pallor of her face as she swallowed it.

"Thank God!" he said, below his breath. He

watched her anxiously, and remained by her side, using every means of restoration, until reaction had become completely established. At last he rose, with a triumphant smile. "She will do now," he whispered. "Keep the room perfectly quiet, and see that she has a little stimulant from time to time. I will see her in the course of an hour."

The letter, which reached Philip a day or two after, was begun on the — of February, on board the Mary Brown, and ran as follows: —

"My dear Son, — It distresses me to think what grief and anxiety you and dear Julia and Aunt Margaretta will feel on reading of the wreck of the Bohemia, if, as I fear, no report of my safety may reach you at the same time.

"I am *saved*, however, and when you know this I trust that the assurance may in some measure repay you for the doubt and apprehension which I cannot spare you.

"I was picked up by this vessel on the night of the — of February, just as I had begun to surrender all hope of ever seeing you again. The captain tells me that he was attracted to the scene of the disaster by cries of distress, and sent out a life-boat, which discovered me and one other clinging to a portion of the cabin steps, which were floating, long after the ship had gone down.

"I was almost insensible. It was the shouts of my companion in misfortune, a sturdy young sea-

man, which had arrested the attention of the
Mary Brown, and secured our deliverance. No
one could have been kinder than this captain, or
more indefatigable in his efforts to restore me from
the state of unconsciousness into which I frequently
relapsed after my first revival ; but when I realized
my delivery and told him of the anxiety which my
friends would feel, and the urgent nature of the
business for which I was going to England, I could
not induce him, by any argument, to change his
ship's course.

"We were bound for Gibraltar, and already three
days out. My worthy rescuer said that he was
in the merchant service of Great Britain. He had
his orders, and they must be obeyed. I offered
him a large sum of money if he would land me
at any convenient point in France or Spain from
whence I could communicate with home, but he
was immovable, and I have surrendered myself at
last to the prospect of several weeks of inaction,
only writing this letter in the faint hope of hailing
some passing ship which will put it in the way of
reaching you."

Then followed a few words of gratitude at the
wonderful escape which he had made, and many
messages to all of them, especially to Julia.
"Would that I could return, myself, with this
letter ! " he added later, in a hasty postscript to
say that they had had the good fortune to come
alongside of a sailing vessel from Bordeaux, bound
for New York, and he therefore hoped that this

missive, which he sent by her, would reach them in two or three weeks, — almost as soon as the telegram, which he would despatch from Gibraltar before returning, himself, to London.

CHAPTER XXX.

"O welcome, pure-eyed Faith, white-handed Hope,
Thou hovering angel, girt with golden wings."
MILTON.

THE first faint promise of young leaves had come, with gray or reddish tints deepening into exquisitely varying shades of palest green, while here and there a more vivid touch of the same color gave expression to the landscape, when Julia was once more taken to drive in the Park. By the middle of April she was to be moved to Herons-ford under the care of Mrs. Wilmott and Char-lotte, while Miss Ruthven bade a temporary fare-well to her charge, and returned to the old-fash-ioned home which she had forsaken for so long.

Edith, too, felt that she must go back to her mother and sister, but she had promised to return in June and make Julia a long visit. Julia's re-covery had been slow but steady. When she was first able to go out again she was still very thin, but had regained her old alertness of manner and brightness of expression. She had received a long letter from Mr. Drayton, telling of his return to London, and of the surprise and disappointment (as he expressed it) of the honorable gentlemen who represented the other side of the lawsuit in which he was engaged at his escape from the machinations of Neptune. Then had followed a half serious and half joking account of the trial, which he knew she would like, and last of all a word or two of tenderest regret at hearing of her illness, as he had done through a letter from Miss Ruthven.

"If I could only give you half the pleasure that my reported loss has given you pain," he said, "I should be very happy."

He wrote to Philip at the same time a letter full of anxious inquiries and urgent instructions as to the care of his "dear little ward," as it pleased him to designate this young woman of twenty. It was in accordance with one of his suggestions that it was decided to move out of town so early, for he thought the country air would be good for Julia; and she submitted to all that was decreed for her, with a new sense of contentment.

A great change had come over her since those awful weeks of darkness and despair, when she lay tossing on her bed of pain. She no longer seemed to herself all alone in the world with but one friend to cling to, and on the brink of losing that one, in whom her whole life centered.

She had been deeply touched by the love and devotion of every one about her in this time of trial, and felt as if she could not do enough for Philip or Edith, or even Miss Ruthven. Indeed, she did not think that she had known this lady's real character before, long as they had lived together; but perhaps her sense of the goodness of all these friends might not have been quickened, and it is almost sure that she never could have lived to realize it fully, but for the crowning mercy, which she believed the direct act of an all-merciful Father, in saving Mr. Drayton's life.

It seemed to Julia that if she did penance forever for her past shortcomings, she never could be grateful enough for this great blessing. She wanted to begin to do something which was very hard to do, at once, in order to prove to herself how sincerely she regretted the spirit of repining to which she had yielded when she fancied that she was forsaken, before the torment had come of losing utterly that which she now told herself that she had had no right to wish for all her own.

Oddly enough, no one appeared to be willing to let her do the smallest thing. Every one was gentle and kind and considerate. Every one thought for her and arranged everything, so that there was nothing for Julia to do but to accept their arrangements, and this at least she did with the best grace.

The parting with Edith was one of the hardest things which she had to look forward to, but even that was sweetened by the hope of her speedy return.

"You will write soon, dear?" she said, as they stood together in the entry, Edith in her traveling dress, while Rogers was taking down her bags to put into the cab, and Philip awaited her on the doorstep.

" Of course I will."

" And often ? "

" Very often."

" I wish thee a very pleasant journey, my child," said Miss Ruthven, whom Edith turned to next, " and although I do not know thy mother, it will please me to be mentioned to her as one who will retain an affectionate remembrance of her child."

Edith kissed the old lady warmly and then came the farewell to Philip. She held out her hand to him, but Philip smiled and shook his head, although he seemed ready enough to take the hand if she had not withdrawn it.

" You do not get rid of me so quickly," he said. " I am going with you."

" Of course, Edith," said Julia, " Philip must see you to the station. You might otherwise have some romantic adventure, such as the one you had when you came to us this winter. Do you not remember? We have found out that you are a young lady who requires very sharp looking after."

Edith laughed and blushed in spite of herself. She had a very tell-tale complexion, which was always producing false appearances, especially for Philip's benefit, as it seemed. He noticed the blush as he helped her into the carriage, and when the last adieus were spoken and they were driving from the door his anxiety got the better of his discretion.

" Did Cecil Wilmott come to say good-by to you? " he inquired.

" Why do you ask me that?"

" In the hope that you will answer me."

" Does that mean for curiosity?"

" It means, rather, for information. I have a reason for wishing to know what I ask."

" What possible reason can there be?"

" It would be hard for me to tell you that, but you will answer me or not, exactly as you please, of course."

" As it happens I prefer to do so. Mr. Wilmott did come last evening," she said proudly, " and I was sorry to say good-by to him."

Her manner puzzled Philip, as it had always.

" I think I was wrong. After all, I am afraid I had no right to ask you these questions," he said. " Will you forgive me?"

He turned towards her as he spoke, but she avoided looking at him.

" Not unless you will tell me why you wanted to know."

" Will it not do if I promise never to offend again?"

" I should like very much to know what your reason is," she answered, playing with the handle of her closed parasol.

" If you will say that you forgive me, I will tell you," said Philip, with a change in his voice; but just at this moment the carriage stopped at the station.

" I am sure it must have been difficult for you to leave your important law business to come with

me to-day," she remarked, when they were waiting
to take the train.

" I wanted to come."

" You are certainly fortunate in one respect,"
she said. " You always want to do amiable things.
You must be naturally benevolent, or perhaps you
have a high sense of duty ; now I am always wanting not to do the things which I ought to do."

" Such as what, for instance ? "

" Oh, I do not know, there are a hundred of
them. I wanted very much not to go to see Mrs.
Davering to bid her good-by."

" I should have had the same wish," said Philip.

" It would have been nothing in you, but it was
shockingly ungrateful of me, after all she has done
for me."

" Granted. What else have you wanted not to
do that was amiable, — or a duty, since you put it
so ? "

" I do not think I want to go home, as much as
I ought," said Edith, gravely.

" Do you not, and why ? "

" I can hardly tell. I believe I am a little afraid
of the changes which I may find, after so long an
absence."

" I hoped that the feeling might have a little to
do with reluctance to leave us," said Philip.

" So it has, of course, but that regret is somewhat compensated by the desire to see my mother
and sister."

" Naturally. We have no such compensation. Are you not sorry for us ? "

" Very, for Julia. I think she will miss me almost as much as I shall miss her."

" And how about me ? "

" You ? oh, you have your books and your artistic employments, I suppose, to say nothing of the all-absorbing affairs at your office."

" They will not fill all my time."

" I thought they would," said Edith demurely; and it suddenly flashed upon Philip that she was intending to punish him for that period of studied neglect, during which he had been so frequently in her society without availing himself of it.

" I suppose a woman never forgives a man who feels her influence for refusing to yield to it," he said bitterly.

" What do you call refusing to yield to a person's influence ? " asked Edith innocently.

" Denying one's self the pleasure of talking to her would be one way," he answered, smiling.

" Well, I should think his doing that might make her a little skeptical of his deriving enjoyment from her society."

" Do you think it would never occur to her that he derived greater enjoyment than he thought it wise to indulge in ? "

" How could it, if he gave her no opportunity of finding it out ? "

" I think women have a wonderful way of finding things out."

"Perhaps you give them credit for too much penetration," said Edith.

"Do you still feel as if you would like to hear my reason for asking you those questions about Mr. Wilmott?" he inquired.

"I do not know," she answered shyly.

"I would tell you now, if I could," said Philip; "but the train is ready and there is no more time for talking."

"Is there not?" she asked, with a sudden upward glance of unmistakable regret.

"I will come to New Rochelle and tell you," he said gently.

"You promise?"

"I promise."

And now the moment was come for parting. Edith was seated in the train which was to take her home. Philip was standing beneath the window. The engine was about to start. He took off his hat and raised his head with the rare, sweet smile which could so transform his grave face. What was it which happened as their eyes met? Edith could not tell. Her gaze suddenly grew misty and she withdrew her eyes, with a vague consciousness that the train which was carrying her off was tearing something which hurt more and more as the distance grew greater between Philip and herself.

CHAPTER XXXI.

" Sweet is revenge — especially to women."
BYRON.

ONE day it occurred to Cecil Wilmott that some one had made him a promise, and that promise had not been kept. He often thought of the fair promiser, but the promise had escaped his memory until now. Immediately he began asking himself why he should not claim this pledge, and when it is explained that it consisted in the simple consent of a young lady to make him a silken purse, it will be seen what a fanciful fellow he was, that such a trifle should appear to him a matter of importance.

His interest in it was undoubtedly due to that which he still felt in Edith Arnold, but it certainly could not be said of him that all this time he was utterly disconsolate, for as the days passed they brought their balm to his hurt spirit. It was pleasant to feel himself able for the first time in his life to order a new coat without a prick of conscience, or to bring a friend home unexpectedly to dinner or to take his mother and Charlotte to the theatre without encountering that hesitation and doubt of the prudence of the step, which on former occasions had gone far to interfere with its enjoyment.

. The month of May found Charlotte and her

24

mother living at Heronsford, while Cecil vibrated as he loved to do between the town and country. He had resumed his old habits of intimacy with Julia, and was as much at home in his uncle's house as in his own, but was never to be depended upon as certain to be at one place or the other.

Strange to say, he had not called upon Mrs. Percy since his return from New York, although he had met her frequently in society. Perhaps his last interview with the widow had led him to dread her searching eyes and direct questions. He felt too sore as yet to wish his wound examined, even with a view to the cure which it was just possible that this lady might have been willing to undertake.

With Julia it was different. He was almost sure that she had read his secret, but she never alluded by word or look to her knowledge of it, and was only a little more gentle and considerate in her manner towards Cecil than she had ever been before. The country air was agreeing with Julia wonderfully. She was losing the angles of her outline, and was not only regaining all that she had lost by her illness, but beginning to look better and stronger than for a long while. A new, peaceful light had come into her face, — a sweetness and contentment which made one wonder whither the dark, defiant spirit which had once looked from her eyes was flown.

Philip, too, seemed happy, but restless. He was never still. He rose earlier and worked later than

ever, often not returning until long after dark, on
these soft spring evenings when every one else was
enjoying the delicious fragrance of the budding blossoms, and Mrs. Wilmott and Charlotte, sitting near
the open windows of the drawing-room, would be
watching anxiously for his return.

Julia was usually to be found at the piano at
such times, and Cecil, if present at all, sitting
dreamily beside her, lost in enjoyment of the music.

It was on a scene like this that Charley Hazzard
entered one evening in the second week in May,
and soon drove Cecil from his favorite corner. He
had come, it seemed, to recall to Miss Prescott her
consent long since given to go with him on a boating excursion. The boating party was to have been
given for Miss Arnold, and Mr. Hazzard, who was
much disappointed to hear that she had gone home,
was anxious to know when she would be with them
again. Quite a lively discussion ensued with regard to Edith's possible movements and whether
she would get back in time for the proposed festiv-
ity, which resulted rather discouragingly, as she was
not expected until June.

" I will tell you what it is, Charley," said Cecil.
" I am going to be in New York to-morrow on business, and I will run up to New Rochelle and see
whether Miss Arnold will not fix an earlier day."
So it was arranged. When he set out on his journey to New York, Cecil was still contemplating the
idea of the promised purse. The more he thought

of it the more he wanted it, until, as was usual with him, the desire wrought the determination to be satisfied. On reaching her house at New Rochelle, however, he was told that Miss Arnold was not at home. There was nothing for it but to leave a card. He scribbled on it a few hasty words embodying his request and telling of Julia's and Mr. Hazzard's desire for her return, and then he turned his steps homeward in a very discouraged frame of mind. His " business " in New York, which was not of grave importance, was soon despatched and then he took the train for Philadelphia.

He found his mother's empty house inexpressibly dreary. It chanced to be an unusually warm evening, and the air seemed close and full of dust, while a sense of loneliness pervaded everywhere. All the furniture in the drawing-room was covered with ghostly gray linen, and all the pictures and chandeliers mysteriously enveloped in muslin bags, and the general effect such as is peculiar to a deserted city house in summer time.

After washing off the cinders accumulated during his journey, he sauntered round to the Club, where he got rid of an hour or so ; but when dinner was over, he found himself much bored with his own society.

It happened that while in this state of dejection he bethought him of Mrs. Percy. Was she at home ? He did not know. He had not kept himself informed of her movements for the last six weeks ; but he began to recall many soft May evenings passed in her company, and almost mechanically he found his hat, and strayed dreamily out in the direction of her house.

Mrs. Percy was at home, the servant said, but she was not in the drawing-room when Wilmott entered, and no lamps were lit. The windows of this room, which looked out back and front, were all open. A vase with some lilies of the valley stood on a little table near one of them, and a basket with some fresh cut roses on the mantel. They were evidently from Mrs. Percy's own bushes and vines, which were blooming and climbing over the fence of the garden behind the house, and filling the air with their sweet odor.

Cecil stepped to one of the back windows, which opened to the ground, and saw the lady herself, half sitting, half lying, in a sea-chair, which had been dragged on to the little grass plot in the centre of the inclosure. A small book lay in her lap, but it had grown too dark to read, although much lighter outside than in the drawing-room, where all was gloom.

"Who is that?" asked Mrs. Percy, without turning her head. She was reclining with her face upturned, as though contemplating the stars. Cecil did not answer for a moment. He had a sudden instinct that his voice would startle her.

Presently she turned, and lifting herself to a sitting posture peered at him questioningly through the twilight. Then he stepped from the window, where his figure had been only faintly visible in the gathering darkness, and came more clearly into view.

"Cecil!" she cried sharply, pressing her two hands together with a sudden movement, and then added, more softly, "Is it you?"

"Yes."

"Why did you not answer me?" she asked, after an instant's pause, quite in her usual tone.

"I was afraid of frightening you."

"How should I have been frightened if you had answered? I was only startled a little because you did not."

"I do not wonder," he said carelessly. "It is growing late; and it seems a long while since I have seen you."

"Does it — to you?"

"Of course it does. I have been meaning to come, but a hundred things have prevented. I hope you are not angry with me."

"Angry! Then you flatter yourself that you have been missed?"

"I suppose I do. May I sit here?" he asked, seating himself, as he spoke, on a cushion beside her chair, with his elbow on the turf.

"If you are not afraid of taking cold."

"The mere suggestion of the possibility is refreshing on such a night as this; but you look cool and comfortable," he said, noticing that she was clad in some soft semi-transparent material, through which her neck and rounded arms were faintly visible.

" I certainly am," she answered, lifting a feather fan and waving it gently to and fro as she spoke.

" How do you manage it?" he asked, lazily watching the gleam of a diamond on her white hand as it passed.

" I dress thinly, as you see, and then I never do anything in hot weather. Now you, no doubt, have been roaming from one end of creation to another, after your usual restless fashion."

" No, I have only been to New York."

" And the rolling stone has gathered no moss. I can read that in your face," she said, turning her own full upon him as she spoke. " Are you sure that you went *only* to New York?"

What wonderful eyes she had! he thought. They seemed to shine out through the twilight, and to shine into him, as he propped himself half reclining on the grass beside her chair, in the same way that he had felt as if they did before, taking away his power of resistance to anything she might demand. No doubt the effect of old habit in yielding had much to do with the fascination she exercised.

" Exactly speaking, I went a little farther," he admitted.

" Can I guess where?"

" I do not know."

" I can gather, at any rate, that your mission was not altogether a success."

" Why so?"

" Perhaps you did not get what you went for."

" I think I shall get it."

"You wanted more than you got."

"How do you know that?"

"How, indeed? We know many things without being able to tell how we know them; but if I were mistaken you would tell me."

"I would tell you nothing on that subject."

"Then I will tell you where you went."

"I do not think you can."

"You must think me very stupid. You went to New Rochelle."

"Perhaps I did."

"Ah, yes, you did. You went to see Miss Arnold, and now you come to me."

"I did not go for what you think," he said, and laid his cheek against the arm of her chair, as he looked up at her tenderly.

"You need not explain. I understand." She turned away her head.

"What, Reta? What do you understand?"

"The situation. It is very complimentary."

"I thought we were done with all this sentimental nonsense!" he exclaimed impatiently. "I thought we were to be friends!"

"I don't know who is sentimental, Mr. Wilmott," she said scornfully. "You looked a little so a moment ago, but certainly I am not."

"You are not very friendly."

"It takes two to make a friendship. You have come to pay me the first visit for nearly three months, and seem quite disappointed that I have not been mourning your absence. That part of your conduct hardly seems friendly, nor have I ever gone so far as to credit you with much sentiment."

"It is not as if we had not met constantly in society," said Cecil. "You could have asked me to come at any moment, knowing me as you do, if you had any reason for wanting to see me."

"It is, perhaps, fortunate for me that all of my friends do not wait to be asked. A woman in my position does not care to be a beggar for their company. I think I can say without boasting that most of my visitors come because they have reason — or think that they have — to want to see me."

"As your 'position' happens to be that of the most popular woman in town, that is quite possible."

"Oh, wish me joy of my popularity!" she exclaimed bitterly. "It is a proud thought that I am sought because it is fashionable to seek me, but at least it gives me the assurance that in accepting a visit I am not accepting a sacrifice. Even yours this evening does not appear to me to be dictated by wholly charitable motives. Am I right, or is it an act of compassion?"

"Compassion? Of course not. Compassion to myself, perhaps."

"So I supposed."

"What do you mean?"

"I fancied that you were a little depressed, a little disheartened, and a little tired of your own company."

"I think I am."

"Well, then, my friend, I advise you to go home and go to bed. It is growing cooler, and I think you will sleep. It is certainly too cool for me to venture to remain in the open air any later." She rose from her seat as she spoke, and threw a soft woollen shawl about her shoulders.

"Will you send me away, then?"

"I counsel you to go, in case you came to me for advice."

"I hardly think that I did do that."

"For consolation, then, perhaps? But you see I have none to offer. I have intimated to you that I am poor in some things, although not a beggar."

He had picked up his cushion and followed her into the house. She was groping along the wall for the bell handle, intending to ring for lights, when his hand unexpectedly met hers in the darkness. He had been conscious of a wish to stay her, to hold her back as it were, as her intention grew more plain of leaving him, but he had not meant to touch her hand, and was startled at the sudden fire which flashed through him at the contact.

"Reta!" he exclaimed softly.

There was no answer.

He felt again for her hand, but it was gone. He touched instead the edge of the cold marble mantel-shelf. Then he heard a light laugh, and the next moment a flaming gas-jet streamed up from the central chandelier. She had found a match and lit it. How he hated the broad, flaring light after the dreamy dusk and darkness!

" I wish you good night, Mr. Wilmott," said
Mrs. Percy, standing in the doorway on the other
side of the room. " I find that it is nearly ten
o'clock, and I am a little tired."

There was no appeal from such a dismissal. He
said good night, and found his hat, and was soon
on his way home.

He whistled softly to himself as he walked along,.
but not for want of thought. " What did she mean
by turning me out?" he was wondering. " Was it
revenge? What do I mean, myself?" He stopped
to light a cigar. At the moment his own situation
seemed as enigmatical to him as it would have
to another. Had he not been thinking of Edith
Arnold reproachfully that morning? And yet she
was in no way responsible for the subtle emotion
which stirred him now.

It appeared to him that there had been an unusual influence exerted over him by Mrs. Percy
that evening. She had seemed different from herself, breathing a sort of suppressed intensity, as if
inspired with some feeling to which she was determined not to yield, which lent her all the more
power while she held it in check. Her very scorn
had attracted him, and she knew it. " She always
had such an extraordinary faculty for understanding me!" he said to himself impatiently. " I think
if I had married it would have been better to keep
out of her way, but as it is it makes no difference."

Since it made " no difference," he did not attempt to resist the impulse which prompted him to

revisit Mrs. Percy the next evening, but when he reached her door he was told that Mrs. Percy was " out of town."

" When did she go ? " he asked, in astonishment.

" She left this morning, sir, by the twelve o'clock train."

" And where was she going ? "

" I really could n't tell."

The person who had answered the bell was quite unknown to him, evidently some one who had come to take charge of the house for the summer.

Cecil turned away with a keen sense of disappointment.

CHAPTER XXXII.

"O suffering, sad humanity!"

LONGFELLOW.

ABOUT a week later Philip had arranged his affairs so that he could "run on to Boston." It was thus that he spoke to such persons as he was obliged to speak to at all of his proposed absence, the ostensible cause of which was the fulfillment of a promise to make a short visit to Lawrence Carey, but the real object which he had for going at this particular time was his intention of stopping on the way at New Rochelle. He stepped into his old office to give some parting directions to Cecil Wilmott, and found him in the act of opening a small parcel, which had just arrived by express.

"Look here!" exclaimed Wilmott triumphantly, as he drew forth a dainty little purse of crimson silk. "Did you ever see anything so pretty as that?"

"Certainly not," answered Philip good-humoredly. "Where did you get it, you gay Lothario?"

"Oh, it was made for me," said Cecil, who, to do him justice, had not the faintest intention of disclosing the name of the donor, but as he lifted the little box in which it had been packed from the table a small card slipped from between the box and the paper, unperceived by him, and fell to the floor face upward. Philip's eyes followed it mechanically, and even at a distance he was startled by a resemblance in the card to one he had seen before. Could it be because a certain name was continually in his thoughts that he fancied he saw it now? He could not bear the doubt, and stooping hastily to pick it up read Miss Edith Arnold's name quite unmistakably. He laid the bit of pasteboard on the table without a word. He dared not trust himself to speak for a moment, so violent was the rush of anger and jealousy and disappointment that surged up in his heart.

Cecil was unconsciously putting away his treasure. He had not seen the card at all. The look of satisfaction with which he stowed the purse in his breast-pocket was too much for Philip's self-control.

" How came Miss Edith Arnold to make you a silk purse? " he asked fiercely.

Cecil started at the mention of Edith's name, and gazed in surprise at Philip's angry face. " She made it because I asked her to," he answered, with a look of cool amazement.

" How did you dare to take the liberty of asking her? " growled Philip.

" How did I dare? " repeated Wilmott, still more astonished than indignant. " I dare do most things which suit my fancy."

" Then I am to understand that you are on such terms with this young lady, that you have only to mention to her your fancies in order to have them gratified? "

" That is not an exact statement of facts," said
Cecil, " but then, I did not make it."

" When did you ask this favor? "

" A week ago."

" Did you go to New Rochelle ? "

" I did."

" What for ? "

" Come, Philip," said Cecil, " I think you have
asked about questions enough."

Philip was silent for a moment, but he was still
so sore and bitter that he soon broke out again.

" Perhaps I had better tell you at once," he said,
" that this is not a subject of playful indifference to
me."

" By Jove ! I should think not," returned Cecil.
" I hope you do not get off jokes in this style."

Philip walked away to the window and stood
looking out, with his back to his cousin, for several
moments without speaking. There was something
so eloquently miserable in its expression that Cecil
began to feel sorry for him, although far from suspecting the extent of his unhappiness.

" What is the matter, old fellow ? " he asked.
" Why have you got so worked up over the idea of
Miss Arnold's giving me a little present ? "

" Are you engaged to her ? " asked Philip, in a
stifled tone, from which and from the question, the
truth flashed upon Cecil. He realized for the first
time that Philip had been a rival, very possibly a
successful one, and the idea did not please him.

" What business is it of yours ? " he inquired,

with sudden asperity. "Have you not known that we liked one another for a long time?"

"I have," came from Philip, solemnly. He took his hat and left the office without another word.

Cecil's feelings, when alone, were not enviable. He had said nothing which was actually untrue, as he kept assuring himself; and yet he was quite conscious that he had conveyed a false impression. He had done it in the heat of anger, and his first impulse was to undo it, but when he came to ask himself how, he did not see what words he could use. Those which he had spoken related to a well-known fact, and could be supported by abundant proof; to attempt to explain them away was to put himself in the wrong, and he soon began to assure his conscience, after his easy-going fashion, that Philip would not be such a fool as to continue to be misled, when this unreasonable fit of jealousy was over.

In spite of the assurance, however, the inner voice would not be silenced. Cecil was accustomed to taking things easily, but he was not accustomed to speaking or acting what was not true; and so he sat down before he left the office and wrote a short note to Philip, which he confided to the post-man, but which, unfortunately, did not reach his cousin before he left home the next morning.

Cecil had not been spending his time satisfactorily to himself for the last twenty-four hours, for he had been trying unsuccessfully to distract his mind from the thoughts and memories which had been so unexpectedly awakened by his last visit to Mrs. Percy.

He tried vainly to discover whither the pretty widow had betaken herself. Many of her plans for the summer were well known among her friends, but which particular one it had suited her fancy to follow was entirely a matter of speculation. Usually Cecil had been the trusted confidant of her last whim, and as day after day went by, and he could learn nothing of her and her whereabouts, he began to feel deserted, and to realize how much he had always relied upon the certainty of her friendship.

He became conscious that her half playful, half affectionate interest in his sayings and doings had given him a pleasant sense of security, and that for a man so constituted that he must always be a little in love, it was a great boon to be able to turn to the coquettish tenderness of such a woman — even if she would give him nothing more — when he was tired of himself, as she had rightly guessed that he had been the last time she saw him. Now, for the first time, her interest failed him. He had been indefinitely deprived of the society of his friend just when he wanted it, and he felt cross.

"Who goes on your boating party?" he asked Charley Hazzard, in a bored tone, as they walked together towards Miss Mortimer's house, where it had been arranged that Mr. Hazzard's guests were to meet, a few days later, —for Miss Arnold had written to decline the kind proposal of postponing

25

the boating party, in case she could hasten her
return.

" Why, Miss Prescott is to go," said Charley,
with such a beaming countenance as proclaimed
that in saying this he was saying everything, "and
Miss Mortimer and your sister. I think those are
all the young ladies. I asked Miss Mildred Davering, but she is doubtful. The men are all members of the club except Drum Kettleby. Only a
certain number can go in the boat, you know."

" Why in the world did you ask me ? "

" Because I wanted you, of course."

" I hate boating."

" That is all fudge," said Charley Hazzard.
" You are out of humor. There is no one who
enjoys that sort of thing more than you do, and
you pull a very decent stroke for a fellow who
does n't practice ; besides you can talk and tell
stories, which is the next best thing to singing."

" Are you in earnest ? It is a tremendous compliment."

" Of course."

" And Mrs. Davering is to keep us all in good
order, I suppose ? "

" Oh ! my mother is away, you know. I have
asked Mrs. Percy to do that."

" Mrs. Percy ! "

" Yes. Don't you think she will make a — a
suitable chaperone ? " asked Charley in a troubled
tone.

" Suitable ? Well, yes, but I thought she was

out of town." Cecil's expression was worth studying.

" Why, so she is, but so are the ladies at Heronsford. I do not think they mind coming in for the night — do you ? "

" I understood you to say the other day that you did not know where Mrs. Percy was."

" Did I say so ? Oh yes, I remember, but I met her in the street afterwards and asked her to join my party. Come to think of it, I don't think she told me then where she was staying. She said she was very tired of people here, and had run away on purpose, without letting any one know whither she was going. I had a good deal of trouble to persuade her to come with us to-day, but at last she consented — and here she is."

They had reached the house, and who should appear on the doorstep but Mrs. Percy herself, in conversation with Mr. Drum Kettleby. She bowed carelessly to Cecil, shook hands with her host, and then they all went in and greeted the other ladies, whom they found assembled.

Miss Mildred Davering was there, after all, looking as pretty as usual ; and then there were Miss Mortimer, and Charlotte, and Julia, who was in her happiest mood. She seemed, even to Cecil, handsomer than he had ever thought her before. Her cheeks fairly glowed with color, and there was a wonderful light in the depths of her dark eyes. Poor Charley Hazzard was quite mad about her. He could not hide his desperate admiration from

the most indifferent of his guests, or keep away
from Julia's side for more than a few moments at a
time. He went humming and blundering round
her, as one has seen a great stupid humble-bee
round a brilliant flower. •

Cecil meanwhile found his way to Mrs. Percy's
side. His mental sky had cleared since she had
come upon his horizon, and he was inclined to take
a more cheerful view of life.

"How abominably you treated me the last time
I came to see you!" he said, preparing for a comfortable scold.

"Did I really succeed in doing that?" she
asked.

"You might have let me know that you were
going out of town," said Cecil.

"It is possible that I might if I had happened to
know it myself."

"Then you had not decided to go before I left
you?"

"I think not."

"And why did you go so suddenly?"

"I hardly remember; I believe I was bored."

"You are very kind to say so."

"Would it have been kind to be bored while you
were with me?"

"If you will let me infer that you were bored
because I was gone, you are really kind."

"Do you think I am?" She suddenly raised
her eyes with a mocking smile.

"I am beginning to hope that you do not mean

to be unkind," he answered, noting as he spoke that the jaunty little boating dress she wore, of dark blue flannel, was an unusually becoming costume.

"I am afraid you are of a little too sanguine a temperament, Mr. Wilmott. If I had really been in despair at the dullness of my own company, after the exhilaration of yours, I fancy that waiting until the next evening would have brought me the renewed delight more quickly than going out of town."

"So you heard of my missing you the next night?" he asked quickly.

"I heard that some one did, and I fancied that it might have been you."

"Then you meant to treat me badly?" asked Wilmott, coloring with vexation.

"I believe I meant a little more than that," she said quietly, and some one else came up to talk to her just then, so that he had to give up the attempt.

In the horse-car on their way out to the boat-house, he talked to Julia, in desperation.

"Do you remember a warning which you took it into your head to give me about a certain young lady, some three or four months ago?" he asked, in a cautiously moderated tone.   .

"A warning?" repeated Julia, with a puzzled expression.

"I think you intended it for such. It was after that evening when you came home and found me talking to Miss Arnold in the twilight. You seemed

very much afraid' that we might get to liking one
another too much."

Julia looked at him and smiled. "Yes, I remember," she said. "Did it do any good?"

"Not a particle, as far as I was concerned, and
with the young lady herself no warning was needed,
as must soon have become evident, even to you."

"*Even* to me? Was I so very obtuse or over
officious?"

"I do not think you were either," said Cecil;
"but things do not always turn out quite as one
would assume from the premises."

"What made you think of it now?" inquired
Julia.

"I was thinking of Hazzard," replied Wilmott,
looking about him as he spoke, to make sure that
their host was out of ear-shot. "I was wondering," he continued, "whether my sensibilities were
unnecessarily aroused on his account. I confess I
cannot help feeling rather sorry for the poor devil."

"Why, has he got into some new trouble?"
asked Julia anxiously.

"I like your innocence," said Cecil incredulously, "but does it strike you as exactly fair to play
fast and loose with a man's feelings as you are
doing with his?".

"What do you mean?" she exclaimed, with a
look of extreme surprise.

"Only to point out to you what any one can see
with half an eye, that poor Charley is over head
and ears in love with you. I thought you must

know it, although it is equally evident that you do not care a rap for him."

"I do care for him, Cecil," said Julia earnestly. "I am very fond of Charley Hazzard. I should feel dreadfully if I thought that what you say were true."

"As for its being true," remarked Cecil, "there is no more doubt of it than that I am sitting on this seat."

Here the conversation was ended by the return of its subject. He would have been much astonished to hear that any one was pitying him.

Cecil could not find another opportunity of talking to Mrs. Percy all the afternoon. She was seated at the opposite end of the boat from him, going up the river, while his neighbor proved to be Miss Mortimer, conversation with whom was never wildly exciting, and consisted on this occasion of small interjections from the young lady, or timorous inquiries as to the danger of accident or the possibility of a wetting.

Wilmott was inclined to curse his fate, but to his great joy Mr. Hazzard made a complete change of arrangement when they started to row home. He asked Miss Prescott to take the seat at the stern usually reserved for the chaperone, and behind which he sat himself as steersman, and placed Mrs. Percy beside Cecil, who chanced to pull the very foremost oar and thus sat farthest from the stroke.

"At last!" exclaimed Wilmott, as he pushed

out from shore. The moon was glorious, — not a silver moon, but a great amber-colored one. Its light made a shining path along the smooth surface of the river, on which one felt almost as if one could safely tread, and the shadows beneath the bushes on the banks looked like black caverns into which one might descend forever, falling through unknown worlds.

" Now you will tell me what you did mean by running away without letting me know where you were going," he said.

" Can you not guess ? "

" I cannot imagine."

" You probably will in time," said Mrs. Percy.

" It suits you to be enigmatical to-day."

" It suits you to call me so. What I said this afternoon was very plain."

" That you not only intended to treat me badly, but meant something more ? "

" Exactly."

" What was it, Reta ? "

" It was simply to show you that I could live without you."

" Strange," returned Cecil, " that you found it necessary to take so much trouble in order to show me that ! "

Just then there was a call to rest upon their oars. The boat drifted with the current. Some one sang a song. Then they began to row again slowly until just as they came beneath the shadow of one of the bridges, where all was dark as night, and looking out from under which the river, the trees, an old forge on the shore near by, and the moonlit sky, with little sailing clouds, formed a charming picture. There was another shout to stop. Cecil seized the opportunity to turn to his companion. Chance had placed them behind every one.

"Why did you suppose that I needed proof that you could live without me?" he asked, in a low tone. "Had I not had abundant proof of it in times past?"

"Perhaps," said Mrs. Percy, "but not lately. I thought you needed another lesson."

"It is not an easy one for me to learn, certainly."

"Are you really so conceited, then?"

"Hardly as absurdly so as you imagine. I should always have supposed my companionship quite a matter of indifference to you if you had not suggested the doubt, but *now* I am really such a fool as to feel like venturing everything I have in the world to disprove it."

"To yourself or to me?"

"To you, I suppose."

"Then you yourself believe that I cannot?"

"Oh! How I wish I did!"

"Why?"

"Because I love you."

There was a long pause.

"Do you know, Reta, that I am not quite sure whether you can live without me, and so in that your proof has failed, but you proved something to

me by going away. You led me to find out that I
cannot live without you!"

Still she did not answer. She was leaning back
in the boat, letting one hand trail in the water.
She did not move or lift her eyes, and very gradually Cecil withdrew his left arm from his oar,
which was resting idly in the boat, and passed it
round his companion, unreproved by word or look.

"Oh, Reta, if you can care for me," he whispered, "after all these years, you will make me the
happiest fellow in the world!"

"How shall I?" she asked softly.

"By giving me what I have most coveted."

"*Most?* Are you sure?"

"I am perfectly sure."

"You will not change your mind again?"

"I never should have changed it if I had thought
you cared for me. Do you love me?"

"I believe I do," she said, lifting her eyes suddenly and looking into his with her bewitching
smile, "but you must take away your arm, dear,
or somebody will see."

Cecil was too happy to be disobedient, so he did
as he was told, and this was fortunate, for just
afterwards Mr. Hazzard sang out to the men to
"make ready," and they were soon pulling down
the stream in a charmed silence.

The charm was not felt by all, for Julia had been
rendered quite unhappy by what Cecil said to her
of Charley Hazzard, and when they pushed off
from Strawberry Mansion on this lovely moonlight

night, her heart was very heavy. She noticed,
with dismay, that Charley's manner gave only too
much ground for her newly-awakened fears, and
turning over many doubts and troubled thoughts
concerning him, she began dimly to recall the
conversation which they had had so long ago at
the Assembly, and to wonder whether he could
really have been in earnest when she thought him
half in fun. Could it be that the poor fellow had
been paying her serious attention all these months
during which she had treated him with the freedom
and the indulgence that she might have granted to
a favorite cousin, whom she had known from childhood? If so, how could she help him? How could
she right the unconscious wrong which she had
done? She felt ready for any sacrifice, and it occurred to her that the hardest thing that she could
do was, possibly, the only thing which would save
him.

Just then he spoke. " Do you remember a talk
we had last winter, Julia? I may call you Julia,
may I not, because we are such old friends? "

" You may, for that reason," she said.

" And the talk? " asked Charley. " It was at
the Assembly. Have you forgotten what I said to
you then? "

" I do not remember exactly what you said," she
replied, in the same low tone in which he had
spoken.

" But you remember what I *meant*, do you not?
and what you answered? "

"I think I said to you then that I never intended to marry," answered Julia gravely.

"Yes, you did," said Charley, "but I hoped you might if I always kept caring for you, as I have done, and never bothered you with saying things. Oh, I know what you mean by that shake of your head; but I am not going to say another word, only to remind you of your promise."

"My promise!" gasped Julia. "When did I make a promise? I do not know what you mean."

"Do you not remember," cried the young fellow, "how I asked you to promise that if you ever changed your mind you would let me know? Do you not remember that you did promise? Oh, you need not think that I am impatient. I am quite willing to wait, if it should be for years; only remember that I am the same always."

"And so am I," responded Julia. "What I said to you before was half in joke, and I had no idea that you were so serious in taking my answer, but it is quite true that I never intend to marry."

"I see," he answered sadly. "You have not changed, but let me hope a little. You may change."

"No, never."

He uttered a sigh which was almost a groan.

"I will not change with regard to you either," she said gently. "You always will be a dear friend, so dear that I am going to tell you the reason why I shall not marry." Her voice shook, and she paused for a moment to gather strength. It was

terrible to her to speak of her inmost secret — that
which had been sacred between her and her God.
Her agitation was contagious, and with intelligence sharpened by his love, he caught a glimmer
of her meaning.

"Do not tell me that you care for some one
else ! " he cried, in a tone of supplication.

"But it is true," she said. " There is some one
whom I have loved all my life."

Julia had spoken in a very low tone. She wondered whether he had heard her, for there was a
long silence. She turned gently round to look at
him, and his expression shocked her. Could this
be Charley Hazzard's — this pale, indignant face
and stiff, straight figure, which sat so rigidly upright
in the moonlight, as if carved out of stone? There
were the signs of such desperate pain and suffering
that she shrank at the sight.

"For God's sake don't look at me ! " he said,
between his teeth.

She turned away her head, but she could still
see him in her imagination. "Will you not believe in my friendship ? " she asked beseechingly.

"I will believe in nothing," he said hoarsely.
" In nothing ever again."

If the little pleasure boat had been sensible of
the load it bore that night, it surely must have
sunk ; but as it was, it glided swiftly down the
moonlit stream, and, not unlike the bark of life,
held side by side a strange, mixed freight of human joy and sorrow.

CHAPTER XXXIII.

" I dare do all that may become a man ;
Who dares do more is none."

SHAKESPEARE.

A BACKWARD April shower, falling in May, had
become conscious of its mistake, and, as usually
happens with shy people, had grown twice as
clumsy and awkward in consequence.

It had spoiled the fresh appearance of Edith
Arnold's pretty morning dress, and driven her and
Gertrude from the lawn tennis ground, where they
were engaged in a delightful game ; and now as
Edith stood gazing disconsolately from the upper
entry window, she saw it flooding the flower beds
all round the piazza and filling the blossoms of the
trumpet vine, which climbed over the roof, so full
of water that they all drooped their heads and
looked utterly forlorn.

It chanced that the approach to the house was
shielded from Edith's point of observation by a
clump of tall young maples, and she was therefore
surprised at this moment to hear a ring at the bell.
Morning callers were not common in the seclusion
of New Rochelle thus early in the season, and
when the housemaid appeared to tell her that there
was a gentleman in the parlor who had asked for

Miss Edith Arnold, she was aware of a slight quickening of her pulses and a faint flutter of expectation.

She slipped down-stairs quietly without going into the room in which her mother and Gertrude were sitting, and paused a moment at the door of the drawing-room, summoning all her courage and self-possession to enable her to offer a cordial and unconscious greeting to the tall, broad-shouldered young man whom she beheld already in her fancy; then she opened the door and saw Philip Drayton standing before her on the hearth-rug, in front of the sweet-smelling boughs of blooming lilacs stuck into the empty fire-place. She was, perhaps, more agitated than surprised. But why was he gazing at her with this stern, sorrowful face? What had happened, that he should look at her so sadly?

These thoughts took her by storm, and held her from speaking until Philip said, —

" I am come because I said I would come to see you. Do you remember ? "

" Yes," she said, still more surprised.

" Do you care to hear the explanation which I said I would give, or would you rather not ? "

She lifted her eyes, which had sunk before his, in another attempt to fathom the cause of his strange greeting.

" I care to hear it if you care to give it," she replied gravely; " not otherwise."

" I should think not," he said bitterly.

"Why do you speak so?" she asked.

"Because I am mad!" he cried passionately. "Do not heed me. I do not mean to blame you, but just now I hardly know what I say!"

"To blame me?" she repeated. "For what? What have I done?"

"Is it possible that you do not know?"

"Of course I do not."

"Not really?"

"Most truly no! Has something happened?"

"You can think of no reason, then, why I should reproach you unless something has happened?" said Philip slowly. "Is it a complete surprise to you, Miss Arnold, to be told that I am in love with you? Have you never dreamed of such a thing as possible? Has there been no look or word of mine to show you that I was struggling with a feeling to which I knew that I must not yield?"

She did not answer. She had fallen to trembling as she stood facing him. Her eyes were sunk on the ground.

"Have you never intended to give me a second's encouragement?" asked Philip, in the same low tone. "Has it been all my own blind infatuation which has led me to hope against hope?"

He paused again. Still Edith did not speak. How could she answer such a declaration of love as this? It was more like an accusation of murder.

"If you can truly tell me that," he resumed

solemnly, "then it is also true that I have no right to find fault with you."

"It is certainly true that you have never given me any right to suppose that — you — you cared for me," she said at last. "Yet even if I had been so vain as to fancy that you did, why should I be so blamed? What have I done?"

"What, indeed?" he cried bitterly. "It is a very little thing to give a man false hope, to reassure him when he fears he is falling into a fatal error, to blind him while you steel his heart to the real state of yours! I know society looks very lightly on these things. Was it all unconscious, then, that light in your eyes when I parted from you?" he asked, in a desperate tone.

There was an instant's pause, and then she said, honestly, —

"No. I thought then — I thought I knew — that you liked me very much."

"And I, poor wretch," cried Philip, "I thought I knew that you liked me much! You see what a fool I have been — and — that I must leave you."

"Why do you call yourself a fool?" asked Edith faintly. "Why must you leave me?"

"Because if I stay I shall do you a great wrong. I ought not, as it is, to have asked you that question, and if I stayed I could not help asking another."

"I wish you would ask it."

"Edith! You do not know what you are saying!"

"God help me!" she cried, "I believe I do not.

26

It is all inexplicable — what you say and what I say — like some dreadful dream."

"As for me," said Philip, "my dream is over, and this is an awakening, — a very bitter one!"

He turned away as though to leave her, in his anger and despair, and not being able to command her voice to speak so as to detain him, Edith took a step forward and laid her hand upon his arm.

"Philip," she whispered.

He turned back instantly and looked again into her face with his stern, sad eyes.

"I believe you are sorry for me," he said, "and it may well be that I am wrong to blame you for the depth of misery into which I am sunk. Give me your hand, for farewell."

Poor Edith could stand no more. As he gave her back the one of her hands which he had taken in his for a moment, she covered her face with both of them and burst into tears, the sight of which moved him deeply.

"I am a brute to have spoken as I did!" he cried. "Do not be distressed at what I said, I beg of you. You should not regard it any more than the raving of a maniac. I told you I was mad, but I swear to you that I bear you no resentment."

"There is some great misunderstanding," she said, withdrawing her hands from her face with a gesture of hopeless mystification.

"Oh no, there is not!" said Philip. "That at least is past, and in my sober moments I do not. think that the misunderstanding was your fault, or that you were responsible for the truth's being hidden from me. We have both been the jest of circumstance. I should have seen the folly of trying to win you from the first. God knows I held back long enough, and then I was deceived, — not by you, but by chance, — into believing that your heart was free. I wish that I might be your friend, and it is possible that I may be yet some day, when this is passed. Good-by until then!"

He stooped and kissed her hand, and then hastened away before she could speak, even if she had been inclined to do so, but she was not. A feeling of utter hopelessness had come upon her, from which she thought that nothing would ever rouse her again.

Her sister Gertrude was much distressed at her altered looks for the next day or two. She told her mother that she thought a " change of air " would be good for Edith, and urged on the preparations for the visit to Heronsford, in which Edith herself did not seem any longer to take the slightest interest. As it chanced, they neither of them knew anything of Philip's visit, for he had come and gone without their seeing him, while the foolish young person whose health they were discussing kept her own counsel and grew more and more unhappy as the days wore on.

CHAPTER XXXIV.

"The clouds that gather round the setting sun
Do take a sober coloring from an eye
That hath kept watch on man's mortality."
                                                WORDSWORTH.

"Is anything the matter, old fellow?" asked Lawrence Carey, as he and Philip sat at dinner on the evening of Drayton's arrival in Boston.

"Nothing that I know of. Why do you ask?"

"You look as if you were very much cut up about something."

"Do I?" replied Philip gloomily. "I am a trifle tired after my journey. I shall be all right in the morning." But he did not seem inclined to retire early, and as the evening wore on they fell to discussing many things in the half personal, half philosophical spirit, which was their nearest approach to confidence.

"Then you will not come back with me to Heronsford?" asked Philip at last.

"No, I think not," said Carey. "There is no use in it. It is all very well to talk about a faint heart and that sort of twaddle, but if a man has given a woman a fair chance to find out whether she can like him, and she does not care for him, there is no sense in fighting against it."

" But," said Philip, " how can one be sure? Might it not be possible for a woman to think that she preferred some one else, and yet to be mistaken? "

" That is her lookout."

" One would say so, if one did not care."

" Oh! if one thought there was any doubt, one would ask the woman, of course. Sometimes a man might have reason to hope from her manner of refusing him."

" How if she had not refused him and yet he knew that she would be bound in honor to do so; would there be any use in his subjecting her to that pain? " asked Philip, with the look of a puzzled judge on his serious face.

Lawrence Carey looked at him with a half surprised, half amused expression.

" I can't tell, my dear fellow," he said compassionately. " It depends so entirely upon the woman. There are some who would misconstrue your delicacy. Few people thank one for trying to bear their burdens. In any case, I think my advice would be to leave the responsibility where it belonged."

" You would ask for her love, then, in any case? "

" I should do it *once*," said Dr. Carey, his mind reverting to his own affairs; " but as to doing it oftener, I am very doubtful. If a woman is cold, she is cold."

" Do you think that is true where there is no

other influence to contend with, or only where there
is some one else whom she likes better?" asked
Philip sadly.

"I really can't tell. It is like speculating
whether the sun will shine on a particular day, to
attempt to inquire into the complex causes of so
simple a thing as personal attraction, or the absence
of it."

"Some men seem born to attract," said Philip.
"Now there is Cecil Wilmott. I remember we had
a talk about him once before; I did not think you
did him justice, and he has come out lately in a way
to warrant my opinion rather than yours; but he is
certainly a light weight in proportion to the influence he exerts."

"Of course he is," said Dr. Carey. "That kind
of fascination is as accidental a gift as blue eyes
or black, but it is less definable. The possession
of it is apt to be generally felt, but not generally
acknowledged. Half the people who yield to it do
so without knowing to what they yield. I do not
care a rap for it, myself, and nothing surprises me
so much as the extent of its power over others."

"I believe the more a person has of it, the more
alive that person is to its influence," said Philip,
musingly.

"Thank you," said Lawrence Carey dryly.

"My dear fellow, I was not thinking of you!"
protested Philip, suddenly awakening to the unflat-
tering implication of his words.

"Oh, I thought you were!"

" On the contrary, I was thinking of a woman," said Philip, reddening painfully at the confession.

" That is all right, old man, you need not tell me any more about it. She is not much of a woman if she does not appreciate you."

" She is a very sweet woman indeed," said Philip staunchly, and soon afterwards they parted for the night.

The result of this conversation, after it had been turned over in his mind with the more active events of the day, caused Philip not only to regret the violence to which his sudden jealousy had driven him, but to wonder whether he had not been foolish in foregoing an opportunity of ascertaining the real state of Edith's affections.

Lawrence Carey thought that it would have been honorable to ask for her love. Why need he have been more scrupulous? Might he not stop again at New Rochelle on his way back and learn the truth? he asked himself as he tossed about on his uneasy pillow that night; but these were not the healthy thoughts of his waking moments, and with the morning his unselfish nature reasserted its strength.

He would take the first opportunity of begging Miss Arnold to forgive him when he could do so as a friend, but he would not take a mean advantage of another man, even to gain what he most wished for in the world ; and so, after passing a day or two in Boston with his friend, he took the night train for Philadelphia that he might secure himself against the temptation of lingering on the way.

He had ordered his horse sent to meet him, but stayed in town all day and rode out that evening much later than usual, to find Mrs. Wilmott, Charlotte, and Julia assembled in the drawing-room.

" Why, Philip! We had given you up!" exclaimed Mrs. Wilmott, as he burst in upon them in his muddy boots.

" Have you seen anything of Cecil?" asked Charlotte. " We expected him, too, this evening."

" Yes, I have seen Cecil," answered Philip gravely. " He came to tell me some bad news."

" Some bad news? What was it?" asked Mrs. Wilmott.

" It was of a friend of all of us," answered Philip, looking meaningly at Julia.

" Not of Mr. Hazzard?" she cried, starting from her seat with a sudden premonition.

" It was. What made you think of him?"

" I hardly know," she said hurriedly. " What is it? What has happened?."

" We are not sure, that anything has," he answered ; " only we do not know where he is."

" Tell us just what you have heard."

" Why, Cecil came to tell me that Hazzard has not been seen or heard of since that boating party which he gave for you."

" How did Cecil hear about it?" asked Charlotte.

" Mrs. Davering telegraphed to him to know where Charley was. She and her husband are at Saratoga, where she expected her son to join her; and not hearing anything from him for more than

a week, she had already written a letter, which came
just after the message, asking Cecil to look him up
and let her know if anything was the matter. This
Cecil tried to do. He went first to the house in
town, and learned that he had not been there since
the afternoon before the boating party. They supposed him in the country. Cecil then took the train
for Wymbleton, not doubting that he should find him,
but learned to his discomfort that he had not been
seen there, either, for ten days. Still hoping that
Charley might have gone unexpectedly to pay a
visit to some friend, Cecil returned to town at
three o'clock and came at once to me; but we have
both spent the whole afternoon in making inquiries
among all the men he knew well, and especially
those who went on the excursion up the river, without being able to find any clew to his strange dis-
appearance."

"Why, what nonsense!" cried Charlotte Wilmott. "A grown man like Mr. Hazzard could not
be stolen like a child. How could he disappear?"

Julia was pale as death, but said nothing.

"It only shows the danger of a young man's
leading that sort of irresponsible life — one foot in
one place and one in another," said Mrs. Wilmott,
with a shake of her head. "There is Cecil himself,
who is only too fond of it. Of course, if no one
knows where he is, he might be anywhere, as I
have often told him; but I never thought of his
being spirited away."

"I remember being quite surprised that Mr.

Hazzard did not walk home with you that night, Julia," said Charlotte. " I thought it odd when he asked Cecil to come with us, especially as the party was given for you."

" When was Mr. Hazzard last seen, Philip ? " asked Julia, almost sternly.

" As far as we can learn, Freeman was the last of his friends who saw him. He says that Charley, after arranging with each one of the men who he should take home, to be sure that all the ladies were safely cared for, accompanied the rest in the horse-car as far as Mrs. Percy's door, when he and Freeman got out together. Mrs. Percy, who was full of gayety, said a hundred pleasant things to Hazzard about the success of his party, the beauty of the night, etc., to which Freeman noticed that he barely replied, but saying good-night to both of them rather abruptly, turned and walked off in the same direction in which they had come. He remembers thinking this strange at the time, as it was the opposite way from the Daverings' house, but thought no more about it beyond the moment."

" Is this the last that is known of him, then ? " asked Julia.

" It is the last that is known with any certainty ; but there are all sorts of reports about already, since it has been known that he is missed. It is said that one of the night watchmen on the railroad bridge across the Schuylkill saw a man put out into the river in a wherry, from one of the boat-houses, between twelve and one o'clock that night, and that when he got into the middle of the stream, the man suddenly disappeared. From where the watchman was posted he could not tell whether he lost his balance, or the boat upset, or whether the man threw himself intentionally into the water. He made his way down to the shore, and after some trouble, succeeded in finding another boat and rowing out to the place ; but when he got there the wherry was floating bottom upwards, and there was no sign of the man anywhere."

" Of course there always would be reports of this kind," said Mrs. Wilmott hurriedly. " It is not worth while to dwell upon any of them when, after all, our young friend may be amusing himself somewhere, and entirely unconscious of the anxiety which he is causing."

" It is bad about Mrs. Davering," said Philip. " Cecil had to telegraph to her to come home ; for if he is not found in another twenty-four hours, the whole thing will be in the papers, although we have tried to keep it as quiet as possible."

Nothing more was said that evening. Even the more cheerful aspects of the subject were not further discussed, for its gloomier ones were uppermost in the minds of all. Julia learned from Philip, after the others had gone to bed, that the river was being dragged, and that he expected to hear the result from Cecil in the morning.

Julia and Charlotte were sitting on a covered veranda which opened from Mrs. Wilmott's bedchamber, the next morning, when the postman came. Julia, who was the first to see him, sprang up and ran down to the front entry, where she met Philip with an open letter in his hand.

"What is it?" she asked. "Has he been found?"

Philip looked at her pityingly. "No, dear Julia," he said, "he is not found for us. He never will be in this world."

"Then he is dead?"

"His body has been found. It is even as you feared."

CHAPTER XXXV.

*"Love took up the harp of Life, and smote on all the chords with might ;
Smote the chord of Self, that, trembling, passed in music out of sight."*
TENNYSON.

"O Philip!" cried Charlotte, intercepting him on his way to his room, the evening after the sad news of Charley Hazzard's death had been confirmed ; "here is a note which came for you the day you went to Boston. I put it into my work-basket intending to give it to you when you came home, but this terrible catastrophe of poor Mr. Hazzard's quite drove it from my mind. I think it is from Cecil."

"All right, Charlotte. You need not be troubled about it. I have seen Cecil three or four times a day since, so that if the contents were of any consequence, I should have been likely to hear."

"I thought the note might have been to tell you some news," said Charlotte meaningly.

"Some news?" repeated Philip, with a sudden frown. "What news?"

"Have you heard of the engagement?" asked Charlotte, beaming all over with an air of mystery.

"No," said Philip savagely. "I do not want to hear of it."

"I beg your pardon, I am sure," returned Charlotte, with offended dignity. "It seemed like the most important thing that had happened since you went away."

" It is important to you, no doubt."

" I fancied that you might take some slight interest in it on Cecil's account," said Charlotte loftily.

" Possibly I should," returned Philip, with a bitter smile, " but the truth is that I would a little rather the subject were not mentioned to me."

" You do not know how cross he was! " grumbled Charlotte, as she described the interview to Mrs. Wilmott a few moments later.

" Ah, well, my dear, I have no doubt that he has the same feeling that I have about Mrs. Percy. He probably dreads receiving her into the family. But although I never fancied her before, I shall try to like her now, and we must make the best of things for Cecil's sake."

" Oh, as for that," said Charlotte, " you always make the best of things. But I had no idea that she cared for Cecil."

Meanwhile Philip, who was very far from imagining this interpretation of his ill-humor, was still smarting under the belief that Charlotte had intended to announce Cecil's engagement to Edith Arnold. His hand tightened convulsively on the note which he supposed to contain the unwelcome tidings, and he thrust it unopened into his pocket.

When Edith received her next letter from Julia she happened to be sitting listlessly in Gertrude's studio, watching the artist put some finishing touches to the portrait of a country peddler, whom she had beguiled into sitting for her. Edith was not thinking of the dirty old man, with his cunning, careworn face and short cuddy pipe. Her thoughts were, indeed, far otherwise engaged, and she suddenly aroused herself from her sad abstraction to perceive that the model had fallen asleep.

"Wake him up!" she said indignantly. "He will spoil the picture."

"Oh, it is a great pity to spoil his nap," replied the placid Gertrude. "I can work on the background for a while. You see the figure is almost done. He only wants another wash over his face."

"I should think he did!" said Edith.

At that moment the postman arrived with Julia's letter, and all the current of her thoughts was changed. She slipped away with it still unopened to a shaded seat in an arbor, at the bottom of the garden, and here she broke the seal. The letter contained a long account of the heart-rending "accident" which filled Julia's thoughts just then to the exclusion of every other subject.

Mrs. Wilmott had received an urgent message from Mr. Davering entreating her to come to his wife. The poor lady had returned to her house in the country just in time to hear the certain news of her son's death, and was in a state of the most terrible excitement, walking her room day and night with sobs and lamentation, refusing to see any one or to receive any consolation, of which, indeed, no one felt that there was much to offer.

Mr. Davering was quite worn out with his efforts to comfort her, and had at last brought her to say that she would be willing to see Mrs. Wilmott, who went to her at once.

"I wanted to go, too," wrote Julia, "I feel so deeply for her, but Mrs. Wilmott begged me not to think of it. She said that seeing me would be sure to awaken painful associations. Poor Mrs. Davering! So here I am with Charlotte and the prospect of a visit from Miss Ruthven, who has been urged by Philip to come and look after us in our unprotected maidenhood. Will you not come soon, dear, and cheer us up a little? We are all very sad, but Philip is as gloomy as a nightmare. I sometimes wonder whether his extreme depression can be entirely due to the shock of our friend's loss, or whether he can have any personal cause of unhappiness which has made him so different from himself ever since his return from Boston. Perhaps he is only very tired. He has certainly had a great deal of care and anxiety since his father went away, and when I spoke of your promised visit the other day, hoping it would give him something bright to think of, he said that he thought he would leave home before then, as he fancied that he needed change of air."

At this point the letter, which had been trembling in Edith's hold, dropped upon her lap, and she covered her face with her two hands while tears trickled silently between her fingers.

Her private desk contained at that moment a

letter partly written to Julia, in which she stated, with many expressions of regret, that she found herself obliged to give up her visit to Heronsford, the day fixed for which was fast approaching. After their last interview her self-respect would not allow her to take a step which might throw her in Philip's society, but now it seemed that she could accept Julia's invitation quite freely, for Philip himself intended to secure her against the possibility of a meeting. He was determined to avoid her, whatever the mysterious cause of his displeasure might be. The thought was infinitely bitter.

At last she dried her tears and rose sadly from her seat to return to the house. She fancied as she did so that she heard the clicking of the front gate, announcing the possible arrival of a visitor, and quickened her pace in order to get to her room without molestation; but as she turned the corner of the house in hot haste, with her straw hat hanging by its strings behind her, and several tresses of her fair hair flying loosely in the wind, she almost ran into some one who was advancing by a converging path.

The broad approach was shielded at this point by the clump of maples which has been mentioned already, and Edith, stepping aside beneath one of the trees with a startled movement, raised her eyes and met those of Philip Drayton.

He came forward eagerly, with an anxious look in his face.

"Have you forgiven me for my rudeness the other day?" he asked. "I do assure you that I am utterly ashamed of my want of self-control. Will you let bygones be bygones?"

She did not answer for a moment. She was evidently very much startled, and, looking gravely at his outstretched hand, just touched it with her finger-tips, which felt as cold as ice.

"I do not wonder that you find it hard to understand me," he said sadly. "I did not expect, of course, to meet you in this way."

"Nor I that you were coming here," said Edith, in a tone which seemed to have changed, since he last heard it. It was quieter than before, and colder. There was no response in her manner to his.

"I thought I owed it to myself and you to ask your pardon," he said humbly; "and then I was afraid that the idea of meeting me might possibly prevent you from visiting Heronsford, so I decided to come and tell you that I was going away."

"You were very kind."

"I meant to be, for I fancied you would like better to hear from myself why I had gone. I wanted you to know that it was chiefly for your sake."

"Then may I ask why?" She turned, as she spoke, and walked slowly along the garden path, and Philip walked beside her for some time in silence.

"It is very simple," he said, at last, in a deep voice in which there was a strong vibration. "I not only imagine that you would probably prefer to have me absent, but it would be difficult for me to so far master myself as to be able to meet you every day as you would wish."

" Indeed ? "

" Why do you say that ? You seem as much surprised as Julia did, when I told her that I should not be at Heronsford during your visit."

" You think then that it ought not to be a mat- ter of surprise to me ? "

" Julia's surprise was based on the fact that she said she thought we had always been good friends," replied Philip gravely.

" I think I have been laboring under the same impression," said Edith dryly.

" I can hardly understand that," he answered ; " for I have not been a very good friend, as I told Julia."

" Did you give her the impression that we had quarreled ? " asked Edith. " I should like to know my cue."

" It seems that if it be to quarrel, you will take it easily," said Philip, with some bitterness.

" I think you can hardly accuse me of having been inclined to do so, although I may have seemed stupid, finding myself unable to guess why you were angry with me."

" When, for instance ? "

" You did not seem very well pleased the last time I saw you."

Philip's face darkened. " Do you not know why ? " he asked. " I told you at the time. Do you want me to tell you over again ? "

"I hardly know," she said, with a slight tremor in her voice. "I should like to understand it if I could, but I would rather that you were not angry with me again. I would rather we were friends."

"Angry! angry!" he repeated, desperately. "Do you call it being angry when a man tells you that he loves you, and shows you his grief that another man has been preferred to.him?"

"Why do you suppose that I prefer another man?" she asked quietly.

"I believe that you do not mean to be cruel," said Drayton slowly, "and I will try to think that you are sincere in wishing to retain my friendship. You have a perfect right to the reserve which you choose to maintain, with regard to your own feelings, from your own point of view, but from mine it is intolerable."

"And from mine," said Edith, "all you say is enigmatical. Whom do you think I care for?"

"Cecil Wilmott has told me, Edith."

"What did he tell you?" she asked, proudly.

"I know now that you are engaged to him."

"Did Mr. Wilmott tell you that?"

"He did not say it, but he implied it. He would not say that it was untrue."

"Then I will say so."

"Take care. He has written to me since. I have the note in my pocket at this moment."

"What can you mean?"

"That it matters little whether you call it an engagement, if there is, as he led me to believe, an understanding between you. Did you not make him a purse and send it to him?"

"I certainly did. Does that constitute an engagement?"

"You are treading on dangerous ground," said Philip. "Will you say in so many words that Cecil told me what was false?"

"How can I, without knowing what he said? I do not believe that Mr. Wilmott would say what was not true," said Edith gravely, "any more than that he said he was engaged to me."

Philip misunderstood her caution. He thought it the deliberate evasion of an acknowledgment which she did not wish to make. An expression of pain and regret passed over his face. He drew a crumpled envelope from his pocket, and handed it to her without a word.

Edith looked at it with amazement. "This note is directed to you," she said, "and it has never been opened. What am I to do with it?"

"Read it," said Philip imperatively.

She quietly broke the seal, and read the following, in Cecil's handwriting: —

MY DEAR PHILIP, — I have been troubled since you left the office lest you may have misinterpreted what I said this morning. I beg, therefore, to state explicitly, in answer to the question which you asked to-day, that I am not engaged to Miss Edith Arnold, who has, as I believe, never entertained towards me any feelings but those of a

friend.   My own to her were once of a warmer nature, but met with the most distinct proof that they
were unreturned.

> Faithfully yours,   CECIL WILMOTT.

As she read the note, a sudden light broke upon
Edith, who perceived that it was dated some weeks
back.   In fact she noted that it bore the date of
the very day when she had last seen Philip, on his
way to Boston.   She raised her eyes from its peru-
sal to the troubled countenance of the young man
before her, with a glance almost of compassion.

"I was sure there was a misunderstanding," she
said, with a sweet, confident smile.

Philip did not know what to make of the smile.
He took back the note from her outstretched hand,
and read it as in a dream, and his whole being
seemed transfigured.

"Dear Edith, is this true?" he cried.

"You should ask Mr. Wilmott.   Did you believe me when I told you that I was not bound to
him in any way?" she said reproachfully.

"I did in part.   I believed the letter of your
words."

"You were kind."

"The truth is," said Philip, "that I was afraid
to believe.   Will you not forgive me now?   Will
you not give me your hand?"

"As a sign that we are friends?"

"No," said Philip.   "I do not ask it as a friend."

She turned a little from him towards the side of

the summer house, into which they had wandered as they talked.

"Edith," he said, "I think you love me."

Still she said nothing.

"Edith! Edith!" he cried passionately, "if you do care for me the least little bit, for God's sake tell me so!"

The terrible earnestness of his tone seemed to move her with a force outside her own volition. She raised her head and held out her two hands to meet his with a sudden impulse, and then as quickly dropped them; but he caught them as they fell.

"You do care a little, do you not?" he asked impetuously.

"Yes."

"Only a little?"

She did not answer, so Philip began to protest.

"I love you more and more every time I see you. Why did you make me believe that you cared for some one else?"

"I did not make you believe it," she said proudly. "It was you who would believe it. I began to think that you never would believe anything else."

"Give me the right to believe something else, and you will find I will do so at any risk. Will you not forgive me?" he entreated.

"Ah, yes," she sighed, "I do forgive you."

"And you love me?" he asked; and then he stooped and took his answer from her lips, which yielded it at last.

CHAPTER XXXVI.

"Be thou the rainbow to the storms of life,
    The evening beam that smiles the clouds away,
    And tints to-morrow with prophetic ray."
                                        BYRON.

CHARLOTTE WILMOTT had a very different office to perform from that with which Philip had credited her. Instead of announcing Cecil's engagement to Edith Arnold, she was called upon to break the news of Philip's engagement to her, to Cecil. Although fully aware that he had surrendered already to other charms, she had prepared herself for a little sisterly consolation on the occasion, and was surprised to the degree of being slightly disappointed at the coolness with which her brother received the information. "I never saw anything in Edith Arnold myself," said Charlotte, "but I thought at one time, Cecil, that you admired her very much."

"So I did," said Cecil, lighting a cigar. "I was in love with her, I think."

"How can you speak of it like that!"

"Why not, since it is over?"

"After all, I don't believe you were worthy of her!" exclaimed Charlotte, with sudden inspiration.

"So she thought," said Cecil coolly.

" Oh, she thought so, did she ? " asked Miss Wilmott, changing sides with female facility, as her indignation took a new turn. " Well, I think her a self-satisfied little minx, and am very sure she is not at all worthy of Philip, however well she may think of herself."

" By which nice gradation of unworthiness one may see exactly how high an appreciation you have of your brother," said Cecil, with something of his old enjoyment of a joke, even at his own expense.

But Charlotte was in no jesting mood. " It is well enough for you to laugh, Cecil," she answered, in an injured tone, " but no one can say that I do not think highly of my own flesh and blood."

It chanced that the young lady who was being thus freely discussed had set forth that very morning from New Rochelle to make her promised visit to Heronsford, and discovered, on reaching Philadelphia, that Philip had come to meet her.

" I have stolen a march upon Julia," he said, with satisfaction.

" How was that ? " she asked shyly. " Did Julia not know of your coming ? "

" I fancy she did not, but I have my dog-cart here and propose to drive you to Heronsford."

" But," said Edith, " I was to take a particular train and Julia was to meet me. She wrote me all about it, and said it left from this same station."

" Well, then, we will send her a telegram," said Philip calmly. " I knew she had despatched Rogers to meet you in town, but not of the rest of her plan. I gave Rogers something else to do, and ventured to present myself instead." There was a quiet confidence in his manner which Edith had noticed there before, in moments which required decision. She inwardly admired him for it, but felt herself called upon outwardly to demur. "I am afraid Julia will be disappointed," she said.

"I shall regret that," replied Philip, "but have you no fear of disappointing me?"

She started and turned to him quickly, with a faint blush and a very tender light in her eyes.

"I think I have a prior right, have I not?" he asked gently, drawing her little hand, as he spoke, within his arm.

"Perhaps you have," she answered, and Philip, taking her answer for consent, helped her into the carriage without meeting with any further objection to such a pleasant mode of ending her journey.

So the telegraphic message was sent, and these two young people began one of life's pilgrimages, which they had determined to make together, with a happy confidence in each other and in the future which it is to be hoped was not to prove the result of inexperience.

Julia meanwhile had risen early that morning, and gone to the garden to gather some flowers to add a finishing touch to the pretty bed-room which she had taken pleasure in preparing for her friend, and after luncheon she proposed to drive herself to the station in a jaunty little village cart which her guardian had provided for her use the year before.

"Hadst thou not better take James with thee, my child?" asked Miss Ruthven, coming out on the doorstep as Julia was about to set forth. "Thou art aware that Frisky hath much of the sprightliness of youth, which may render him difficult to control, and is also not patient under the approach of railway trains."

"Oh, no, dear Miss Ruthven. You must not be anxious, for I know Frisky's ways, and Edith and I will be quite enough of a load for him."

"There thou art right," said Miss Ruthven thoughtfully, "for it is not well to load a young horse too heavily. Only remember thy promise to be careful." The old lady stood shading her eyes as she looked after Julia, who drove off in the best of humors. She knew that one of the "ways" of the spirited black pony which drew her Liliputian equipage was to *back* when he saw a locomotive, and remembering his antipathy she turned him off into a grove of evergreens at a short distance from the station, to wait until the train in which she expected Edith had come and gone. Then she threw the reins over his neck and left him among the trees while she ran out to look for her friend, — but no Edith was there.

She walked all round the little square wooden station-house with a keen sense of disappointment, peeped into the waiting-room, where she only saw two severe-looking old ladies wearing the American livery of gray linen dusters, and was about to return to the wagon when the station-master said, in answer to some inquiry, —

"There 'll be another train along, Miss, just in a minute. It 's an express train, but it 'll stop for a flag or a passenger, and your friend may be in that."

"Perhaps she may," said Julia, with renewed hope. "I must go back to Frisky or he will be over the traces," was her next remark; and Frisky was inclined to verify it, for she just reached him in time to prevent that enterprising animal from making various new discoveries in the art of harnessing.

Whiz! Whiz! Whiz! came the express train, flying and flashing past with such uncurbed velocity that she gave up hope again. It did not seem to her to pause an instant, certainly not long enough to deliver a passenger, before it was whirling away in the distance; but she was mistaken.

One person had got off the train, and was coming briskly across the railway track before she had time to turn Frisky's head homeward and emerge from the friendly shelter of the grove. The solitary passenger came and stood in the opening of the green hemlock boughs and gazed upon her with a surprise and pleasure in the meeting which hardly dared trust its own origin.

Julia was dressed in a light summer costume consisting of some gay-colored chintz, much puffed and looped as to the skirts, in shepherdess-like style, but fitting closely to her waist and shoulders, with a delicate white muslin kerchief crossed about the throat. She wore a broad-brimmed straw hat, round which a dark red silk scarf was twisted carelessly, and was bending forward, as she sat in the village cart, trying to disentangle Frisky's tail from the reins. Her back was towards the spectator, and he drew a step nearer before he spoke her name.

" Julia ! "

She started and dropped the reins, but did not look round until he repeated the word. Then she turned her head very slowly with an expression of fear, but one look was enough to change it into joy.

It was in very truth Mr. Drayton who stood close to her with a smile on his lips and the glow of health on his cheek. It was no midnight vision, born of hopeless longing, which was thus suddenly presented to her in the morning sunshine, and with a cry of happiness she sprang toward him.

" Were you afraid I was a ghost ? " he asked, tenderly drawing her to him and looking down at her with a gleam of his old humor.

But she did not answer. She stood for a moment gazing up into his face as though she could not see enough of him.

" I am too glad," she whispered, and laid her head upon his shoulder with a long sigh.

His face suddenly changed. " My sweet, sweet child," he said, pressing her to his heart. " I do not deserve this happiness. Shall I tell you all the things which I have been thinking of while I have been away?"

"Yes," she said, "tell me everything."

"Where shall I begin?"

"Begin with that night," she answered, lifting her head and looking up again.

"The night of the accident?"

"The night I saw you! Did you think of me?"

"You mean when" —

"When you were so nearly lost."

"Of course I thought of you — and Philip. It was most natural that I should."

"But did you see me?" she persisted. "Did you see me when I saw you?"

"Do you mean that you thought you saw me on that night?" he asked slowly.

"I did see you, and there was water all around you, and you were holding out your arms to me!" she answered, and as she spoke his face grew pale and his eyes darkened with excitement.

"I can hardly believe this, Julia," he said in a trembling voice, but Julia cared for nothing but the truth.

"Did you see me?" she said.

"Yes, dear, I thought I did. It seemed to me in that awful moment, when consciousness was passing from me, although I still clung to a fragment of the wreck, that for one instant the greatest longing of my heart was answered, and I saw your face! I had believed it to be the hallucination of a drowning man."

They were both silent for a moment. Julia had never withdrawn her eyes from his. She did so now, with a look of profound contentment, and rested her chin thoughtfully upon her hand.

"I knew it," she murmured.

"My darling! What would I not have given to spare you the shock and suffering you had! I think the hardest time for me was when I was in that sailing-vessel, carried along night after night over the dark water."

"After you were *saved?*" she said.

"Yes. When I was being taken to Gibraltar against my will, with such a strange sense of helplessness and isolation from all my world, to which I did not doubt that I was already as one dead."

"Hush!" she whispered, shuddering, and put her hand up as though to close his lips, but he caught the hand and kissed it, with a vehemence which brought the color to her cheeks.

"I made up my mind to two things while I was abroad," he said. "What do you think they were?"

"I do not know."

"The first was to come home just as soon as the duties to others which I had undertaken would permit," he said, with a merry smile.

"And the second?" asked Julia.

"The second decision," he replied more gravely, "was not reached until after I returned to London, and received Philip's long letter telling of all the anxiety which my reported loss had brought, and above all, of my little girl's illness. Then I determined — look at me, dear Julia."

She raised her head obediently, and looked gravely into his face.

"I determined that come what would, you should know my love, and that it was love alone which had driven me from you — even if you turned from me with dread a moment after!"

She opened her eyes with sudden astonishment.

"What can you mean?" she asked. "Have I not always known that you loved me, tenderly and truly?"

"You have indeed," said Mr. Drayton, "but I love you more, now. I love you desperately — absorbingly; with a love which claims you for its own!"

She turned away her head, and drew her hand from his with gentle dignity.

"Is it strange," he continued, "that when I was mastered by such a selfish feeling as this, I should have felt that my only manly course was to leave you?"

"It seems strange to me," she said.

"I felt, that I could not stay, Julia, without asking you to be my wife."

To this she did not answer by word or look. She was intensely still. The lids were drooped over her eyes, but her half averted face spoke to him in spite of herself. It seemed that there was a silent reproach in it.

"Do not fancy that I was afraid to bear the pain of a refusal," he said hurriedly.

Still she answered nothing.

The minds of men and women travel by such different methods that even where most sympathetic they sometimes reach quite opposite conclusions from the same premises.

"The truth was this," he said at last, with an effort to speak out all that was in his mind, let it cost what it might in the way of misconstruction. "I knew that in answer to the protecting love which I had had for you so long, my child, and of which we have just spoken, you loved me too as a daughter might love a father, and I feared to shock that love by offering you a feeling so different; or that by the gradual influence which my mind had acquired over yours in the years we had lived together, I might persuade you to believe that you cared for me more than you did, and then, too late, might come the true hero who could have filled your dreams, and I should stand by in despair to see my darling's life made wretched."

Julia turned her face towards him now with one long reproachful look.

"You are my hero," she said.

"I thought that in your exalted fancy you might have imagined me very different from the reality," he answered. "It seemed best to remove my influence and let you see more of others."

"If I never see you again from this moment," said Julia, with a strange courage which had come to her as he talked, "or if I spend all my life with you, it will be the same thing with me, and as for your being a hero, that is proved, and there is no more room for fancy in the matter."

"My love! My love!" he cried passionately, and caught her in his arms. "Will you be my very own?" he said, bending over her.

"Did you not wish to forget me?"

"I never hoped to do so. I knew it was impossible."

He spoke almost sadly. His eyes were looking into hers which suddenly grew bright with triumph.

"Say again that you love me," she whispered.

And he did say it in more ways than one, so that at last she was convinced; and by and by they perceived that Frisky had eaten up all the bushes in his neighborhood, and proceeding to get his head the other way they drove slowly towards Heronsford, but when they had gone about half the distance Julia drew in the reins with a sudden jerk and a little exclamation.

"What is the matter?" asked her guardian, looking about them vainly for the cause of this abrupt stoppage.

"Why, what can have become of Edith?" she cried. "I expected to have met her at the train!"

"Are you sure that you met the train she told you?"

"Oh! she did not tell me, it was I who told her."

"What do you mean, dear?"

"I wrote her last week just what train to take, and I sent Rogers in to meet her this morning."

"Probably she has made some change of plan, and when we get home you will find a letter explaining it."

"Perhaps I shall," said Julia, and there was every reason now why she should have driven on, but still the cart stood still in the middle of the country road, and Frisky had begun his favorite habit of browsing by the wayside.

"There is something else which — which troubles me," she said presently, examining the lash of her slender driving whip with great interest.

"What is it?" asked Mr. Drayton, very gently.

"It is about my mother," she said, blushing all over as she spoke.

"You mean about telling her?"

"Yes."

"Leave that to me."

"But will she — will she *like* it?"

"I think she will, when she fully understands. She shall be told first, before any one else. Is not that what you would wish?"

"Oh, yes! I wish no one else need know at all!"

Mr. Drayton laughed. "There is no need of their knowing for the present, at any rate," he said.

"Mr. Drayton" — timidly.

"Are you going to call me that always?"

"I don't know," she said, blushing again; "but I want to tell you something."

"Well, dear?"

" When you were away and that dreadful news came, and afterwards when I was ill and was getting better, Philip was so true and kind and thoughtful for me, that I never can forget it. I have always felt to him as towards a brother, but I do not think I quite appreciated before all the strength and tenderness that there was in him."

For answer Mr. Drayton put his arm about her and pressed her to his side.

" Thank you for telling me," he said, after a moment, and then Frisky was reminded of the error of his ways.

www.ingramcontent.com/pod-product-compliance
Lightning Source LLC
Chambersburg PA
CBHW032300280326
41932CB00009B/640